AF556133

Digital Research in Library and Information Science

Digital Research in Library and Information Science

Neelesh Kashyap

RANDOM PUBLICATIONS
NEW DELHI (INDIA)

Digital Research in Library and Information Science

ISBN 978-93-5111-564-9

Published in 2015 in India by

RANDOM PUBLICATIONS

4376-A/4B, Gali Murari Lal, Ansari Road
New Delhi-110 002
Phone : +9111-43580356, 011-23289044, 011-43142548
e-mail: sales@randompublications.com,
info@randompublications.com, randomexports@gmail.com

Reprint 2021

Type Setting by : Friends Media, Delhi-110089
Digitally Printed at : Replika Press Pvt. Ltd.

Preface

Researchers have recently reviewed the status of some digital libraries from around the globe. These reviews reveal that while the digital libraries have very good information access and retrieval mechanisms in place, there is almost no provision for quality reference and information services.

However, these studies show that there is a trend towards the personalisation of digital library service, as in case of HEADLINE and GEMS (presently called iGEMS, a digital library developed at Nanyang Technological University in Singapore). Some recent research efforts have been directed at building personalised digital library environments. These studies can be grouped into three categories: user needs assessment, personalised user interface and personalised digital library, researchers reviewed literature on user interfaces, particularly in a digital library environment, and suggested the need for a task-based digital library.

Researcher discussed the personal digital library (PDL) that acts as a front-end to other electronic library systems and manages the user's information needs. Barry and Barbara discussed the creation of personal digital libraries. The North Carolina University Library developed MyLibrary @NCState as a portal application to the NCSU Library's information resources. This portal allows user profiling to build a dynamic, customised gateway to both general and discipline specific resources. MyLibrary is a Cornell University Library initiative to provide personalised library services to their students, faculty and staff on the basis of a focus group study to gauge library users.

Although the book covers a wide range of technical, economic, social and organizational topics, the focus is on the actual working components of a digital library..

I would like to thank my team for standing beside me throughout my career and writing this book. My special thanks go to "Random Publications" who have published the book.

–Neelesh Kashyap

Contents

1

Research Techniques in Digital Library

INTRODUCTION

Researchers have recently reviewed the status of some digital libraries from around the globe. These reviews reveal that while the digital libraries have very good information access and retrieval mechanisms in place, there is almost no provision for quality reference and information services.

However, these studies show that there is a trend towards the personalisation of digital library service, as in case of HEADLINE and GEMS (presently called iGEMS, a digital library developed at Nanyang Technological University in Singapore). Some recent research efforts have been directed at building personalised digital library environments. These studies can be grouped into three categories: user needs assessment, personalised user interface and personalised digital library, researchers reviewed literature on user interfaces, particularly in a digital library environment, and suggested the need for a task-based digital library.

Researcher discussed the personal digital library (PDL) that acts as a front-end to other electronic library systems and manages the user's information needs. Barry and Barbara discussed the creation of personal digital libraries. The North Carolina University Library developed MyLibrary @NCState as a portal application to the NCSU Library's information resources. This portal allows user profiling to build a dynamic, customised gateway to both general and discipline specific resources. MyLibrary is a Cornell University Library initiative to provide personalised library services to their students, faculty and staff on the basis of a focus group study to gauge library users.

The MyLibrary project has two components, MyLink and MyUpdate. MyLink allows patrons to save useful information resource links that they found themselves or those suggested by the librarians via a targeted notification in their personal space. Users can access this personal space from any place. MyUpdate periodically queries the online catalogue and notifies users, utilising a pre-defined user profile.

Headline is one of the eLib Programme's Phase 3 projects, developing a hybrid library system called the HeadLine Personal Information Environment (PIE), This PIE uses portal-type technology to present an information environment that is personalised to the user's needs and allows user customisation. This project presents users with pages of resources relevant to their courses/department. PIE users are also provided with an "all resources" page that contains all the library resources.

Users can create their own lists of resources on their own pages. Meyyappan reported on ongoing research at Nanyang Technological University in Singapore on the design and development of task-based digital library organisation and a digital work environment (DWE). The major objective of these research projects is to allow users to personalise digital library access so that they can view their preferred resources, and hence, information is automatically filtered. These projects aim to select automatically a subset of the DL collection based on the nature and characteristics of a user.

The user then can add new resources, or delete recommended resources, to his or her page. The DWE project is somewhat different from others in the sense that the main objective of the DWE is to provide filtered access to the local digital library collections, to remote digital libraries, as well as to traditional libraries, and,most importantly, to the vast information resources on the university intranet. The system also allows users to create their own personal workspace to store selected information resources for future use.

GROWTH OF DOCTORAL RESEARCH IN INDIA

Elsewhere in India other individual librarians and library science teachers eager to earn doctorates were hampered by the non-existence of programmes. In the 1960s and 1970s some doctorates on library-related topics were earned by library professionals from some other faculties such as sociology, history, law, economics, management, and the like. The mantle of reviving and furthering doctoral research facilities was assumed by J. S. Sharma, then the university librarian and head of the library science department of the Panjab University, Chandigarh. Under his guidance the second *de jure* Ph.D. in library science was awarded in 1977 after a gap of full two decades. Thereafter, there was no looking back. Many universities followed with mostly individual efforts and enthusiasm. Doctoral research got a fillip in the 1980s. India maintained its Third World leadership in library research as well as in library education and literature. Ph.D. programmes have rather mushroomed even despite the lack of facilities or adherence to standards.

FACILITIES FOR RESEARCH

A conscientious university teacher is always in a dilemma over how to divide the time between teaching and research. Teaching is a primary compulsive and urgent duty to be performed. Students expect their teachers to give them time and personal attention. There may be appreciation in good teaching but the rewards lie in research. The university expects its teachers to do research for its prestige and fame lie therein. But when it comes to supporting of research many universities in India are neither generous nor unambivalent. Ordinarily piecemeal research, especially in social sciences, is not supported financially. Internal support for research trickles through a tedious and off-putting bureaucracy and political manoeuvring. Colleagues are unsupportive. They are unappreciative, intolerant and jealous. Library facilities are poor. Thus most of the teachers are driven to the passivity of guiding doctoral research instead of doing postdoctoral work.

THE DETERIORATION OF STANDARDS

The University Grants Commission (UGC) preconditions for faculty employment and promotions have prompted many library professionals to acquire Ph.D. degrees, though many may not have the aptitude and the intrinsic ability to do research. Standards have not only been diluted but have been kept at abeyance. Supervisors and the examiners have become obligingly compromising. The cut-off date of December, 1992 for obtaining the Ph.D. degree to get an exemption from the national level test for teaching jobs in universities/colleges has done incalculable damage to research standards.

An eminent academician has corroborated the ill effects of this policy:

> "They were required to submit their theses before the deadline regardless of the date of registration. Some of the candidates on whom Ph.D.'s were conferred were not fully acquainted with the contents of their dissertations. In some cases even the supervisors were innocent of any knowledge of what the theses were about. The incitement came from the UGC".

Programmes for Ph.D. research have been introduced and expanded mindlessly. As a result, there has been a bit of doctoral boom – a spectacular rise in Ph.D. awarding universities and awardees – though many institutions lack utterly the resources of people or material or both. A 1987 bibliography listed 41 Ph.D. theses written from 1957 to 1985. In a recently published bibliography of doctoral dissertations in India from 1950 to March 1997 about 340 titles have been listed. This record of 340 dissertations, though not wholly authentic, is reliable by and large. In productivity the Panjab University, Chandigarh, led up to the mid-1980s. Thereafter, it lost the number game to the universities of the south.

The universities that have so far awarded up to ten degrees are ranked below:

- Karnatak University, Dharwad 44
- Jiwaji University, Gwalior 27

- University of Rajasthan, Jaipur 26
- Andhra University, Visakhapatnam 25
- University of Delhi 17
- University of Pune 16
- Gulbarga University 15
- Utkal University, Bhubaneswar 11
- University of Burdwan 10

The universities in Bangalore, Banaras Hindu University in Varanasi, and Nagpur University are picking up in research.

THE CONTRIBUTIONS MADE BY RESEARCH

Contrary to expectations, dissertations are not fountain heads of the rest of the literature to grow and mature. These primary sources of information are distanced from relevance. The National Social Science Documentation Centre systema-tically procures one copy of each research dissertation in social sciences to preserve and make them available to researchers for consultation within the premises of its library. Retro-spective bibliographies of LIS dissertations in India are available.

The latest information on theses awarded, Ph.D. degrees and Ph.D. research in progress is available in the featured column of the weekly University News of the Association of Indian Universities, New Delhi. It is a major source to keep track of the dissertations awarded Ph.D. degrees by Indian universities in all disciplines. In spite of availability, other researchers do not adequately use these dissertations; nor are these works cited or quoted by teachers or textbook writers.

Working librarians rarely use research results to solve their professional problems. There is no precedent of a library inviting a library school to do research on a problem confron-ting them. At the risk of calling attention to a red herring, it is worthwhile to have this idea corroborated from a veteran library leader.

Professor P.N. Kaula candidly observed:

- That LIS departments have little or no understanding and cooperation with the central library . . . The problem is more psychological than academic . . . Much harm has been done to the teaching of library science by the disharmony....

Librarians go in for local, *ad hoc* and *pro-tem* solutions for their practical problems. Researchers consult a teacher or a fellow researcher for a topic of research rather than a practitioner. It is not only true in India but elsewhere too. Thus research has become divorced from reality–a theoretical exercise at best. This seems a universal phenomenon in our profession. Carl Keren doubting the value of research in information science daringly suggests that "It would be worthwhile to find out how much of it has really contributed to our body of knowledge and to the methods used by practitioners." He himself understands that "As suggested, probably be rather disappointed".

American teacher Margaret Steig endorses this notion:

- Research done by library and information science educators seems to receive little respect from professionals, and if they do not find it of value one has to wonder who will.

RELEVANCE OF RESEARCH

In a developing country like India, there could not be a dearth of research problems to be investigated. But there seems a lack of perception to visualise and identify valid problems for research. A cursory glance of the topics worked on will at once reveal that the topics chosen do not have a problem or hypothesis but merely survey the state of the art or the existing conditions. The popular areas for research have been, in order of popularity: university libraries, bibliometrics, library use and user studies, information seeking behaviour, information systems, classification and indexing, special libraries, library history, reference service and sources, and library science education.

Document selection and procurement, cataloguing, and experimental designs in library management are the least popular topics — though these seem practical and relevant to present day needs. That basic research is the most neglected area is endorsed by other surveys of doctoral research. Library automation, library software, networking and information technology are just emerging. There is need to revive research in classification especially in context of OPACs, information networks and the electronic information environment in general. The Curriculum Development Committee (CDC) on Library and Information Science of the University Grants Commission rehashed the importance of research, though it did not dwell at length on this aspect in its report.

The blue document listed some areas for research, which are no less broad than the current courses being taught at the Master's level:

- Structure and development of knowledge.
- Classification, cataloguing and indexing.
- Infometric studies.
- Computer applications.
- Historical studies.
- Social and economic aspects of librarianship.
- Library and Information management and systems analysis.
- Applications of techniques of library and information science to evaluate other disciplines.

The list could have been more specific. Though not much revered, the report rightly lays emphasis on standards in research. It uncompromisingly asks for a clear declaration from Ph.D. candidates that the "work is based on the discovery of new facts by the candidate or the new relations of facts . . . and how the work tends to the general advancement of know-ledge". While it is normally expected of every completed piece of research, yet it rarely happens. The evaluation process, however formal, is easily manipulated without qualms. Examiners are obliging on a reciprocal basis.

In a small profession like ours this interplay of mutual usability comes in easily. It is often said jocularly that the degree is recommended more for the supervisor than for the candidate. We must admit that the library profession has failed to lure the best brains and even more to retain them. Mediocrity thrives; hypocrisy reigns. But this is not to overlook the genuine research and researchers. Apart from not so relevant topics, theses have contributed little towards pushing the frontiers of knowledge; few are models of methodology. Indian library research seems to have no moorings in the prevailing realities.

Topics are ideal, superficial and bookish. Even experi-enced librarians keen on earning the Ph.D. degree rarely come with an important problem for research. The supervisor who shies from controversial topics usually suggests the topic. Criticising individuals in formal black-and-white mode or exposing harmful tendencies of a class are not for them. Even a mild and healthy criticism is not tolerated in India. Feudal norms still lie deep in the Indian social ethos.

In addition, there is a dire paucity of data archives and reference works. Collecting data and information is considered a satisfactory end to the job — the goal of the research exercise. It is very difficult to collect data by questionnaire in a vast country like India. Each researcher has a bag full of woeful tales to tell. Library associations at all levels seem to have washed their hands of the research responsibility. These do not even collect and compile statistics of the professional activities pertaining to their areas. Their libraries are poor. They have no research budget. For quite a time professionals have been talking, writing and conferencing about library education and research in India.

Every year the Indian Association of Teachers of Library and Information Science (IATLIS) holds a seminar on topics of library education and research. That it is the most popular topic with the teachers and librarians can be gauged from the fact that the FID/ET seminar was the largest of all the 49th FID pre-conference seminars held in India. The literature on library education and research is enormous, though repetitive and inflated. We have given lip service to the change of curricula and the raising of standards of research. But the needed change has not come through. The blame is wholly put on the lack of infrastructure and unavailability of funds. That is not the entire reason. The lack of effective collective efforts to safeguard the standards seems no less major cause.

DIGITAL LIBRARY OF INDIAN BIOMEDICAL JOURNALS

Digital Library of Indian Biomedical Journals medIND has many functional and process components.

Selection of Journals

The scope of the Collection development policy is well defined to include only those Indian Medical Journals that are either indexed in IndMED or in PubMed database. The selection policy of IndMED is to include peer reviewed journals having at least published on time for the last three years.

At present, IndMED covers 77 Indian biomedical journals. All the articles are assigned metadata using data input worksheet based on Common Communication Format of UNESCO. These articles are indexed using controlled vocabulary 'Medical Subject Heading (MeSH) list of US National Library of Medicine.

It is being updating on an ongoing and timely basis can be accessed at <http://indmed.nic.in> which is searchable through web interface. The securing of intellectual rights has been easier due to rapport existing with the publishers of these journals. To remove any ambiguity and to reach clear understanding with the publishers, a formal Memorandum of Understanding (MOU) was signed with the journals [represented by their editors] to make available their contents for the medIND project.

At present, 37 Indian biomedical journals have signed a formal MOU with NIC. The aim of this understanding is to provide a rights framework under which cooperation is established between NIC and joutnals to provide their full content to the end user free of cost.

The journal publishers provide the content and NIC does all the other activities like conversion, organization, hosting and providing access to the end users. The salient features of MOU are given as below:

- The resulting materials will be stored and hosted on NIC server;
- No fee will be payable to either party for providing content to NIC or converting into digitization;
- On termination of the agreement, NIC shall provide continuing access to the digitized completed up to the date of such termination;
- The copyright of the data would remain with the respected Editors.

Acquisition of Source Materials

The acquisition of material is the important part of project management. The content is of three types - printed version, born digital, and online existing journal archives. This heterogeneous material is converted into homogenous digital content as given below:

Converting Existing Print Media into Digital Format

Bulk of the archival and back volume content received is in form of printed copies of the journals. Each article, editorial and case study is scanned and stored as PDF (multi page) files. The files related to issue of a journal is put in a separate folder. File names are assigned as per a file naming policy that is based on bibliographic properties of content. The journal's content page of each issue is scanned, OCR and converted into HTML file. The content page in HTML format has all the links to the respective PDF files holding the articles.

Converting "Born Digital" Journals

These days, it is common to find journals being composed in DTP packages like PageMaker before they are printed. For such journals, the composed material is acquired with the cooperation of the editors/publishers of the journals. This is directly converted into the PDF files without the need of scanning.

The quality of such PDF files is of much better quality. The name of the files is converted in accordance to the file naming convention. The content page of the issues is converted into HTML format and links are provided to the PDF files containing the full text articles.

Archives of On-Line Journals

There are few Indian journals that are already available on-line on the web. However since they are presently hosting on commercial web servers, it may not economical for them for continuing hosting back-volume of the journals.

In such cases the archive can be moved to medIND after suitable conversion according to the policy of file names and file organization. This would ensure unique and persistent address for the contents in such archives.

File Naming and File Organization Policy

Unique and persistent URLs for each article are most desirable for such a project. To achieve this there has to be suitable policy for file names and file organization. Such a policy was formulated and adopted. This formed the core on which cross linking between references in IndMED and their corresponding full text file under medIND has been done. Salient features of the policy is as follows:

Directory Structure

The directory structure is as follows: <http://medind.nic.in>/Journal Folder/.../Year-Folder/.../Issue Folder/...Article Files .../Article Folder/

Journal Folder

There is a folder under the site domain for each journal. The name should be unique for each journal folder. A unique three alphabet code has been created for each journal under MedIND called as MJID. This folder contains Year-Issue Sub-Folders and default (index.html) and other html files constituting the home page for the journal.

Year (Sub) Folder

This folder contains the issue subfolders. The Year folder is of three character format 'cyy' whereas c is for century and yy stands for last two digit of the year. For example, Year 2002 would be t02.

Issue (Sub) Folder

This folder is named as "Inn" format having at least two character long. Each Issue folder contains a table of content html file with same name as folder name.

Article File Naming Policy

The file names of articles are given as per the format given below: *<MJID><Century-Year><Issue No.><Pagination> <DOT><File Extension>*

- <MJID>: It is a unique identifier for each journal in IndMED and MedIND. It is of three alphabetical characters.
- <Century-Year>: It represents the year of publication and of three characters. The first character represents the century and is an alphabet. Next two characters are numeric representing the year (first year would be taken if it is a block year).
- <Issue No.>: A variable length of characters, starting with "i" followed by numerical characters represent the issue number.
- <Pagination>: A variable length of characters, starting with "p" followed by numerical characters represents the starting page number of the article. In case more then one articles starts on the same page then a alphabetic character is suffixed to qualify each article sequentially.
- <DOT>: The name portion of the file ends with a dot (.).
- <File Extension>: Three character extensions are suffixed after the dot to represent the common file types.

DIGITIZATION

Thirty-seven journals have signed MOU till now and given the consent for putting their contents under medIND project. The content is being received in hard as well soft copies formats. Each format requires digitization process. These processes are described below:

Conversion from Hard Copies

Steps Involved in OCR to PDF document

- Scanning the document: Resolution has been fixed for text as 300 dpi whereas for table and image, the resolution is 600 dpi;
- Each table is marked as an image as OCR most often distorts table;
- The remaining document is OCRed and saved as Word Document;
- Necessary corrections are performed such as spellings, special characters, colour changing, layout of the text and references;

- Quality checks: Each document is verified and passing quality test, is converted into PDF using Acrobat.

Steps in creating Table of Contents from scanned document

- Scanning the content pages of a journal, OCR and save in Word;
- Necessary corrections are performed such as spellings, special characters in the Word document;
- To design table of content in the same layout as given in the journal, it is designed in HTML format and saved as per naming convention. Hyperlink is given to each article;
- Quality Checks: Each link is being checked for correctness.

Conversion of Born Digital Contents

Steps in converting born digital contents to PDF document

- Content is being received in the form of Page Maker format;
- Converting from Page Maker format to pdf document and save it as pdf file as per the naming convention adopted;
- Checking the completeness of the document;
- In case, image or page(s) are missing, these are scanned locally for completeness.

DESIGN OF DIGITAL LIBRARY MEDIND WEB SITE

The medIND project is having its own domain name at the Internet (http://medind.nic.in). It has pneumonic value and stands for Medical Journals on Internet [from India]. Home page gives details of the project listing of the participating journals.

This listing is hyperlinked to each participating journal home page at the medIND web site. The site provides two approaches to access the journal articles.

Browsing

Journals are hyperlinked and arranged in alphabetical order. Such hyperlinked list leads to pages giving details of selected journals such as editors, instructions to authors, contact address, parent body etc.

Further, this leads to listing of issues of the journal by years/volume wise. The content page provides hyperlinks to the individual article.

Searching

The searching is being provided through the bibliographic database IndMED. Each record of the IndMED has been linked to the individual article in the MedIND site. The searching of the articles can be achieved through from http://indmed.nic.in as well as from http://mednic.nic.in web sites.

The references will display icons indicating the availability of the full text. In developing digital collection, issues of intellectual property rights have been dealt to strengthen the cooperation between editors and content service provider to facilitate access to digital content through Internet to end users in the area of biomedicine on non-commercial basis.

The design of digital collection should be usable, flexible and simple enough to accommodate future changes and also enables other applications to utilize data for development of future applications.

The naming convention of digital collection is acted as bridge between metadata base and full text of content. This project fulfills the demand of providing full text of documents to health professionals free of cost throughout the world.

It serves as a model for the development of similar collections in others S&T areas, medIND is a step in the process of making it as an open archive source where Indian journals covered in Medline database as well in IndMED database will be stored and will be provided access free of cost to health professionals throughout the world.

This will give enough visibility and exposure to Indian biomedical journals and demand for Indian literature would be met through the medIND project. In future, more visibility to articles included in medIND journals would be provided by adopting and exposing metadata in OAI-PMH and RSS protocols.

DEFINING THE DIGITAL LIBRARY CENTRE

Before proceeding, it is necessary to define what a UK higher education-based digital library research centre is. As one reply to this question put it:

"It's one of those things that is obvious when you see it you can quickly say whether something is a digital library research centre or not. Trying to define an authorative catch-all definition that every centre and non-centre is happy with, is another thing altogether."

By its very title, such a centre is a place where research into 'the digital library' is carried out. However, both 'research' and 'the digital library' are themselves vague, all-encapsulating terms; the phrase 'digital library' alone signifies remarkably different things to different people.

In addition, it could be argued that many university, and some FE college, departments carry out some kind of digital library research. For example, identifying the right database system to store information relevant to the subject domain of a department could constitute 'digital library research', as could designing a web site in order to provide access to content produced by the department, or providing department-wide access to a range of third-party electronic information services.

Because of the fuzziness of terminology, and the pervasiveness of digital library technologies in most aspects of education and information systems, acceptable synonyms of 'digital library centre' could include 'electronic library centre', 'information management centre', 'virtual library unit', 'learning technology unit' and many others.

However, there are a number of groupings and departments in UK academia that explicitly promote themselves as digital (or electronic, networking, learning technology or IT) research, development or service-oriented centres. These include centres such as the CDLR, CERLIM, CIRT, ILRT, LITC and UKOLN.

There are also distinct groupings of projects within UK higher education departments of information science (more commonly known as 'library schools') such as the Information Management Research Institute, which promote themselves as some variation of a 'digital library (research)' centre.

We looked at a number of these centres and groupings in order to identify the activities they conducted. The ten most common were:

- *Digital library services*: Creation, maintenance, enhancement.
- Evaluation of digital library projects, services and programmes.
- Consultancy in digital library matters.
- Developing digital library demonstrators usually, but not always, as part of a funded project.
- Research in a variety of aspects of digital/electronic library matters.
- Training in some aspect of ICT, or digital library usage.
- Fund raising for the centre.
- Digital library project and service coordination either as the sole partner, or as the lead partner of a consortium.
- Digital library centre, service and project-oriented publicity and promotion.
- Organising and promoting digital library events.

As an added complication, it could be argued that there are a number of centres carrying out most of these activities that do not market themselves as digital library (research) centres. For example, EDINA provides a wide range of electronic data-oriented services, in addition to events, service coordination, promotion and so forth.

In addition, the JISC-funded Resource Discovery Network coordinates a number of 'hubs' *i.e.,* centres that provide a range of internet resource discovery and related electronic services in specific subject domains; these are either based around a long-established service, such as EEVL, OMNI and SOSIG, or are based around newly established resource discovery systems.

These hubs, though service-oriented as opposed to research-oriented, are typically involved in seven or more of the aforementioned ten activities. In addition, as one subject gateway research officer put it:

".even though we maintain a service, we still need to carry out research on a continuous basis. Better interfaces, methods of integrating our service with the RDN and others, faster information download, techniques to increase recall and precision, monitoring usage."

For the purpose of this article, we will drop the word 'research', so as to include those centres that provide mainly digital library services, therefore leaving us with the 'Digital Library Centre', or DLC for short. We will define the DLC somewhat unscientifically as being:

'A centre containing two or more digital library-oriented services or projects, where the services and projects interact in technical, personnel, promotional or other ways, and where the majority of activities in the aforementioned list of ten are carried out.'

The Benefits and the Drawbacks

What are the benefits of running a DLC?

- The skills and experience of staff can be used across a range of projects, and the non-project components of the centre, as opposed to being used on one discrete project. This benefits both the development of the staff, and the development of projects and services.
- The centre will have a higher profile than a disconnected collection of projects, therefore (theoretically) attracting potential funders and skilled staff.
- The more staff there is, the greater the pool of contacts and collaborators (through those staff), and the more people who may become aware of the more obscure sources of funding.
- Proposals can be submitted for work based on previous or current work in the centre, therefore increasing the chances of those proposals being funded.
- The centre should have more 'clout' within the host institution, and is therefore able to fight for better/adequate accommodation and other institutional resources.
- With good (and independent) financial manage-ment, there is more flexibility in moving monies between projects, services, initiatives and other budgets within the centre.
- Some activities can be carried out more efficiently; for example, a number of closely-related projects or services could carry out joint dissemination activities.

Obviously, there are drawbacks to establishing a DLC; otherwise, most HE institutions would possess one, and all DLCs would succeed and prosper.

Significant problems encountered by such centres include:

- Funding non-project staff, such as centre administrators and directors; many conventional funding sources will only fund staff directly employed on a project or service, and will expect the bidding centre or institution to provide appropriate administration, directorial and other non-project based staff out of its own funds.

- In the same vein, funding non-project activities, such as centre-oriented PR (web site, leaflets, presentational expenses).
- Finding increasing amounts of funding in order to retain staff who are increasing in experience and skills.
- *Accommodation*: This really should not be a problem; a successful DLC can bring in substantial funds to the host institution, raise the institutional profile, provide a range of services and information to other units within the institution, and assist in raising the RAE rating of several departments. You would therefore assume that Higher Education institutions would happily provide sufficient accommodation. This is not the case; most UK HE DLCs have fought a permanent struggle to gain satisfactory accommo-dation of anywhere near the standard of similarly sized units in the same institution.
- You will need to speculate before you can accumulate. Before hiring staff who will secure funding, the aformentioned accommodation has to be located for them, in addition to desks, PCs, stationary and the like; this will easily run into several thousand pounds of spending before any member of staff of the new DLC actually starts to write the first funding application or proposal.

The 'Vision' of the Centre

Before establishing a DLC, you essentially need some kind of vision, agenda, remit or plan. This is useful when dealing with sponsors, funders, incoming staff, PR-related issues and so forth; it is not enough to mumble "we do digital library stuff" and leave it at that.

The vision of a DLC is usually oriented around one or more of the following:

- *Some subject domain or spectrum*: For example, a centre could offer a range of services including electronic journals, resource discovery access and internet training in a specific subject.
- *Some type of digital library service*: For example, a centre could specialise in providing services, research and consultancy in various aspects of electronic journal creation, maintenance, access and charging.
- *A geographic area*: A centre could aim to become the main higher education institution based centre of digital library research activity within its particular region of the country.
- A particular funding source or 'seam'.
- *Some particular user domain*: For example, a centre could research digital library issues applicable to teachers, lecturers, librarians, schoolchildren or some other type(s) of user.

The vision will be partially determined by the existing projects (and proposals for future projects currently submitted) which will form the new centre. In addition, the skill set and experience of staff who will work in the centre can be a significant factor in the scoping of the vision, as well as those digital library-related resources and services (usually within the host institution) on which the centre can rely. The vision (which needs to be updated as projects and services come and go) can be used to provide the basis of the centre mission statement and several other PR elements.

Funding the Centre

Unless your centre has several projects that involve large amounts of digitisation work, or invests in some hugely expensive specialist piece of hardware, then the large majority of expenditure will be on staff wages.

Focusing on the 'Vision' or the 'Money'

The two extremes of funding a digital library centre seem to be:

- Carefully evaluating the resource, skill and funding requirements necessary to fulfil a well-defined digital library centre vision, followed by locating and pursuing the appropriate funding sources.
- Throwing together a speculative proposal for every call or tender that contains a phrase similar to 'digital libraries'.

Most centres fall somewhere between these two extremes; if you work in a senior position in a DLC, it is an interesting exercise to (honestly) see what proportion of proposals submitted in the last year more closely match either of the two extremes.

In an ideal world, a DLC would firmly adhere to the first extreme. However, the culture in which typical DLCs are embedded is based upon short-term contracts, where there is a constant quest to find funding to keep individual staff members 'on' for as long as possible. Therefore, unless your DLC has managed to develop a successful financial mechanism for retaining significant reserves, it may need to step outside of the 'vision' and acquire funding via whatever means in order to retain key staff. As one ex-director of a DLC replied:

"I felt like a hamster on a wheel; as soon as funding was secured to extend the contract of one member of staff, it was time to secure funding for another. And before long, I was back to the first member of staff. So, we would 'squeak' to various funders on a regular basis, and every now and then one of them would throw us a bit of cheese to give us the energy to carry on running a while longer. That's quite a cynical way of looking at it, isn't it? Four whole years of my life and it reads like the lyrics of a Radiohead song."

In addition to acquiring funding to retain key staff, there is also the burden of perpetually funding a continuous service. Whereas a research project usually has some finite end, digital library services carry on until they are either sold, bought out or taken over, or are integrated into some other service, or become financially unviable. In addition, services can become obsolete in terms of either the content or the supporting technology, though this should not happen in a

DLC which sufficiently maintains and upgrades its services.

Even if a service is discontinued in some manner, there is often a need to make available some publicly-accessible archive of the content, which in itself raises issues of continuous maintenance and cost. This is not always considered by people who submit proposals to create digital library services.

The Diversification of Funding Sources

One of the more interesting aspects of studying digital library developments in UK HE is that of seeing where the funding comes from. This is relatively easy, as most funders demand branding or mentions of themselves in the publicly-accessible deliverables of the project or service.

Looking at the completed projects and services of DLCs from the last decade, we see that the large majority were funded from three sources:

- The JISC (Joint Information Systems Committee) funded a large number of research-oriented projects, as well as a smaller number of more service-oriented developments. Many of these projects were funded under large programmes such as eLib and JTAP, through which much of the funding was awarded to groups working in HE institutions.
- Public organisations and bodies concerned with library and library-content development, such as the British Library.
- European funding programmes.

However, a cursory examination of recent and current projects and services in the more successful DLCs in the UK (in terms of personnel growth) indicates that funding now comes from a more diverse array of sources, many of which were not targeted explicitly at higher education institutions.

For example, recently funded projects in DLCs include 'providing ICT services aimed at benefiting disadvantaged communities', 'providing training for staff in public libraries', and 'providing work packages for secondary school ages'. Non of these needed to be provided by HE institutions in particular and were not advertised as such, being open calls to any appropriate public or private organisation. So, why are DLCs now locating funding from a wider range of sources?

Some of the more sensible answers put to this question were:

- The change in focus of traditional sources of funding. A key example is the JISC; though the JISC still fund a number of exploratory and research-based projects, the focus of many calls has moved to developing and sustaining integrated services, through initiatives such as the Distributed National Electronic Resource.
- The increase in collaborative ICT and digital library funding for, and work with, Further Education. This is a drive encouraged by a number of organisations including the JISC.

The FE sector brings with it a range of characteristics starkly different to those of HE; for example, the number of institutions involved, the subject domains and qualifications, the network configuration, and the skill-set of staff. These and other factors often present interesting challenges when HE and FE organis-ations work together on digital library and ICT initiatives.

- *More commercial project sponsorship*: Companies are realising that providing funding for projects involving computers, training, networks, digital information and education reflects positively on themselves. For example, the BT-sponsored 'Lifelong Learning Awards' aims to "support lifelong learning projects which use ICT to promote access, innovation and teamwork".
- Same cake, more slices. There are an increasing number of organisations not all of them DLCs applying for the same grants and pots of money: ".maybe it's just me getting older, but there seems to be many more people bidding for the same funding nowadays". Several funders now process proposals and responses to tender in a multi-stage manner; this is partially so all of the unsuccessful bidders do not have to submit a final, full (and time consuming) proposal, but also so that the funding organisation does not have to judge a large number of these full proposals in one go.

A holistic Approach to Funding

So, what are these diverse sources of funding that the more successful DLCs seem to be tapping into? The rest of this section lists eleven types of income; the more established DLCs use most, if not all of these in some form or other.

Source 1: conventional Digital Library Project and Service Funders

There are a surprisingly large number of funding organisations who either issue calls or tenders with a fixed deadline, or who take a 'submit whenever you want for consideration' approach. Though the competition for funding from many of these sources is quite steep, they are worth considering, especially if you can argue your case around relevant experience (through completed works or through staff). However, beware of creating your own tight deadlines on calls and tenders:

Example: Leaving it to the last meeting A DLC became aware of a call with a closing date seven weeks distant. As this was more than a month away, the call was not deemed to be 'urgent' and did not make the AOB section of several strategy-related meetings.

With three weeks to go, a meeting was called the following week for people interested in submitting a proposal to the call. At this meeting, all of the attendees stated that short term commitments ruled them out of writing part or all of the proposal. Eventually, the DLC director cancelled three external meetings, wrote a proposal overnight without the help of the more knowledgeable staff, and the proposal did not succeed.

Source 2: European Funding

European funding proposals can result in substantial amounts of money, and lead to working relationships and trips abroad to interesting cities and countries. However, such proposals often require an preposterous amount of paperwork; it is common for a member of staff to spend the best part of a month, and often more, working solely on such a proposal.

Source 3: Own Institution

There may be sources of funding within your own institution, especially if the project or service either raises the profile of the institution, or has a real chance of attracting future income.

The summative evaluation of phase three of the eLib programme (findings, point 16), states "Some of the eLib phase 3 projects have become self sustaining with funding provided by the host institutions themselves".

Source 4: E-commerce: Sell things on the Net

While lagging behind the more commercial sectors, there is an increasing awareness, and use of, e-commerce systems in higher education.

This leads to two opportunities for DLCs; either to use e-commerce to sell whatever they can, or to build, advise on, research and maintain the digital library components of such commercial systems within their own institution.

Source 5: Training

ICT and digital library-related training has been carried out within and by academic departments and projects for many years. Currently, public libraries and schools by the thousand are currently being connected to the Internet, resulting in a need for training. In addition, the recent emphasis on life-long learning, and the large increase in public PC ownership, should result in a substantial demand for good quality training in these areas for some time to come.

Source 6: Consulting

If your DLC contains staff that specialise in a particular subject, technology, user type or sector, then there are possibilities for offering their services on a consultancy basis. Academic consulting has the advantage of often being short-term, and therefore a contract-filler (and staff retainer) between longer periods of project or service funding.

Source 7: Commercial Funding

Most universities actively forge links with commercial organisations, especially those based nearby. The resident 'business opportunities' unit should indicate which commercial organisations that the university are chummy with would be interested in funding digital library research or services.

Source 8: Advertising and Affiliate Funding

This relatively controversial approach to fundraising is usually referred to in the context of placing advertisements and banners on web-based services and resources. A steadily growing number of UK higher education based services raise revenue in this manner.

However, a recent JISC-commissioned report on advertising on JANET highlights concerns at institutional and other levels regarding the implications of this approach, as well as the realistic amounts of revenue that could be generated.

Source 9: Sponsorship

Sponsorship is a more acceptable form of visible commercial involvement, whereby an organisation does not necessarily plaster your web site with adverts in return for monies. Sponsorship can take many forms, such as sponsoring a piece of equipment, a session at an event, part of the salary of one member of staff, or print-based PR materials.

Source 10: Hosting Events

Workshops, seminars and conferences can generate profit, though generally not substantial amounts especially when the final amount of staff resource used by an event is calculated.

Unsurprisingly, the key factor in many profitable DLC organised events seems to be whether the host institution has appropriate facilities that can be hired at attractive rates. However, events hosted by a DLC can be a great showcase for the projects, services and products produced by that centre.

Source 11: The RAE (Research Assessment Exercise)

The RAE occurs every four years. Very generally speaking, departments submit details of research they have undertaken, from which a panel in the subject area decide on a research rating (from 1 to 5 and 5*).

This rating determines the amount of core research funding that is awarded to the department. One of the main determining factors in the last few RAE exercises has been the amount of output published by researcher in peer-reviewed journals.

Therefore, various DLCs that are part of, or affiliated to, information science departments have often entered those staff who have published several such papers into the RAE, so as to maintain or increase their RAE rating and secure more core research funding.

STAFFING THE CENTRE

The Required Staff

As indicated throughout this article, a wide range of staff roles need to be filled in order to maintain a fully-functioning digital library centre. The core staff of a DLC may include:

- A director, with optional 'vision', who acts as a figurehead and 'public face' of the centre.
- Project management and coordination staff.
- Technical staff, for individual system and service maintenance, and PC and networking maintenance.
- Administration staff.
- Financial administration staff.
- Centre promotional staff *i.e.,* people to create the centre web site, leaflets and so forth.
- Staff familiar with copyright and IPR issues.
- Staff experienced in fund raising and proposal writing.

...and, of course, staff to work on the individual projects and services.

It is important not to 'scrimp' on administration staff:

Example: "The director is busy emptying the bins" A DLC centre submitted a number of proposals for funding. Non of these included an element for administration staff; in addition, the centre had no dedicated staff due to budget cutbacks passed down from higher authority in the host institution. Most of the projects were funded, but immediately fell behind as the research staff, mostly unskilled in administration, had to carry out these tasks.

The (highly paid) director of the centre spent an increasing amount of time dealing with tasks such as emptying bins and rectifying the lack of paper in the toilets, when ideally he should have been negotiating with potential funders of the centre. The situation was exacerbated by several research staff leaving, partially as they viewed doing administration tasks as a demotion.

Analysis of staff roles and numbers in UK DLCs indicate that, for every non-admin staff member, between 3.5 and 5.5 admin staff are required to fulfil core, project and financial administration roles in order for the centre to function at these levels.

Hiring Staff

Most digital library projects and a large number of services within the UK HE sector directly employ a very small (4 or less) number of people. Therefore, just one member of staff can have a large positive or negative effect on the progress of a project/service.

Hiring staff is therefore a risky business. These issues are not new; various projects in programmes such as eLib suffered delays due to difficulty in obtaining, and retaining, staff with sufficient technical abilities. These and related issues will be analysed by 'The Human Element', a study which aims '.to learn about the issues surrounding the recruitment, development and retention of project staff in UK HE libraries and archives, with special reference to RSLP and JISC projects.'

One ex-DLC co-director referred to staff hiring as: "...Russian roulette with five bullets, and the funders insisting you pull the trigger because the clock is ticking on the project and you cannot afford a further delay in order to re-advertise if all of the candidates are disappointing. What else can you do?"

The Digital Library Officer Skill Set

In August 2001, I asked a number of people who have been involved in selecting staff for DLCs to identify the most important criteria for a *good member of staff working within and across a Digital Library Centre.*

The criteria mentioned by several different people were:

- A 'team player', at both.
  - — The level of the centre and
  - — The level of the projects that they work on.
- Does their job with the minimum of supervision, and with no disruption to their (project and centre) work colleagues.
- A networker.
- Uses their skills to help other projects in the centre
  - — Even ones with which they have no connection
  - — Even if it does not benefit their own project.
- Promotes the centre as part of his/her project.
- Does not object to travel and overnight stays.
- Good communicator.
- Can produce good written and verbal English.
- Produces what they are supposed to produce, and on time.
- Iidentifies and 'grabs' opportunities for the centre as they arise.
- Is genuinely productive or as one reply stated, "...spends more time working than talking about working...".
- Is correctly motivated *i.e.,* is politically oriented to support their project and the centre, as opposed to solely advancing their own career and reputation.

It is interesting to note that most of the criteria are concerned with communication, both within the centre and beyond.

Burrowing deeper: identifying the correct staff

Several people suggested techniques that can be used to identify the correct staff with a greater degree of accuracy. These include:

- Taking more time over the interview stage. This is a somewhat controversial measure, as several people strongly objected to spending "time I do not have" on long interview procedures.
  The counter argument to this is "hire in haste, carry someone at leisure" more time spent selecting the correct candidate can avoid the aggravation caused by hiring an unsuitable person.
- Interviewing as a group (in additional to individual panel interviews), over half or most of a day. As the aforementioned skill list has shown, communication is valued highly within DLCs. There are many scenarios where DLC staff have to deal directly with strangers, often with little or no warning; for example, meeting a potential funder at a conference. In addition, staff within a DLC typically have to negotiate and work with other staff in the centre, on the same project and different projects, and a range of people within the host institution of the centre. Therefore, interviewing in a larger group, and involving group activities such as role-playing or a meal, can provide a better indication of relevant communication skills.
- Asking direct non-abstract questions, as opposed to traditional questions such as "Where do you see yourself in five years time". For example, if someone has worked for a period of time on a research project, then ask what they contributed to the project in terms of resource or effort.
- Giving the candidate some opportunity to demonstrate knowledge of relevance to the post that they are applying for; it is surprising how infrequently this occurs. For example, if a candidate is being interviewed for a post in a metadata registry service, then ask questions about metadata, contemporary metadata standards, where metadata research appears to be heading, and so forth.
- Asking other people who know the candidate, or their work. The digital library community in UK higher education is highly people-network oriented, and it is common to encounter current or previous work-colleagues of a specific person at an event such as a conference or workshop. If the timing is right, ask their opinions though be careful not to break the confidentiality of the job application procedure, for obvious legal and moral reasons.

Do not feel under pressure to take the 'best available' if none are suitable. This can be difficult, when dealing with a short-term project for a funder with whom you wish to forge a reputation for reliability. Have a back-up plan and schedule for quick re-advertisment of the post.

Keeping Good Staff

Good staff usually want to increase their experience and skill set, take on more senior roles in coordination and management, and see a subsequent increase in salary levels. Keeping good staff is vital, not only in terms of progressing the services and projects that they work on, but in terms of bringing in new funding most conventional digital library funding calls demand the CVs of relevant staff. Techniques for keeping good staff include:

- *Visibly rewarding good staff*: If someone is producing a good piece of work, encourage them to produce a paper concerning the work and submit to a digital library conference. An all-expenses paid trip to *e.g.,* San Francisco in 6 months time can help to encourage staff to stay:-). In addition, such publications can count towards the RAE (thus increasing chances of funding through this route), and postcards from staff in exotic locations can often make other staff think "How can I get some of this conference action?"
- *Ensuring that staff roles in proposals have some element of flexibility*: A real example is that of a proposal for a resource discovery service, where the deliverables and schedule were based on staff doing nothing but cataloguing (at speed) 8 hours a day. Subsequently, the service had a relatively high turnover of staff, partially as the cataloguing staff had no opportunity to develop new skills through undertaking other tasks or roles.
- *Supporting and encouraging staff to write proposals*: Ideally, details of calls which may be of interest to staff should be circulated on internal mailing lists. Staff (especially those nearing the end of their contracts) should be supported via administration, training, and/or extra time to write proposals in subjects which interest them.
  This has the advantages of sustaining staff, bringing more funding into the centre, and staff moving onto projects and services in which they are directly interested.
- *Having a flexible work culture*: Two DLC director, on my first day of work, informed me that (paraphrased) "I don't care what hours people keep, so long as they get the job done". This is healthy, as to many people one of the attractive elements of academic research is the informality; most of the time you do not need to wear a suit, do not need to be sitting at your desk at 9am sharp, and do not need to schedule coffee or meal breaks (or, compared to some call centres, need to put your hand up when you want to use the toilet). Accentuate this culture.

THE RELATIONSHIP WITH THE HOST INSTITUTION

While most, or all, of the funding for projects and services in a DLC will come from outside the host institution, the relationship with that institution is often the most important one for the DLC to cultivate.

Unless the DLC manages to acquire large amounts of excess revenue (this is unlikely), it will rely on the host institution for a diverse range of services and facilities, such as accommodation, financial system support, networking support, electricity, sanitation, interlibrary loans, and so forth.

Or, as one ex-DLC director put it, ".all the things that you don't notice while you are working in a digital library centre, until they break, leak, explode, go missing or become unavailable without notice."

Good relationships between the DLC and various units within the host institution are therefore essential. It is recommended that key DLC staff forge good working relationships with key staff in the following support units:

- Estates for everything to do with building, infrastructure and accommodation.
- Finance for receiving timely and detailed information about the financial state of projects and services, and answering financial queries.
- External relations for publicising the DLC in university publications.
- Print and reprographics for producing PR materials.
- Computing services for networking issues that impact on your digital library services.
- Catering so people at meetings, workshops and seminars are fed and watered.
- Room booking for space and facilities at meetings, workshops and seminars.
- Core institutional management senior principles, heads of departments and faculties so that people who make the key strategic decisions are aware of your centre, and it doesn't miss out on any internal digital library related work.
- Security especially useful when you start to possess expensive servers and other hardware.
- Personnel for contract renewal issues, and hiring new staff.
- The library for journal and book needs, as well as being a source of new staff who want to move into all things digital.
- Business opportunities for locating commercial partners and opportunities.
- Research support for project and service proposal approval.

Publicising the DLC throughout the institution on a regular basis is a wise option, as:

- Digital library work in various departments may come your way, if these departments are aware of you.
- Other departments are dissuaded from setting up such a centre if the university already hosts one.

RESEARCH IN LIBRARY AND INFORMATION SCIENCE

The roots of research in our profession are not very deep. Research in library science is a twentieth century occurrence ushered in by the library school of the University of Chicago in mid-1920s. The visionary efforts of the Chicago School bore abundant fruit and offered leadership to the world in library science research. The pace of library research is picking up everywhere today due to social pressure as well as inspiration. In justifying the Ph.D. programme in our profession, it has been urged that "if librarianship aspires to become a profession, it should depend upon research to develop its knowledge base and its theoretical framework".

RANGANATHAN'S WORK

The credit for the formal institution of the doctoral degree programme in library science in India goes undeniably to Dr. S.R. Ranganathan. In 1951, he started one at the University of Delhi surmounting many difficulties and facing personal ridicule. The University of Delhi awarded the first de jure degree in library science in 1957 to D.B. Krishan Rao who worked on a faceted classification for agriculture. Doctoral research remained in the wilderness when Ranganathan shook the Delhi soil off his feet in 1955. The *Documentation Research and Training Centre* (DRTC) in Bangalore, founded by Ranganathan in 1962, is technically not empowered to award the Ph.D. Therefore, for the rest of his life, from 1962 to 1972, Ranga-nathan only advocated solo and team research with stress on quality, relevance and basics.

No big research projects were taken up at DRTC though individual teachers and students maintained both the quality and the tempo of research. Since the death of Ranganathan almost the entire DRTC faculty has earned Ph.D.s from other Indian universities on topics of research relevant to DRTC. Now the DRTC teachers are approved Ph.D. guides in many Indian universities, and they have already produced many Ph.D.

THE INDIAN CONTEXT

In India following British tradition and American precedent as established by Asa Don Dickinson, Librarian, Panjab University, Lahore, 1915-1916, library schools for advanced professional education have remained attached to universities. The growth of universities in Independent India ensured their constant growth. In a university, apart from teaching, a teacher is expected to do and guide research. The third function of a university, namely service and consultation, has always remained weak in India despite many newly established universityindustry linkage programmes.

SEMANTIC RESEARCH FOR DIGITAL LIBRARIES

During the DLI, which ran from 1994 to 1998, significant research was conducted at all six projects in the area of semantic retrieval and analysis for digital libraries. Among the semantic indexing and analysis techniques that are considered scalable and domain independent, the following classes of algorithms and methods have been examined and subjected to experimentation in various digital library, multimedia database, and information science applications:

Object Recognition, Segmentation, and Indexing

The most fundamental techniques in Information Retrieval involve identifying key features in objects. For example, automatic indexing and natural language processing (*e.g.,* noun phrase extraction or object type tagging) are frequently used to extract meaningful keywords or phrases from texts automatically. Texture, colour, or shape-based indexing and segmentation techniques are often used to identify images. For audio and video applications, voice recognition, speech recognition, and scene segmentation, techniques can be used to identify meaningful descriptors in audio or video streams.

Semantic Analysis

Several classes of techniques have been used for semantic analysis of texts or multimedia objects. Symbolic machine learning (*e.g.,* ID3 decision tree algorithm, version space), graph-based clustering and classification (*e.g.,* Ward's hierarchical clustering), statistics-based multivariate analyses (*e.g.,* latent semantic indexing, multi-dimensional scaling, regressions), artificial neural network-based computing (*e.g.,* backpropagation networks, Kohonen self-organizing maps), and evolution-based programming (*e.g.,* genetic algorithms) are among the popular techniques.

In this information age, we believe such techniques will serve as good alternatives for processing, analyzing, and summarizing large amounts of diverse and rapidly changing multimedia information.

Knowledge Representations

The results from a semantic analysis process could be represented in the form of semantic networks, decision rules, or predicate logic. Many researchers have attempted to integrate such results with existing human-created knowledge structures such as ontologies, subject headings, or thesauri. Spreading activation based inferencing methods often are used to traverse various large-scale knowledge structures.

Human-computer Interactions (HCI) and Information Visualization:

One of the major trends in almost all emerging information systems applications is the focus on user-friendly, graphical, and seamless Human Computer Interactions. The Web-based browsers for texts, images, and videos have raised user expectations of rendering and manipulation of information.

Recent advances in development languages and platforms such as Java, OpenGL, and VRML and the availability of advanced graphical workstations at affordable prices have also made information visualization a promising area for research.

Several digital library research teams including Arizona/Illinois, Xerox PARC, Berkeley, and Stanford, are pushing the boundary of visualization techniques for dynamic displays of large-scale information collections.

The Illinois DLI Project: Federating Repositories of Scientific Literature

The Artificial Intelligence Lab at the University of Arizona was a major partner in the University of Illinois DLI Project, one of six projects funded by the NSF/DARPA/NASA DLI (Phase 1). The project consisted of two major components:

- A production testbed based in a real library
- Fundamental technology research for semantic interoperability (semantic indexes across subjects and media developed at the University of Arizona).

The Testbed

The Illinois DLI production testbed was developed in the Grainger Engineering Library at the University of Illinois at Urbana-Champaign (UIUC). It supports full federated searching on the structure of journal articles, as specified by SGML markup, using an experimental Web-based interface.

The initial rollout was available at the UIUC campus in October 1997 and has been integrated with the library information services. The testbed consists of materials from 5 publishers, 55 engineering journals, and 40,000 full-text articles. The primary partners of the project include: American Institute of Physics, American Physical Society, American Astronomical Society, American Society of Civil Engineers, American Society of Mechanical Engineers, American Society of Agricultural Engineers, American Institute of Aeronautics and Astronautics, Institute of Electrical and Electronic Engineers, Institute of Electrical Engineers, and IEEE Computer Society.

The testbed was implemented using Soft Quad (SGML rendering) and Open Text (full-text search), both commercial software.

The Illinois DLI project developers and evaluators have worked together very closely on needs assessment and usability studies. The production testbed has been evaluated since October 1997.

Six hundred UIUC user subjects enrolled in introductory computer science classes have used the system; and their feedback has been collected and analyzed. We expect to have collected usage data for about 1500 subjects at the end of the study. Usage data consists of session observations and transaction logs.

After four years of research effort, the testbed successes include:

- Willingness to build custom encoding procedures for SGML. This enabled the testbed to succeed in federating journals from different publishers with differing use of SGML, where Elsevier and OCLC failed.

- Canonical encoding for structure tags. The testbed can federate across publishers and journals.
- Willingness to build custom software for searching. The Illinois DLI system is able to show multiple views on the Web and has advanced structure search capabilities.
- Production repositories for real publishers. The project became the R&D arm of several scientific publishers and generated valuable contributions to the scientific publishing industry.
- Changing the nature of libraries with research. The project enables a research prototype to become a standard service capability for engineering libraries.

However, in the nature of research, we also have experienced many testbed difficulties:

For the user interface, the project originally planned to modify the Mosaic Web browser (which was developed at UIUC). When the Web became commercial, Mosaic was quickly taken out of the control of the developers. Custom software is hard to deploy widely: the Web browser interface has widespread support, but the functionality was too primitive for professional full-text search and display.

Several practical difficulties were found in using SGML for this project. Plans to use standard BRS as full-text backend had to be abandoned. It proved essential to use an SGML-specific search engine.

Good-quality SGML simply was not available. We had to work with every publisher, since nothing was ready for SGML publishing.

SGML interactive display proved not to be of journal quality. Physics requires good-quality display of mathematics, which is very difficult to achieve.

As the project comes to its end, several future directions are being explored:

- Technology transfer to publisher partners: Several partners have expressed interest in receiving the testbed technologies. A contract has been developed with the American Institute of Physics to clone the testbed software and processing. A similar contract is under development with American Society of Civil Engineers.
- Testbed continuance by university library: An industrial partnership programme has been established between the UIUC Library and publishers. A UIUC spin-off company has been formed to provide software and future services.

Semantic Research in Illinois DLI Project

The University of Illinois DLI project, through the partnership with the

Artificial Intelligence Lab at the University of Arizona, has conducted research in semantic retrieval and analysis.

In particular, natural language processing, statistical analysis, neural network clustering, and information visualization techniques have been developed for different subject domains and media types.

Scalable Semantics become Feasible

Statistical and neural network clustering proves useful and feasible interactively and for large-scale collections. Specifically, the AI lab has developed a noun phrasing technique for concept extraction, a concept space technique for building automatic thesauri, and a self-organizing map (SOM) algorithm for building category maps. More details are provided below.

Semantic indexes for large collections

Two large-scale semantic indexing simulations were performed in 1996 and 1997, respectively. We analyzed 400,000 Inspec abstracts and 4,000,000 Compendex abstracts to generate about 1,000 engineering-specific concept spaces (automatic thesauri) using the NCSA supercomputers (Convex Exemplar and SGI Origin 2000). Results of such computations could be used for semantic retrieval and vocabulary switching across domains.

FUNCTIONALITIES FOR FUTURE DIGITAL LIBRARIES

We are interested in the problem of *distributed resource sharing* in future digital libraries. We adopt a pure P2P architecture but our ideas can be easily modified to work in the case of hierarchical P2P networks, as in. *Information providers* (DLs) and *information consumers* (users) are both represented by peers participating in a peer-to-peer (P2P) overlay network. There are two kinds of basic functionality that we expect this architecture to offer: *information retrieval (IR)* and *publish/subscribe*. In an IR scenario a user poses a *query* and the system returns information about matching resources. In a pub/sub scenario a user posts a *subscription* to the system to receive notifications whenever certain events of interest take place. In this extended abstract we concentrate on the latter kind of functionality and sketch how to provide it by extending the distributed hash table Chord. *Distributed Hash Tables (DHTs)* are the second generation *structured* P2P overlay networks devised as a remedy for the known limitations of earlier P2P networks such as Napster and Gnutella.

We present a set of protocols, collectively called *DHTrie*, that extend the Chord protocols with pub/sub functionality. We assume that resources are annotated using a well-understood attribute- value model called *AWPS* in. Thus publications and subscriptions will also be expressed in *AWPS*. *AWPS* is based on *named attributes* with value *free text* interpreted under the Boolean and vector space (VSM) models. The query language of *AWPS* allows Boolean combinations of comparisons *A op v*, where *A* is an attribute, *v* is a text value and *op* is one of the operators 'equals', 'contains' or 'similar'. The following is an example of a publication in *AWPS*:

{ (Author, "John Smith"), (Title, "Information dissemination in P2P..."), (Abstract, "In this paper we show that ...") }

The following is an example of a query:

(Author = "John Smith") $\wedge$ *(Title* $\sqsupseteq$ *P2P* $\wedge$ *(information [0.0] alert))* $\wedge$ *(Abstract* $\sim_{0.7}$*"P2P architecture have been...")*

This query requests resources that have *John Smith* as their author, and their title contains the word *P2P* and a word pattern where the word *information* is immediately followed by the word *alert*. Additionally, the resources should have an abstract similar to the text value *'P2P architectures have been...'* with similarity greater than 0:7.

THE DHTrie PROTOCOLS

We implement pub/sub functionality by a set of protocols called the *DHTrie protocols*. The DHTrie protocols use *two levels of indexing* to store queries submitted by clients. The first level corresponds to the partitioning of the global query index to different nodes using DHTs as the underlying infrastructure. Each node is responsible for a fraction of the submitted user queries through a mapping of attribute values to node identifiers.

The DHT infrastructure is used to define the mapping scheme and also manages the routing of messages between different nodes. We use an extension of the Chord DHT to implement our network. The second level of our indexing mechanism is managed locally by each node and is used for indexing the user queries the node is responsible for. In this level, each node uses a hash table to index all the atomic queries contained in a query by using their attribute name as the key.

For each atomic Boolean query the hash table points to a *trie*-like structure that exploits *common words* and a hash table that indexes text values in equalities as in. Additionally for atomic VSM queries an inverted index for the most 'significant' query words is used as in. In this abstract as suggested, focus on the first level of indexing and present the sub- scription, publication and notification protocols that regulate node interactions. Protocols for query updating and removal are omitted due to space. The local indexing algorithms we use and their experimental evaluation are thoroughly discussed in.

The Notification Protocol

Once all the matching queries have been retrieved from the database, *P* creates notification messages of the form Q NOTIFICATION (*l*(*c*)*r*) and contacts all the nodes that their queries where matched against *p* using their IP address associated with the query they submitted. If a node *P'* is not online when *P* tries to notify it about the published resource, the notification message is sent to the *successor (p')*. In this way *P'* will be notified the next time it logs on the network. The modifications to the join and leave protocols of Chord to achieve this functionality originally presented in the non-DHT system P2P-DIET are omitted due to space considerations. To utilise the network in a more efficient way, notifications can also be batched and sent to the subscribers when traffic is expected to be low.

Frequency Cache

In this part, we introduce an additional routing table that is maintained in each node. This table, called *frequency cache* (FCache) is used to reduce the cost of publishing a resource by storing the IP addresses of the nodes responsible for frequent words contained in published documents. FCache is a hash table used to associate each word that appears in a published document with a node IP address. FCache uses a word w as a key, and each FCache entry is a data structure that holds an IP address. Thus, whenever P needs to contact another node P' that is responsible for queries containing w, it searches its FCache. If FCache contains an entry for w, P can directly contact P' using the IP stored in its FCache. If w is not contained in FCache, P uses the standard DHT lookup protocol to locate P' and stores contact information in FCache for further reference. Using FCache the cost of processing a published resource p is reduced to $O(v + (h — v) \log N)$, where v is the number of words of p contained in FCache. FCache entries are populated as follows. Each time a resource p is published at a node P, P contacts the nodes responsible for storing queries with words contained in p. After this process is over, P knows the contact information of those nodes, and stores it to FCache along with the word each node is responsible for. After that, for each publication taking place at P, P maintains this routing information for the most frequent words contained in resources published to it. Notice that the construction and maintenance of FCache is based only on local information and that the only extra cost involved is FCache misses and the routing information discovered is also cached for further reference).

BRIEF PRESENTATION OF EXPERIMENTAL RESULTS

We have evaluated DHTrie experimentally in a distributed digital library scenario with hundreds of thousands of nodes and millions of user profiles. For our experiments we used 10426 documents downloaded from CiteSeer and also used in. The documents are research papers in the area of Neural Networks and as suggested, refer to them as the NN corpus. Because no database of queries was available to us, our queries are synthetically generated by exploiting 2000 documents of the corpus. The remaining 8426 documents are used to generate publications. Our experiments show that the DHTrie protocols are *scalable*: the number of messages it takes to publish a document and notify interested subscribers remains almost constant as the network grows. Moreover, the increase in message traffic shows little sensitivity to increase in document size.

We demonstrate that simple data structures with only local information can make a big difference in a DHT environment: the routing table FCache manages to reduce network traffic by a factor of 4 in all the alternative methods we have studied. Since probability distributions associated with publication and query elements are expected to be skewed in typical pub/sub scenarios, achieving a *balanced load* is an important problem. We have studied an important case of load balancing for DHTrie and present a new algorithm which is also applicable to the standard DHT look-up problem.

THE NEW WEB PARADIGMS AND THEIR IMPLICATIONS FOR E-RESEARCH IN THE SOCIAL SCIENCES

The Future of the Web is yet unclear, but some approaches like Social Web, Semantic Web, and Cloud Computing have been used widely and can still be substantially improved. In this part as suggested, describe the new scenarios enabled by them in terms of e-research in the social and behavioural sciences, and as suggested, also glimpse at the possibilities offered to social scientists by future Internet proposals.

THE SOCIAL WEB

Despite of the fact that even from its first stages of development at the early 1990's the *World Wide Web* (WWW) had a flexible and collaborative design that allowed users to create new links and content, it was not until the beginning of the 21st century that this possibility became true by virtue of the technological and methodological evolution popularly known as the Web 2.0 or the Social Web. For the last two decades, Web users have moved forward from simply carrying out hypertextual data transfers to the socialization of many aspects of their lives. The Web has evolved towards the "Read/Write Web," achieving one of the goals initially proposed by its designers.

Describing this new stage of the Web as the "Social Web" seems more appropriate, since the adoption of the new technologies and methodologies involved has not been as abrupt or revolutionary as the term "Web 2.0" might suggest, but through a progressive process of socialization. There may be differences between both terms when explaining the origin of the change, but there is no such discrepancy when considering its effects. O'Reilly defines Web 2.0 applications as services that get better the more people that use them. Over the last 15 years, the Web has grown from an information-centered network into a people-centered social media in which user-generated content is crucial.

This trend is likely to continue further, considering that Future Internet aims at favouring user-empowerment. Two are the foundations of this Social

Web: users and data. Users generate content with different levels of implication, attract more users, and reshape platforms and Web services in terms of content and purpose. Data is the fuel that drives social media, regardless of whether it is generated by users or by other online services. Instead of conforming vast repositories of unrelated information, the Social Web's data is available in several standard formats, ready to be remixed, completed or updated by third-party services. As stated by Engeström, people do not just connect to each other using social media.

They connect through "shared objects," and good online services allow people to create social objects that add value to the rest of the users, and subsequently to the whole social media. Both these aspects of the Social Web can enhance e-research in social and behavioural sciences in two different ways. On the one hand, the Social Web allows using methodological approaches that would be unfeasible otherwise, providing cheap and effective ways to engage people in participating in experiments, or taking advantage from the sharing features of social media to distribute and process experimental data. On the other hand, the success of the Social Web has significant consequences from a psychological point of view, in terms of new or implicit behaviours in social media. Thus, the Social Web can be a good means for improving research methodology and, at the same time, an object of e-research in psychology.

IMPROVING RESEARCH METHODOLOGY THROUGH THE SOCIAL WEB

Many authors agree that the popularization of computational technology provides a new way to do science. Wolfram remarks the power of using computers when facing complex problems, even through simple programmes, delegating the tedious calculations to machines. Shneiderman, new kinds of science are needed to study the integrated interdisciplinary problems at the heart of socio-technical systems. This Science 2.0 combines the methods of traditional science with the opportunities offered by the Social Web to collect and process real-time empirical data. E-research in the social sciences is also involved in this evolution. In addition to academic social networks, general purpose social networks can be used to spread scientific findings or even to discuss them.

The idea of achieving insightful conclusions through open debates in social media is still very controversial for many reasons. Nevertheless, there is no such debate about using the social media as a way to recruit participants for experiments. Many social science experiments can take advantage from the wide range of ways to push information provided by the Social Web. It is easy to publish information regarding the experiment or to recruit potential participants using tags, categories, recommendations, groups, or fan-pages, without annoying other people with unsolicited notifications that could be considered as spam. Due to all the hints provided by user-generated content, the Social Web is able to hit very specific targets and avoid general and ineffective ways of promotion.

Thus, e-researchers in social sciences can reach very specific participants in studies that would be extremely difficult or even unfeasible without the social features of the Web. Apart from the increase in the number and prevalence of participants in social sciences experiments, the Social Web provides several techniques to analyse and exploit user-generated content. Virtually all social media services allow interacting with their data through *Application Programming Interfaces* (APIs). APIs allow consuming a Web service without using a browser to browse through service's Website contents. Features derived from APIs are often underestimated by non-programmers.

Using a real-life comparison, APIs can be shown as "delivery services" of a restaurant. If a family does not want to prepare dinner, they can either go to a restaurant or call to a delivery service. There are also mixed alternatives, like going to a restaurant and order a take-away meal, or even pay for a catering service at home. Coming back to Web services, the meal is the content that users need, and the delivery service is the API. There are some restaurants without delivery service that force customers to go to their place for a meal, as API-less Web applications do; and there are some other restaurants which provide both alternatives, and customers can decide whether it is worth going to the restaurant or it is better to have dinner at home.

Moreover, by using APIs, third-party developers can aggregate social services to create new ones, called "mash-ups". Another interesting feature of social media APIs is that they allow to access, collect, and analyse huge amounts of useful information. Older methodologies, like traditional offline experimentation or even online experimentation with no use of social media, can handle tens, hundreds, or thousands of participants. But using the APIs provided by social media, millions of interactions can be handled in real time. Eventually, the range provided by the API is able to cover the whole target population of the study, but it can sometimes be more limited in wide-range studies due to technical and economic reasons. Nevertheless, going from thousands to millions of interactions is a significant leap in e-research. For instance, Twitter's public APIs allow to access to the 1 per cent of all real-time 'tweets'—messages sent via Twitter—to third-party applications.

The third-party applications using Twitter APIs can apply to be whitelisted, which allows upgrading their quota and access to the 10 per cent of all Twitter content. This means a huge number of 2 to 20 million tweets per day for regular and whitelisted applications, respectively. Providing ways to build a third-party applications' ecosystem is at the core of all successful social media platforms. The case of Facebook is particularly remarkable because it enables the creation of successful business models within the social network, boosts the use of the

Facebook fan-pages by companies, and provides several interfaces to publish outside-generated content in Facebook, or *vice versa*, Facebook content in third-party platforms.

If Facebook's benefits from interconnectivity are considerable, Twitter's are outstanding. Although it is still unclear whether Twitter can be considered a social network like Facebook or not, Twitter describes itself as an "information network" where users find, curate, and deliver content, rather than socialize. Twitter users focus less on their social graph and more on information broadcasting. Paradoxically, Twitter's limitations are its biggest strengths: Its home page is extremely simple compared with other social media, text-based content and 140-character limitations encourage focusing on crucial information and the subscription-based social graph allows asymmetric relationships between users. Contrary to Facebook's symmetric relationships, where "friendship" is always bidirectional, a Twitter user can follow another user, while not being followed by her.

The simplicity of Twitter's Web interface contrasts with the large set of rich clients that extend the capabilities of the platform through an intensive API usage. Metaphorically, we can see Twitter as a government that builds highways, sets the regulations to use them and provides standard and simple vehicles. Users can choose to drive these standard vehicles or get others more adapted to their needs, as long as they fulfil the regulations. This is a standard feature of most social media platforms, but it is more evident in Twitter because of the extreme simplicity of its Web interface and the myriad of third-party clients. As Cheng and Evans found, in 2009 TweetDeck was the most popular non-Twitter.com publishing tool with a 19.7 per cent market share, and more than half of Twitter users used something other than Twitter.com. In 2010, as stated by Twitter's CEO, just 25 per cent of the content is generated from Twitter.com.

That is, 75 per cent of traffic comes from outside Twitter.com through the ecosystem provided by public APIs. Twitter is a good example of the success that public APIs can reach, but the rest of social media are also seizing the opportunity to offer content outside their platforms and enabling mixing their contents: Facebook users can share Youtube videos in their fan-pages or walls, blog editors can embed slideshows from Flickr and add social media links at the end of each post to share it across the Social Web, LinkedIn users can include Slideshare presentations in their resumes. Using APIs is not exclusive for social media, though. Wherever a dynamic map is needed, Google is providing it through Google Maps API. Social sciences e-researchers must take into account the fact that most of the Social Web's data is being heavily used and reused. Accounting reused information should be done carefully.

On the one hand, researchers should avoid populating their local databases with multiple copies of the same information. On the other hand, information reusage may imply relevance, and should be analysed on its own. Suh, Hong, Pirolli, and Chi studied the variables that predict Twitter content reusage. Agichtein, Castillo, Donato, Gionis, and Mishne question the simple metrics used when analysing social media, and introduce a general classification framework for combining the evidence coming from different sources of information, that can be tuned automatically for a given social media type and quality definition. The Social Web's public APIs are not the panacea to all problems related to content. Sometimes they are inadequate, insufficient or too complex to use. In those cases, e-researchers should look for third-party APIs with extra functionality or a wider range of provided information formats. GNIP.com is probably the best example of a third-party API provider, as it supplies its own APIs for more than 30 different social media.

For instance, GNIP. com provides several Twitter-related APIs with interesting extra features, like access to the 50 per cent of all Twitter content, delivered in real time, a stream of all Twitter statuses containing URLs, delivered in real time too or statuses that mention any given user. The main drawback of this kind of services is its price, not suitable for low-budget research initiatives. Even so, there are academic institutions that offer third-party social media APIs for free, but under some restrictions due to the costs involved in maintaining the service. Finally, when no API is provided to access relevant information from service providers, e-researchers still have some alternatives.

The first one is to take advantage from "Web feeds", if they are available. Web applications use web feeds to publish updated content in a standard way. Newspapers are probably the best example to illustrate the Web feed concept. In a newspaper's Web site, information is arranged by relevance and topicality. If someone wants to be informed, she should periodically access that Web site and look for new content. As this can be very difficult for some news, newspapers offer a publicly available time-ordered news list as a Web feed. Gathering the new content of a Web site is extremely easy when Web feeds are available. The main difference between API-based queries and Web feeds is that using the former allows advanced queries, whereas the later is limited to the last updates. Coming back to the previous comparison between APIs and pizza deliveries, a Web feed would be like a delivery where customers cannot order the pizza they want, but the last pizza that came out from the oven.

The second alternative when no API is provided is a technique called "Web scraping." Using Web scraping techniques, a researcher can convert human-readable data provided by a web site and defined in *Hyper Text Markup Language* (HTML) into raw data defined in an XML dialect or other data formats, and subsequently store and process it by means of a content analyser.

There are many problems related to Web scraping:

- The HTML code of some Web sites is not easy to parse to extract valuable data,

- Small changes in Web site's HTML code have large impact in the gathering process, and
- Extracting data from Web sites and using it in third-party services can sometimes violate Terms of Use and content license of the service provider.

In conclusion, there are many interesting features of the Social Web that can be very useful for e-research. Firstly, the Social Web is an excellent platform to promote ongoing experiments and to disclose findings, encouraging discussions about them and reaching a large-scale pool of people interested in participating in experiments. Secondly, the Social Web's stress on data reuse allows researchers to collect and process huge amounts of original information, using social media public APIs, third-party APIs, or even more complex techniques like Web feeds or web scraping.

THE SOCIAL WEB AS THE OBJECT OF E-RESEARCH IN PSYCHOLOGY

Over the last decade, the Social Web has gone through various stages. The social component of the Web is a key factor to understand why so many technologies are now considered obsolete, and why the findings of research studies conducted a few years ago no longer apply to the current situation. Linden and Fenn created a graphic representation of the maturity, adoption and social application of specific technologies to characterize the over-enthusiasm or "hype" and subsequent disappointment that typically happens with the introduction of new technologies.

As shown in Figure, a typical "hype cycle" consists of five phases:

1. *"Technology Trigger"*: The new technology is presented to the public with a proof of concept, trying to achieve media coverage.
2. *"Peak of Inflated Expectations"*: Everyone wants to use the new technology. Media organisations show it as the solution to every problem. There may be some successful applications of a technology, but there are typically more failures.

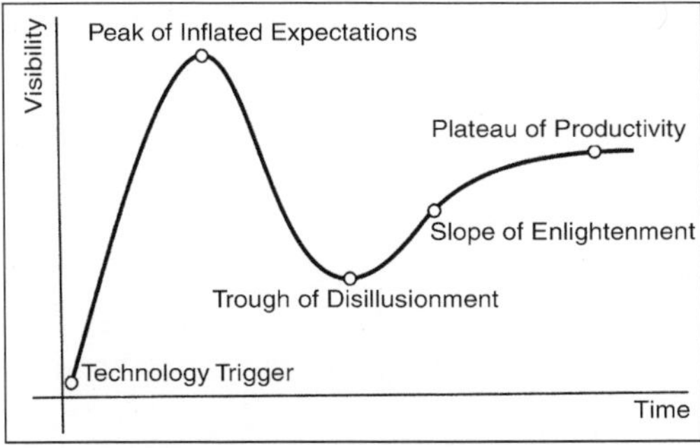

Fig. Gartner's Hype Cycle Phases

3. *"Trough of Disillusionment"*: Overenthusiasm vanishes and technology fails to be successful in all proposed scenarios. Media usually abandons the topic and the technology.
4. *"Slope of Enlightenment"*: The technology is improved and adapted to those specific situations where it was successful.
5. *"Plateau of Productivity"*: The benefits of using the technology are widely demonstrated and accepted. The technology becomes increasingly stable and evolves in second and third generations.

Blogging, like all technologies related to the Social Web, passed through the different phases of adoption, very similar to this "hype cycle." The number of blogs was consistently doubled every 6 months from 2003 until 2006 but needed 320 days to double in 2007. In 2008, there were 600,000 blog posts per day, less than in 2007. Did blogging reach the "Peak of Inflated Expectations" at the end of 2006? It is very likely that the success of Facebook and Twitter influenced in this decrease of blogging usage, but this can also be related to the fact that blogs were presented as the solution to all Web needs during the period from 2003 and 2007.

The over-enthusiasm was answered with the creation of companies focused in blog analysis but some of them changed their target when blogging became less popular. Nowadays, blogs are close to the "Slope of Enlightenment," as they are being used for the specific purpose they were created for. This crazy growth of expectations around the Social Web was described by Engeström as "butterfly flights," as they fly higher and higher, and suddenly descend to the floor. The same happens with social media adoption when they lose the users' interest. Thus, exponential growth rates should be considered cautiously in the Social Web, because they can be a sign of being at the "Peak of Inflated Expectations."

E-research in psychology has dealt with blogging by studying the causes and consequences of being a blogger. Even though there are diverse motivations for blogging, some authors suggest that it can be predicted from the big five personality traits: People who score high in openness to new experience and high in neuroticism too are more likely to be bloggers. Similarly, Hsu and Lin proposed a model based in the *Theory of Reasoned Action* (TRA) where ease of use, enjoyment, and knowledge sharing explain 78 per cent of the variance of being a blogger; and social factors and attitude towards blogging explain 83 per cent of the variance of continuing to blog.

In relation to the consequences of being a blogger, Baker and Moore found that intending bloggers were more psychologically distressed and more likely to use venting and self-blame to cope with their stress than non-bloggers. Intending bloggers also scored lower on measures of social provisions and were less satisfied with their number of online and offline friends when compared to non-bloggers. Consistent with the similarities between blogging and writing a diary, many of the benefits related to writing a diary have been found to also be present in blogging.

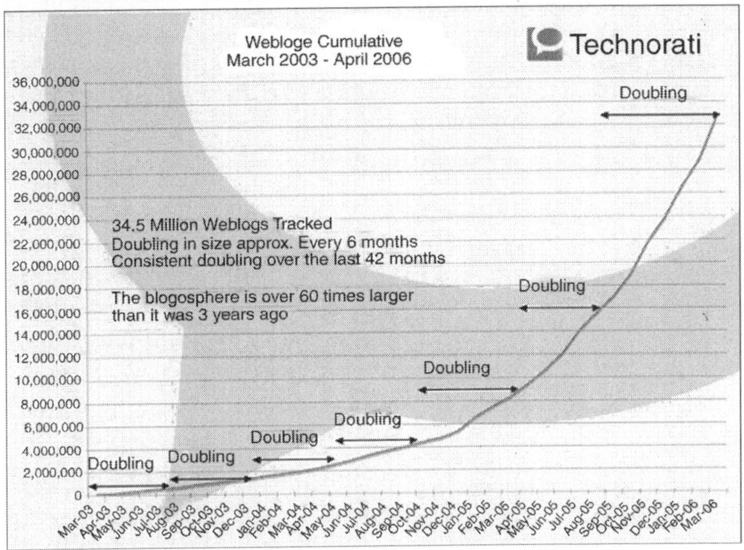

Fig. Weblogs Cumulative

Despite the fact that wikis did not attract the attention of many e-researchers in psychology, Amichai–Hamburger, Lamdan, Madiel, and Hayat studied personality characteristics of Wikipedia members and found that Wikipedia members locate their real me on the Internet more frequently than non-Wikipedia members. They also found significant differences in agreeableness, openness, and conscientiousness, which were lower for the Wikipedia members, and an interaction between Wikipedia membership and gender: Introverted women were more likely to be Wikipedia members as compared with extroverted women.

There is no doubt that online social networks have been hot topics for e-research in psychology. MySpace was the first online social network to reach an audience of more than 100 million people, creating huge expectations for this new way to socialize. Thelwall studied the motivation of MySpace members, finding significant differences between male and female. Female members tended to be more interested in friendship and males more interested in dating. As expected, female and younger members had more friends than others, and both genders seemed to prefer female friends, with this tendency more marked in females for their closest friends. Regarding privacy, females were more likely to maintain private profiles. Due to the extensive use of slang there are difficulties in parsing the messages shared on MySpace. However, Thelwall, Wilkinson, and Uppal found that two thirds of the comments expressed positive emotion, and that just a minority contained negative emotion. Perhaps unsurprisingly, females were more likely to give and receive positive comments than males, but there was no difference for negative comments. Torkjazi, Rejaie, and Willinger remarked the "hype cycle" of MySpace analysing the number of members.

The growth of allocated user IDs in MySpace was exponential until 2007 followed by a sudden and significant slow-down in 2008 motivated by an increase in the popularity of Facebook. Hargittai verified the struggle for new members between Facebook and MySpace and found significant differences according to their socio-economic situation. Students whose parents had lower levels of schooling were more likely to be MySpace members, whereas students whose parents had higher levels of education were more likely to be Facebook members. Facebook offers a reasonable trade-off between standardization and customization for members' profiles. Both characteristics are interesting from a researcher perspective: Having standard features makes profiles easily comparable, and customizations can be correlated with many other variables. Zhao, Grasmuck, and Martin found differences between anonymous online environments and social networks like Facebook, where most members use their real identity. Facebook members claim their identities implicitly rather than explicitly.

Other studies agree that Facebook profiles reflect actual personality rather than selfidealization, and can be used to predict owner's personality, especially for extraversion, but not so accurately for emotional stability. Rosen studied the tendency to publicly trumpet one's online friendships, and characterized it as a narcissistic quest for social status. Several authors came to a similar conclusion. For example, Buffardi and Campbell found that higher levels of social activity and self-promoting content in Facebook can be predicted through narcissistic personality self-reports. Ellison, Steinfield, and Lampe found a strong connection between Facebook use and perceived social capital. Social networks help to maintain relationships as people move from one offline community to another.

Such connections could have strong payoffs in terms of jobs, internships, and other opportunities, even in online environments. Lerman and Galstyan found evidence of it analysing the impact of the "social graph" in social news Websites: Users tend to like stories submitted by friends and stories their friends read and liked. Another important issue related to Facebook is privacy. There is a tendency for social media users to value privacy, security, and trust, but there are still inconsistent concerns about them.

For instance, Acquisti and Gross found that social networks users are mildly concerned about who can access their personal information and how it can be used, but not concerned about the information itself, mostly because they are the publishers of the content shared on the social network, and because they believe to have some control on its access. Moreover, there are many social motivators against privacy when using social networks, like having fun or allowing the social network to be a useful tool by sharing enough information.

Fogel and Nehmad concluded that general privacy and identity information disclosure concerns are more salient to female than male. Social media around "social objects" offers a wider range of alternatives to deal with privacy. Lange analysed social relationships among youth on Youtube, identifying various degrees of "publicness" in video sharing. Considering the anonymity and the access restriction as factors, four combinations could happen.

Lange remarked the use of two strategies to leverage anonymity while sharing content:

1. "Publicly private," in which video maker's identities were revealed, but content was relatively private because it was not widely accessed, and
2. "P rivately public," where content was widely accessible, but detailed information about video maker's identities was limited.

However, anonymity and privacy are not the same thing,and social media users should realise that both are important. Twitter is not really a social network, but an information network.

Perhaps the most interesting issue regarding Twitter is related to the fact that users reshaped the network, creating new ways of using it:

- When users needed a short way to answer a message, they added an "@" to the username to mean it;
- "RT" or "retweet" was unofficially created to express that the content is not original, but forwarded from other user; and
- As there was no tagging system on Twitter, users started to prepend a "#" to words to be considered as tags by other users.

Months later Twitter administrators realised that these new codes were "de facto" standards among the users and implemented them as official features. Taking into account its fast evolution in less than 5 years, studies published in the last years should be considered within its context, as their conclusions are not likely to apply to current Twitter activity. For instance, Java and Song concluded that the most common use of Twitter was talk about daily routine. This could be true in 2007, but nowadays people use Twitter with other purposes. Moreover, other particular characteristics of Twitter, like its text-based only content, asymmetric relationships or similar functionality for mobile users, make Twitter a great platform for e-research in social sciences. Cha, Haddadi, Benevenuto, and Gummadi analysed influence in Twitter and found that popular users who have a large number of followers are not necessarily influential in terms of spawning retweets or mentions.

Furthermore, a concerted effort seems to be the best way to gain influence in Twitter. Conversely Suh, Hong, Pirolli, and Chi found that the number of followers and "following", as well as the age of the account, seem to affect influence in Twitter in terms of "retweetability," while, interestingly, the number of past tweets does not predict retweetability of a user's tweet. It is also interesting the fact that URLs and hashtags have strong relationships with retweetability, confirming the shift of typical Twitter activity from daily routine to information sharing. Perhaps some of the controversial issues can be explained examining the topology of the social graphs. Mislove, Marcon, Gummadi, Druschel, and Bhattacharjee stated that online social networks have structures that differ from other networks, in particular the Web.

Social networks have a much higher fraction of symmetric links and also exhibit much higher levels of local clustering. *Location Based Social Networks:* (LBSN) go further in the real-time social media mobility. As LBSN users tend to be Twitter members, all of them are tightly connected with it, providing multiple ways to automatically publish their content on Twitter. This can be also problematic. Humphreys, Krishnamurthy, and Gill found that about a quarter of tweets included information regarding when people are engaging in activities and where they are. Educating users about the ways in which personal information can be used for alternative purposes is an important step in media literacy. Given the privacy and security issues in social networking, several radical approaches for social media are being tested. For example, Diaspora is a distributed social network that provides a decentralized alternative to services like Facebook.

The project is currently under development by Grippi, Salzberg, Sofaer, and Zhitomirskiy, and works by letting users set up their own server of the social network, or by using a server of a trusted organization. Diaspora servers interact to share status updates and other social data. Being open source software, it can be audited by security experts and checked for backdoors or other privacy leaks. With a decentralized schema, the members of an institution concerned about privacy, security, and trust can use the Diaspora server set up by their own IT department, and still socialize with the rest of the social network with no risk. Path.com offers another new concept: The personal network. Each path member creates her own personal network limited to her 50 closest friends.

This limit is based on the "Dunbar's number," a theoretical cognitive limit to the number of people with whom one can maintain stable social relationships. Although, Dunbar's research suggested 150 as the maximum number of social relationships, the network expands in factors of roughly 3. It is still too soon to assess such revolutionary approaches, but all of them suggest that there is much work to do in the Social Web in terms of privacy, security, and trust.

THE SEMANTIC WEB

When Berners-Lee, designer of the World Wide Web, described the Semantic Web with Hendler and Lassilla, the evolution of the Web appeared to be targeted towards a machine-readable World Wide Web, and not through the socialization of the technologies involved. Initially, Berners-Lee underestimated the Web 2.0 phenomenon, considering that most of the alleged new features were already present in his original World Wide Web design. He dreamed about a new Web where machines would be able to understand and work with the data transferred on interactions between people or other machines and prevent people from tedious and repetitive procedures that could be accomplished through machines talking to other machines. If so much data is already published on the Web, why do we still need to compare or aggregate it manually? For instance, a Semantic Web approach of "buying the cheapest flight from one place to another" would provide the automatic mechanisms to gather all the information from diverse sources, understand and integrate it into a semantic reasoner, and get the best offer among all processed ones.

Although the Semantic Web is a much bigger step compared with the Social Web, its current development status is promising but limited. The main reason is technological. Adapting a Web designed for humans to a machine-readable one is not a trivial task. The Social Web is the Web of people. Social media users generate, consume and share content. The Semantic Web is the Web of data. Semantic data provide enough meta-data to allow for automatic processing. Old hyper-text formats are too limited for this purpose, so new formats are needed. Semantic web formats should be able to describe data, define data properties, relationships among data, data classes or models, and logic rules to process data without human help. The *World Wide Web Consortium* (W3C) launched the Semantic Web Activity, where a big number of Working Groups are developing and adapting the Semantic Web standards. Designing the standard formats to build the Semantic Web is very important, but more actions have to be taken towards achieving a machinereadable World Wide Web.

The next step should be to start describing Web data using semantic formats, creating ontologies that explain and describe relationships between concepts. Under the field of the Semantic Web, an ontology is a formal representation of knowledge about a specific domain. Within an ontology, concept properties and relationships between them are explicitly described using a restricted vocabulary that allows automatic reasoning about them. Thus, defining and using ontologies are key factors for the Semantic Web's success, but it is not an easy task and experts are needed to supervise and correct the ontology defining process. Besides, in most of the cases experts cannot formally describe their domain of expertise and the formalization process may lead to a loss of accuracy. Ontologies are valuable tools used to process large amounts of data.

They are often confused with taxonomies—hierarchical, experts-made—or even folksonomies—nonhierarchical, amateurs-made. Both taxonomies and ontologies need experts to be precisely defined, but while taxonomies are focused on classifying, ontologies provide enough semantic metadata to enable automatic reasoning about the data. Perhaps, recurring to a widely-used example is the easiest way to understand ontologies better. There are different versions of the beer ontology, but regardless the semantic format used to describe it, all of them are very similar.

Figure shows a beer ontology that describes almost everything related to beer: Types of beer, ingredients, regions where beer is produced, awards and associations related to beer brewery, beer festivals, and so on. Expert knowledge about beer brewery is needed to create the beer ontology, because it has to be able to accurately describe every concept related to beer. Combining the beer ontology with a semantic reasoner and other Web services, a Semantic Web service would be able to fulfil complex queries like "show me the closest bars serving a pale ale beer with caramel, ordered by distance and beer price." Considering that data is the raw material of scientific research, the Semantic Web is tightly related to e-research.

Indeed, Engelbrecht and Dror suggest that cognitive psychology can contribute to the development of ontologies for semantic technologies and the Semantic Web in two different ways:

1. The efficiency with which activities that involve domain experts are carried out and the utility of the resulting ontologies can be improved by considering human information processing and its limitations, and
2. The human cognitive system, in general, and human knowledge representation, in particular, can act as a model for the structure of ontologies.

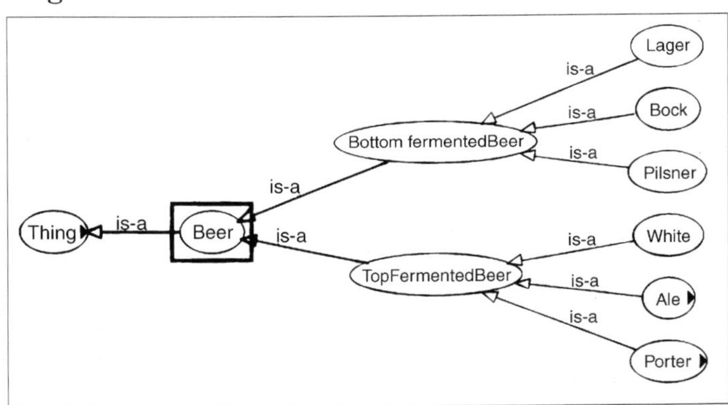

Fig. Partial View of a Beer Ontology

While it is essential to take into account the cognitive abilities of experts to create ontologies, it is also important to consider the opportunities that the Semantic Web could provide. Bairoch pictured the current situation: "It is quite depressive to think that we are spending millions in grants for people to perform experiments, produce new knowledge, hide this knowledge in an often badly written text and then spend some more millions trying to second guess what the authors really did and found." If all scientific knowledge published in thousands of peer-reviewed journals were stored using semantic formats, automatic reasoning could be used to infer vast amounts of new implicit knowledge, refuting established models, completing preliminary studies, or foreseeing new fields of research. W3C's Scientific Publishing Task Force was created with this goal. Actually, Aleman-Meza went further in reanalysing published data when they proposed a Semantic Web application that detects *Conflict of Interest* (COI) relationships among potential reviewers and authors of scientific papers.

W3C decided to encourage the use of Semantic Web technologies for Health Care and Life Sciences, for many reasons:

- These domains have to process huge amounts of complex data,
- There is a high level of interaction in managed data,
- Data sources are very heterogeneous and diverse,
- The benefits are crucial for humanity.

However, there are still some bad practices related to "in silico" experiments. Good and Wilkinson criticized researchers that prefer to develop their own and lesser-quality technological solutions in order to increase the number of publications and citations, which is precisely the opposite of the main goal of the Semantic Web. Having more and better applications using *Life Science Identifier systems* (LSID), *Resource Description Framework* (RDF), *Web Ontology Language* (OWL), and Semantic Web Services should discourage the use of non-standard technologies. What would be the psychological equivalent of large genomic databases? There is no direct equivalent, but as explained before, the Social Web generates millions of single interactions among social media users that could be semantically analysed to extract opinions, emotions and feelings and to infer new knowledge from them. Opinion Mining or Sentiment Analysis are two promising fields of research specialized on content analysis.

Some Web-focused companies are currently developing semantic parsers for social media content and many researchers are applying data mining techniques to information shared in social media. In two similar studies, Mislove and colleagues created cartograms based on the evolution of political topics on Twitter through time. Sakaki, Okazaki, and Matsuo proposed an algorithm to detect earthquakes in real time by social sensors. In a similar way, Asur and Huberman found significant correlations between box-office revenues of movies and social media activity prior to their public release. Finally, many other authors have worked on the integration of the Social Web and the Semantic Web, trying to take advantage of the best features of both approaches. Despite being so promising, the Semantic Web will not be widely available within the next few years, due to the technological and human resources involved. However, "Linked Data" is an attempt to progress towards a more realistic application of Semantic Web, where a cut-down data model empowered by the rich expressivity of new semantic standards is used to define vocabularies and instance data which are interlinked.

Thus, a global knowledge graph is being enabled under the auspices of Linking Open Data initiative, linking and bringing together concepts and relationships about different knowledge domains. An interdisciplinary and global science could arise from Open Data. In the meantime, less ambitious approaches, like microformats or "lowercase semantic web"— also known as "decaffeinated Semantic-Web" or "lower-s semantic web"—, can provide semantic features to the Web through simple semantic annotations. These annotations are often invisible to users but enable valuable third-party web applications and e-research initiatives. For example, each message or "tweet" transferred via Twitter contains not only the 140 characters sent by the user to the social network, but also tens of metadata fields regarding dates, location, user preferences, scope of the message and so forth. Reips and Garaizar used geo-location related metadata of millions of Twitter messages to create iScience Maps, a service that allows researchers to assess via Twitter the effect of specific events in different places as they are happening and to make comparisons between cities, regions, or countries and their evolution in the course of an event. Web-based research should be aware of this kind of solutions and apply them, when available.

NEW PARADIGM ADDRESSED BY FUTURE INTERNET

The current Internet, with billions of users worldwide is a great success in terms of connecting people and communities, but it was designed in the 1970s for purposes quite different from today's heterogeneous needs and expectations. The current Internet has grown beyond its original expectations and beyond its original design objectives. Many partial solutions have been progressively developed and deployed to allow the Internet to cope with the increasing demands in terms of user connectivity and capacity.

There is a growing consensus among the scientific and technical community that the methodology of continuously "patching" the Internet technology will not be able to sustain its continuous growth, and to cope with it at an acceptable cost and speed. The current Internet architecture is progressively reaching a saturation point in meeting increasing user's expectations and behaviours, as well as progressively showing inability to efficiently respond to new technological challenges.

Future Internet is a new term which summarizes the efforts made by international associations to progress towards a better Internet, either through:

- Small, incremental evolutionary steps, or
- Complete redesigns and architecture principles.

It should offer all users a secure, efficient, trusted, and reliable environment, that allows open, dynamic, and decentralized access to the network and adapt its performance to the users' needs and context.

Figure illustrates how the 4 pillars of Future Internet rely on the Future Internet networking infrastructure foundation:

1. Internet by and for people,
2. Internet of contents and knowledge,

3. Internet of services, and
4. Internet of things.

All the elements of the Future Internet need each other and are mutually dependent. New services and applications are a prerequisite for investments in new infrastructure, since Infrastructure without necessary capabilities cannot support new services and applications. New infrastructure technologies open new opportunities for new services and applications. Therefore, cooperation between all stakeholders is required for a successful Future Internet. Considering how all of these new approaches redefine the relationship between users and technology, their implications for e-research in Social Sciences are clear: Not only because of the methodological changes that will come, but also because of the wide range of new scenarios and their psychological and social implications.

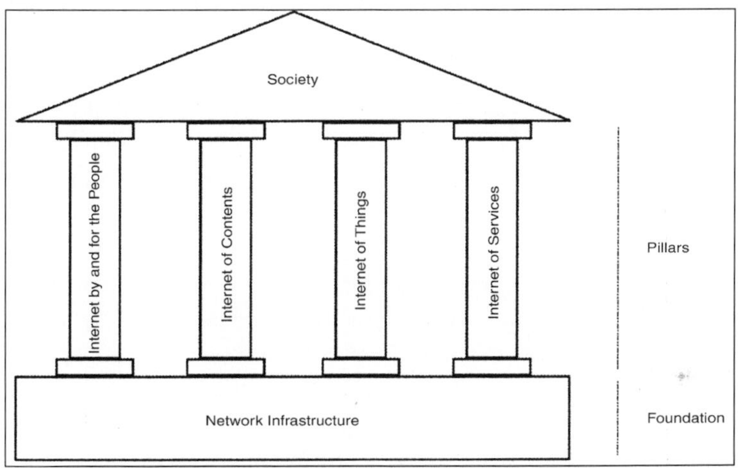

Fig. Future Internet Foundation and Pillars

THE WEB AS A PLATFORM

The most recent advances in the architecture of the Web allow using it as an excellent platform to deploy social science experiments over the Internet. In this part as suggested, discuss the specific implications for e-research in social sciences of those improvements, both on the server and the client-side.

SERVER-SIDE TECHNOLOGY: WOA, REST, CLOUD COMPUTING

The Web as a platform defines its services using *Web Oriented Architecture* (WOA), a design and modelling methodology that extends *Service Oriented Architecture* (SOA) to web applications. WOA represents information as resources that will be handled by user-agents and Web servers through a simple *Representational State Transfer* (REST) mechanism. In other words, simple interfaces using XML and *Hyper-Text Transfer Protocol* (HTTP). Regarding the infrastructure, Cloud Computing provides a platform to develop and deploy Web applications offered as services that can be consumed without knowledge about its use and the implementation of its resources. This set of technologies and design methodologies fosters the vision of the Web as a platform to develop and deploy all kind of applications, including social science e-research ones, empowering them with distributed, scalable and underlying technology agnostic services.

Although Web 2.0 has more commonly been known as the Social Web, some researchers have also highlighted another important facet of it: It transforms the Web into an application platform. This is explained by the fact that there are numerous services or functions published on the web as proven by the site programmableweb.com, where thousands of services, mainly offering easy to consume *Representational State Transfer* (REST) interfaces—a well-know approach to export functionality through the HTTP protocol—and smart combinations and aggregations of them in the form of Web mash-ups are published.

Learning this publicly available web-accessible functionality is very easy at first, developers only need to understand the methods, parameters and results returned by its *Application Programming Interfaces* (APIs). Therefore, they have given place to remarkable innovation in mash-up creation from the active Web developer community. Furthermore, the emergence of a new computing paradigm, namely Cloud Computing, where data and services lie in highly scalable data centers which can be ubiquitously accessed from any Internet-connected device, is addressing two key aspects for reliably pushing application functionality to the Internet: scalability and ease of deployment. Cloud Computing can be defined as a pool of abstracted, highly scalable, and managed compute infrastructure capable of hosting endcustomer applications and billed by consumption. Interestingly, Cloud Computing makes available a service hosting infrastructure for Web application server-side deployment through easily consumed REST interfaces.

Remarkably, Cloud Computing is designed to make more computing and storage resources available in a dynamic manner as the demand for the consumption of a given Web application grows in time. Big companies such as Google, Microsoft, and Amazon offer compelling Cloud Computing solutions on top of which e-research applications could be easily and scalably hosted.

CLIENT-SIDE TECHNOLOGY: FROM BROWSERS TO WEB APPLICATION PLAYERS

Thanks to the last decade's technological and social developments, the Web is progressively becoming something that cannot only be browsed, but also used for specific purposes. At present, it is becoming less and less frequent to use a Website just to have a look at news or to "jump" from one site to another, with no particular purpose in mind. Instead, many traditional desktop applications are being replaced by equivalent programmes offered as Web services that can be accessed by Web user-agents, now more similar to "application players" than to simple Internet browsers.

As we have already discussed, part of this evolution from static websites to current Web applications can be seen as the result of the natural development of the technologies that support the Web. However, the evolution of web user-agents has played an important role too, providing an execution environment increasingly similar to that of the traditional desktop applications. Many of these improvements have been made possible by the Hypertext Application Technology Working Group, an initiative of the developers of the main web useragents aimed at extending and updating the hypertext definition language used to design Web sites so that it can support the main functionalities of most applications, such as local storage, exchanging messages between documents, drag-and-drop features, browsing history management, or 2D immediate sketching, among others. The efforts made by the WHATWG, with the support of the W3C, gave rise to the specification of HTML5, which includes many of these improvements.

Let's analyse in detail the most important implications of HTML5 for e-research in social sciences. First, the "canvas" object for 2D sketching, the drag-and-drop events or the timed multimedia playing allows social science researchers to design experiments that, until this very moment, could only be conducted with desktop applications.

Given that the Web is increasingly being accessed from mobile devices, one can achieve several goals by being able to drag-and-drop elements directly with the fingers or by synchronizing the interaction with multimedia elements:

- The development of more attractive experiments,
- The possibility of interacting with the experiment almost anywhere and in any circumstances, thanks to the use of Web standards, and, most importantly,
- The study of psychological processes that can hardly be explored with the limited interactivity of traditional PCs.

HTML5 also offers interesting possibilities for Internet-based surveys, as it provides a new API for web forms that allows to edit documents, send data from one form to another, or even manage browsing history. Both types of studies, either interactive or form-based, can benefit from the local-storage functions offered by HTML5, so that experiments do not depend on the users' connectivity, which can facilitate longitudinal studies and also naturalistic experiments conducted outside the laboratory. An additional contribution of these standards to the new Semantic Web is their support for microdata management, brief semantic labels that can help to make inferences about the type of experiment being conducted, its published results or the relationship between that experiment and similar ones conducted by the same research team or related people.

In spite of these new possibilities, both WHATWG and W3C continue working on new specifications that allow Web user-agents to better compete with desktop applications. For instance, Web workers have been designed to accomplish background tasks. Similarly, Web storage, Web sockets, and serversent events can be used for a better integration of Web applications. The Geolocation API allows to place on a given map any web interaction in an automatic manner.

Finally, other data formats can be imported to HTML by means of SVG or MathML. The implications of all these tools for e-research are promising, not only because of the specific contributions made by each of them, but also because of the more general transition from an hypertext- and form-based Web to a different Web in which almost everything in a desktop is possible and the Web user-agents provide all the necessary functions to simplify this task.

CONCLUSION

Throughout this chapter, the different approaches of the Web as a platform for the development of social science experiments have been fully considered, from simple standalone web experiments to Cloud Computing based services accessed by Web application players. Researchers cannot only run their traditional experiments on the Internet to get larger and more representative data, as has become usual during the last decade, but they can also benefit from the new Web technologies and the increasingly social character of the Web. The Social Web can be used as a research platform to collect data that can be used to contrast psychological or sociological theories on how people interact, reason and feel in different settings. Likewise, the recent developments in Cloud Computing and in the design of Web-user agents will allow conducting more interactive and realistic experiments on the Internet.

Moreover, the way people interact and behave on the Internet may not be a mere reproduction of the offline social behaviour. The peculiarities of this medium and the impact it might have on behaviour, as well as the personal factors that influence their use, are becoming important issues in current social science research. Psychological research can also make an important contribution by endowing people with the cognitive skills necessary to grasp knowledge in this vast universe of information, while protecting their privacy.

Although our discussion has focused mainly on our own area of expertise, experimental psychology, other social sciences, such as marketing, sociology, politics, economics, education, or anthropology, should benefit to a similar extent from these new technologies. During the next years, the combined efforts of these disciplines and computer scientists will surely provide new and intriguing insights on human behaviour.

2

Design and Development of Web-Enabled Databases

Application of computers certainly has improved the ways in which we acquire, process, store and disseminate information in libraries. As a result, we have automated house-keeping operations, catalogue and, user services in libraries. Moreover, with the advancement in the network technology during last decade, we have started providing user services through various online modes *viz.,* e-mail, FTP, Telnet, etc. These static/interactive modes of data/ information sharing over network have improved the library services and, their popularity among the users. During 1994, libraries began to show their presence on the internet by setting up their web sites. In the beginning, libraries built their web pages by providing mainly static information.

However, in the late 1997, libraries began re-engineering their web pages with the intention of providing information from databases in a dynamic manner . Today the advancements in web and database technology have enabled the libraries to share/publish the data/information directly from the databases over the internet. Now web has become a dynamic platform for information delivery over the internet and very useful for libraries to provide various user services. This paper intends to provide an overview of the database tools available for designing in-house databases in the libraries as well as the web technology for publishing such databases over the web. Besides, the paper discusses the need of developing in-house databases in libraries, advantages of web-enabled databases, and selection of database tools from RDBMS commonly available.

DATABASE SEARCHING IN CENTRAL UNIVERSITY LIBRARIES

In consequence of the recommendation of the National Knowledge Commission, each of the Indian states has at least one fully-funded central university. Now there are 39 central universities. Privately funded and owned statelegislated universities are also being established to cater to the increased demand for higher education. In between there are many universities that are not legislation-based but are authorized by the University Grant Commission to award degrees. Central universities are better-equipped in terms of financial resources, faculty, and infrastructure, and thus have an edge over the usually fund-starved state universities. The libraries across the globe are challenged to integrate e-resources into their collection, services, and patrons' lives and academic libraries face obstacles when virtual learning environment (VLEs) become "the primary means of interaction between students and universities.

Providing access to electronic journals and other e-resources is an important area of librarianship. The design of usable online interfaces is a crucial issue. Traditional library services and printed material are still more effective to researchers in Indian universities than web-based information and resources. Barriers to progress in this area in university libraries in India cannot be overlooked.

NETWORK INFRASTRUCTURE AND STRENGTH

Fast and effective information retrieval to support information sharing requires sound and wide network with adequate bandwidth. The UGC-sponsored Infonet is the mainstay of the academic info-network infrastructure. The UGC has constituted a national committee called the Central Monitoring Committee (CMC) for smooth implementation and execution of information infrastructure. The CMC has chosen ERNET India (Education and Research Network) to establish information network in universities. The committee has recommended high bandwidth campus wide networks for Internet and external connectivity. So far 149 universities have been provided connectivity with raw bandwidth ranging from 512 KBPS to 20 MBPS. The Inflibnet is administering and funds its cost for all these universities.

Retrieval Techniques

Net Server and CD-ROM mirror servers are very popular among the universities. The university libraries under study no longer provide CD-ROM services. Multimedia databases are available only in DU and JNU, while all the eight libraries own and provide access to full text and bibliographic databases. For academic libraries the two most important consortia are the UGC-Infonet and Indest. All the libraries have self-subscribed as well as consortia based databases, whereas the DU and JNU have also developed in-house databases.

Being traditional and general universities under the preview of the UGC, all are members of the UGC-Infonet, while DU is also member of AICTE Indest consortia. All the universities use commercial as well as open source databases while DU and JNU have also their home grown databases. Open source databases are also available there, but the study found that only DU, BHU, IGNOU and JNU host important open source online databases on their websites. Other universities are not able to create this kind of facility for their users merely because the staff of these libraries are not conversant with open access sources on the Internet.

Databases can be accessed through login and password, but the misuse of these is a common complaint. Therefore, IP access is more suitable. Now most of the universities allow online access to databases either through their intranet or directly from the Web. Experienced librarians prefer a campus-wide facility for providing access to databases. AU, IGNOU, Jamia, JNU and Viswabharati allow access from limited and specified terminals within campuses. Assam, IGNOU, Jamia, JNU and Viswabharati allow access through campus wide Intranet or Internet with identification and password. Many busy scholars and faculty have less time to visit the library. Therefore, access to online information must be provided on their desktops. This requires campus wide Internet accessibility. Further it was found that AU, BHU, DU, Jamia, JNU, PU and Viswabharati allow IP enabled access while IGNOU databases are password based.

Download Facility

Downloading of the required files is a critical issue. In case of commercial databases it is costly as the host library has to pay per download. But indeed it is an essential facility. It has been found that all the libraries provide downloading of PDF and HTML files, while image downloading facilities are available in all except at BHU and DU. RTF downloading is not permitted by BHU, DU and Jamia Millia Islamia, Whereas word file are not downloadable at BHU, DU and Jamia. DU and JNU provide DBMS software to download the data oriented information.

Data Retrieval Techniques

Some of the universities provide common databases linked through federated search. Only DU has the federated search engine GIST find. In this survey, only DU and PU revealed their online search techniques while the other libraries kept these confidential. DU uses Boolean, Interactive, and Proximity searches, while PU uses quick search.

Simple search Advanced/Boolean search in addition to menudriven searches are provided by their vendors. Both these libraries provide facilities for further refinement of large chunks of search output to make the search more precise and relevant. Nevertheless, none of the universities use data mining.

Complexity of Information Retrieval

Indeed information retrieval techniques vary from university to university system. It depends upon both internal and external factor of database. In the questionnaire about 48 aspects or facilities for information retrieval were identified and the users of these eight libraries were asked to mark their ease of use on the Likert scale as:

- Easy 3
- Challenging 2
- Difficult 1

User Orientation

For optimum use of all resources and services of a library, user orientation programmes, especially of new users, are a proven effective measure. User orientation is the most important component in the online databases for the users to gain knowledge and enhance usability of databases. All the university libraries in this study have positively voted for provision of such programmes to help users in the effective use of the retrieval system for information access. This survey found that orientation programme are conducted by all except AU, BHU, IGNOU, and Viswa Bharati. It is important to note that regular orientation programmes are required to make the users familiar with new feature of new databases. DU conducted programmes as "How to search the online databases," while the Pondicherry library provides instructions in the use of library resources including eresources and effective online searching. BHU conducts programmes on Science Direct and Proquest. DU provides need-based instruction and PU provides general instruction in effective search and the publishers also conducted such programmes to faciliatets searching of their supplied databases.

DU conducts such programmes throughout the years, while PU organizes orientation of the users at the beginning of the academic years. PU also offers need based person to person training. It is clear that there is no uniform pattern of conducting user's orientation programmes. Indeed we need a dedicated library staff for online training of library users, especially in the electronic environment. There are posts of information scientist in universities funded initially by the by UGC. Those hired are mostly from computer science and not conversant with library philosophy and routine.

There is an urgent need of a designated post for an online librarian who can provide assistance in using e-resources and may also take care of any aspect of user orientation for sharing and dissemination of library e-resources. The survey showed that none of the library staff has any formal education and training in online searching. Most have learned it on the job, and most have learned by trial and error.

IN-HOUSE DATABASES IN LIBRARIES

There are a number of ready-made library automation software packages in the market which can be used to automate the library functions and user services. However, many of these packages lack web interface and, thus, do not provide library database access (OPAC, etc.) through web. Moreover, these commercial packages provide less flexibility to librarians for making desired changes to the existing databases and to publish the same on the web.

An in-house designed database system provides full flexibility to the developer/administrator/librarian and is simpler to install, maintain and, use without having to rely on external support, and also is highly customizable and can be designed to meet local needs. Librarians can also participate in design/ development process as now a days easy and user-friendly database tools are available with in-built web interface. As per the survey conducted in order to get a clear understanding of the current role of library web master, 100 percent of the respondents felt that librarians should have some role in web site design and maintenance .

BENEFITS OF WEB-ENABLED DATABASES

Web-enabled databases have certain advantages over other means of sharing/publishing information over internet. These advantages are common to bibliographic databases also where libraries can put their OPACs and other databases on web. According to L.J.Haravu ; Kristin Aantelman and; Chong Ho Yu , the benefits of web-enabled databases are as follows:

- Global/wide ac cess to data with a sin gle user in ter face
- Format in dependent ac cess of data (text, graph ics, au dio, video, etc.)
- Up-to-minute up dated ac cess of data in real time
- Dynamic updation of data from many locations
- Cost-effective way of data sharing
- Instant feedback from users
- Seamless links from resource to resource
- Unlimited download/printing
- Environmental friendly.

Besides, Ortiz-Repiso and Norm Medeiros have written excellent papers on differences between traditional v/s innovative means (web OPACs) of library catalogs, while B. Ramesh Babu, *et al* have presented an overview of web OPACS with their advantages in libraries.

DATABASE TOOLS

In the early days of database development, it was the flat-file system to store data in a single file by using field separators and record separators. Later, such flat-file systems were facilitated by an index in which a single index file stored keywords and pointers to the records that were stored in main file. This made retrieval more efficient, still flat-file systems were seriously inefficient. It showed data-redundancy, poor data control, and did not supported complex data types (audio, video, graphics, etc.) . After 1960s, two database models were developed in quick succession to solve the limitations of flat-file systems. These database models were Hierarchical Database Model and Network Database Model. The Hierarchical Database composes of a root segment, parent segments and child segments. This model depicts a set of one-to-many relationships between a parent and its children. However, this model has number of limitations. It does not include ad hoc querying capability and, a multi-parent relationship is difficult to implement, as in a many-to-many relationship.

The Network Database Model attempted to deal with many of the hierarchical model's limitations. The network database structure easily accommodates the multiple child, although, its structural complexities often limit its effectiveness and efficiency. Both of these database models are obsolete now mainly because of their incompatibility with web environment and have been replaced by RDBMS. RDBMS is the current database implementation standard being used for publishing information on the web. It includes the following features which make it suitable for web environment:

- Provide extremely useful tools for database administration;
- Adhere to powerful query language SQL (structured query language) developed by Microsoft Corporation;
- Compliant with ODBC/JDBC and other database interface tools;
- Work in client/server mode;
- Offer distributed database and distributed processing options; and
- Have referential integrity controls to ensure data consistency and, thus, suitable for web environment.

It is easier to design applications in RDBMS due to the following features:

- Requires less programming skill
- Availability of third party tools, and
- Inbuilt web interface.

These all features of RDBMS have made them ideal for library applications to setup bibliographic database solutions and publishing them over the web. In the early days of library systems development, vendors have designed library applications software by using pre-relational database technology. Still some library systems suppliers are continuing to maintain and develop such products.

These proprietary library applications software have their own advantages and disadvantages. However, in the library management systems marketplace, there is a growing trend towards the use of RDBMS. Some of the common RDBMS which can be used to design in-house databases in libraries are *MS Access, SQL Server, Oracle, Informix, Sybase, File Maker Pro, SAS,* etc. However, the selection of suitable RDBMS for library applications depends on the particular library requirements, kind of applications (bibliographic/full-text/ numeric), the application level (database level/data warehouse level), magnitude of data (number of records/length of fields), nature of data analysis (basic statistics, *i.e.,* sum, average, mean/advance statistics) and, comprehensiveness and inter-operability.

Other points to be considered while selecting database tools for library applications are easiness, user-friendliness, flexibility and low cost. In most of the cases in libraries where bibliographic databases are dealt with, commonly available consumer database products such as *MS Access*, and *File Maker Pro* are sufficient. These products can support up to 1GB of data and provide cheaper solutions. However, these database tools are suitable for small databases and not useful for large databases, hence provide limitations in web environment.

There are specific database solutions for large databases available from *MS SQL Server, DB2, Oracle, Informix, Sybase,* etc. These database tools support up to several terra byte of data; permit thousands of simultaneous users; work in client/server mode; show natural affinity towards web environment and, thus, suitable for large bibliographic, web-enabled databases in libraries. However, to design full-text databases in libraries where large files are to be stored and retrieved, these tools do not offer good solutions as most of these tools support 200-255-400 characters field length. Although, many of these tools allow unlimited entries in memo field, the data inside a memo field are not searchable and thus, offer limited utility.

In this respect, *MS SQL Server* has extended the searchable field length up to 8063 characters and thus, provide solutions for moderate full-text databases. As a common trend , a number of libraries have been using open source software available either free or on nominal prices. These database management systems include the most common *mySQL, mSQL* and, recently updated *PostgreSQL*. These database tools are easy to work and run on various platforms such as UNIX, Lynux, NT, etc. Besides, there are some library specific text retrieval database tools for management of full-text large files, generally known as 'Free Form Databases', provide powerful search engine. Although, in some ways they are at the opposite end of the RDBMS, little database structure imposed on the designer and, thus, provide an easy and readymade database structure. However, they provide some limitations in achieving integration in the modules other than searching such as cataloguing, classification, management module, etc. These software are *BRS/Search, Basis Plus, Status,* etc.

WEB TECHNOLOGY

World Wide Web or WWW or web, sometimes wrongly mentioned as synonymous to internet, is a sub-set of it and is a most promising mode of publishing/sharing of data/information. Now, the web has emerged as the dominant protocol over internet due to its special features like easy interfacing of diverse platforms/technologies; provision to incorporate text, graphics, audio and video, etc.; permitting to access data/information in a non-linear way and; jumping from one document/resource to another through hyperlinks.

The superiority of www over other modes of online sharing *viz.,* e-mail, FTP, Telnet, Gopher, etc., has been well explained by Paul Scully . In fact, web has provided a single user interface to facilitate the user interaction with the databases or systems resources. The web uses unique URL (universal resource locator) address which facilitates the access of information seamlessly across the diverse platforms in a client-server mode. The actual data represented in a structured way reside in a powerful computers called server, while the latter is equipped with server tools/software to populate the information over web.

The client/user equipped with web browser such as Microsoft Internet Explorer (MSIE) and Netscape Navigator, etc., which interact with the server through common communications protocol TCP/IP over high speed network/ internet. In fact, the client/user sends its query to the server while the latter processes the request and gets the response/results from the database and sends it back to the client/user over the web.

COMPONENTS OF WEB-BASED SYSTEMS

WEB BROWSER

It is a software that helps users to interact with the server for sending queries and getting results over the web. MSIE and Netscape are the most popular web browsers, both of these are available free.

Web Server

Web server is the software that helps in sharing the system resources/ files over the internet through web browsers. The latter communicate with a web server via the standard Hyper-Text Transfer Protocol (HTTP). In fact, web servers receive queries from the client, process it, get data from databases and send it back to the client over web. The popular web servers are Apache, Microsoft IIS, iPlanet from Sun-Netscape alliance, and newly developed *Zeus* from Zeus Technology Ltd. Although web servers are increasingly found as components within full-featured server operating systems, there are some basic selection points that should be highlighted. These points are scalability and performance; high availability and reliability; interoperability and open standards; system administration and; security . In fact, there are not much choice in the web server segments as many of them come along with database tools, show natural affinity with the database tools from same vendor, and some other work better with certain platform/operating systems. According to the widely followed Netcraft web survey, approximately 60 percent of web servers run Apache, with Microsoft's IIS and the Netscape/iPlanet web server as its major competitors. However, Gartner studies have given Netscape/iPlanet a larger share of public web sites, followed by Apache and Microsoft/IIS. Apache is being used for the public sites of companies such as Merck, American Express, Texaco, Chrysler, and others.

However, it is easier to find both Microsoft/IIS and Netscape/iPlanet as the servers for large corporate public web sites when using the lookup facility offered by Netcraft. Also, for intranets, most counts credit Microsoft/IIS and Netscape/iPlanet as the leaders, followed by Apache, IBM's Lotus Domino Go server, and others. Among hot e-commerce sites, E*Trade runs the Netscape/iPlanet server, eBay runs Windows/IIS, and Amazon runs Apache (the Apache-based Stronghold Secure Server), according to the Netcraft web survey .

WEB AUTHORING TOOLS

Basic web server software does nothing except it sends HTML data in response to a browser request. However, certain other web-authoring and scripting tools are required to extend the functionality of web server to extract the data from databases. These web-authoring tools (*HTML* and its derivatives; and other Markup languages, etc.) and scripting tools (*Perl, C++, Java Script, JScript, VBScript,* etc.) are required to write web pages and scripts to interact with back-end databases. In early days of web-based applications, *CGI* (common gateway interface) Programmes were used extensively to extend the server functionality by allowing web users to interact with the web server to request specific data from the databases. Although, writing *CGI* program is difficult and requires programming skill, however, it works with high reliability.

Now a days, a number visual editors are available to generate the web pages and write scripts automatically. The common editors are *Microsoft Front Page, Visual Interdev, Netscape Composer, Web Builder,* etc. Besides, other technologies have been introduced to communicate with the back-end databases. These technologies are Microsoft *Active Server Pages (ASP)* and *Java Server Pages (JSP)* from Sun Micro Systems. Both the technologies have combined the HTML codes with the scripts in a single page and thus, making it easier to interact with back-end databases. During last few years, object-oriented and component based solutions were added to further make it easier to interact with the back-end databases. These solutions include:

- Microsoft COM/DCOM,
- ActiveX Data Objects (ADO);
- OMA and CORBA (Common Objects Request Broker Architecture) from Object Management Group;
- Sun's EJB (Enterprise Java Beans),
- Java Applets (for client) and
- Java Servlets (for server), etc.

Besides, some database connectivity tools such as ODBC and JDBC have also emerged as in-built features of operating systems, etc.

FREE WIZARDS AND THIRD PARTY TOOLS

Writing HTML codes and scripts for database interaction is the most difficult part, requires programming skill, systems logic and manipulation planning, especially for non-computer professionals. However, a number of free wizards and third party tools are available on internet which can generate hundred of lines of codes automatically with a single click, thus, making it easier for non-skilled users to set up web-enabled database solutions in libraries. Some of the free wizards are Rule Zero, Power ASP, Active Server Pages Tools and Components, etc. Besides, *Microsoft FrontPage* also provides database wizard to generate *ASP* pages/*VBScripts* automatically to interact with back-end databases, while *Visual InterDev* provides a visual interface to develop a web-enabled web site with minimum efforts.

XML AND RELATIONAL DATABASES: USES AND OPPORTUNITIES FOR LIBRARIES

Extensible Markup Language (XML) is becoming an indispensable tool for virtually every type of content that is digitally produced. The advantages of XML for libraries have been well described by others. On a general level, XML has at least three key advantages:

- *XML is standard*. XML is a subset of Standard Generalized Markup Language (SGML), a well established and highly regarded ISO standard. XML also offers mechanisms (document type definitions, and more recently, XML Schema) to encourage and enforce common definitions of the logical structure of a document so that standards for the documents themselves are easier to apply.
- *XML is extensible*. XML has no limits on the number of markup languages that can be defined using it, and each of these languages can consist of an unlimited number of tags. This flexibility is essential for fostering the widespread adoption of XML and helps explain why XML has been utilized for markup languages in every conceivable subject area, ranging from chess playing to mind reading.
- *XML is well supported*. It seems that almost every serious Web technology is now expected to define its relationship to XML, and XML has fostered an explosion of related technologies. The W3C has made many tools and toolkits freely available to Web developers, and utilities and applications for XML are being developed by a worldwide community of vendors, open source contributors, and other groups that seek to move information across the Web.

XML has been used extensively for authoring standalone documents, but database solutions for storing and managing large collections of materials in XML format are becoming more common. As Bourett, a researcher who tracks developments in XML databases, points out, choosing between an RDBMS and other database options for storing XML often comes down to whether you are working with data or documents. If the XML content is usually manipulated at the individual field level, needs to be accessed with standard query and reporting tools, and pulls together information from sources that are updated and maintained separately, then a Relational Database Management System (RDBMS) approach may make the most sense. Examples of this kind of "data-centric" content include purchase orders, flight schedules, and scientific data.

If the XML content is largely contained in individual documents, and the content will be edited and updated at the document level, then Object Orientated Databases (OODBMS), Object/ Relational Databases, and other solutions that can maintain XML documents as a more complete unit on the backend will be preferred. Data housed in an RDBMS are typically based on individual rows in tables, using "keys" or "ids" to pull together content dynamically. Most RDBMS solutions for storing XML assemble XML representations of the data on the fly. Object relational databases and some RDBMS addons, such as Oracle's Internet File System (IFS), step slightly outside of the standard RDBMS tables to work with Binary Large Object (BLOB) or other mechanisms built into the database to store whole XML documents without parceling pieces of it to separate tables.

This allows the document to be stored with all tags and ordering preserved. Of course, the data and document distinction is not absolute, and there are other factors that can influence the choice of a database. An organization may have built up a high level of Oracle experience, for example, and that would have a huge impact on any data management decisions. Libraries are also in a somewhat unique situation in that they house collections of both data-centric and document-centric materials that may require database solutions. For example, libraries with finding aids in Encoded Archival Description (EAD) format or full text materials marked up with Text Encoding Initiative (TEI) are more likely to favour "document-centric" solutions and require extensive full text searching capabilities that are more prevalent in OODBMS and Object/ Relational Databases. Libraries are even more likely to deal with content that is "data-centric", such as purchase orders and circulation records; they may already have RDBMSs in place to support the processing activities associated with this data.

MARC AND XML

The difficulty in separating data from document-based content can be seen in the Machine Readable Cataloguing (MARC) format, one of the library community's most successful and durable standards. Like many document-centric formats, MARC records can carry a lot of text-intensive information. Libraries may even choose to convert MARC records to standalone XML documents in order to take advantage of mainstream XML tools for indexing or for presentation purposes. On the other hand, MARC records are "data-centric" in the sense that they can often bring together data sources that are maintained outside of the bibliographic description of an item. Authority, holdings and item records, for example, play a key role in helping to define the bibliographic view of the physical and virtual objects in the library's collection, yet these records are often processed and updated separately. Libraries have begun to explore the use of XML for MARC. Lane Medical Library at Stanford University has created a DTD and released conversion software for converting MARC records to XML documents in an initiative called XMLMARC. K.T. Lam has also proposed a DTD for MARC and suggests that the use of a decentralized authority repository may one day be possible with XML linking technologies.

This would allow libraries to "point" to established names and subjects that could be maintained remotely rather than replicated by each individual library. Clearly, there is interest on the part of libraries in bringing MARC fully into an XML environment. The challenge is to define an XML infrastructure that can handle the amount of materials that libraries catalogue without isolating the content from the transactional processes that libraries use for acquiring and circulating the collection. Cataloguing records are typically maintained by dozens of library staff and are linked to ordering and circulation processing procedures that involve many updates. Any application of XML that is tied directly to where cataloguing records are maintained and use XML as a means of updating content may need to be "transaction aware" and support a high level of multi-user access.

MIDDLEWARE ALTERNATIVES

A number of middleware mapping tools exist for layering XML representations of information that is housed in an RDBMS on top of individual tables, such as IBM's DatabaseDOM. The middleware typically uses Structured Query Language (SQL) to pull together the fields needed for the XML input/output. The advantages of this approach are that this greatly increases the number of database systems that a library can select from because all major RDBMSs support SQL, and that this allows great flexibility for moving from one database to another. For formats like MARC, these tools also offer the possibility of using XML technologies without losing the robustness of relational databases for maintaining content and linkages that are updated by multiple users. The disadvantages of this approach include the overhead required to assemble and disassemble XML documents as they move in and out of the database, and the extra groundwork to define an XML representation that takes full advantage of both the RDBMS and XML technologies.

A good example of an XML mapping tool for relational databases is Castor, an open source project from Exolabs. The mapping file in Castor determines how the XML will be produced from the contents of the RDBMS. In addition to defining whether a field in the RDBMS is to be rendered as a node or an attribute, an ID reference is provided that identifies the records in the appropriate table. Castor is very "Java-centric," which can be an advantage or disadvantage depending on how comfortable an organization is with the Java platform. By working with Java, a developer can use Castor to render the records in an RDBMS accessible and updatable as XML documents. Databases that can be used with Castor include Oracle, MySQL, and PostgreSQL.

CURATED DATABASES

The term 'curated' comes from the Latin curare–to care for. Of course, all valuable data sets are cared for in some way or other, but the term curated database is normally re- served for those databases whose content has been collected by a great deal of human effort through the consultation, verification, and aggregation of existing sources, and the interpretation of new raw data.

Many curated databases act as publications and are currently replacing the traditional reference works found in libraries such as dictionaries, encyclopedias, gazetteers, etc.

Some notable examples of curated databases include:

- UniProt, which forms the standard reference for protein sequence data in molecular biology. It currently consists of over 300,000 entries. This database has a large team of dedicated curators and is typically regarded as a 'gold standard' of protein databases.
- The CIA World Factbook, which is probably the most widely used source of demographic data. It was first published as a book around 1990 and was there- after released annually. For the past 8 years or more the Factbook has also been published on-line. Recently, the interval between releases of the on-line version has been reduced to two weeks.
- The IUPHAR receptor database, which describes the molecules that transmit information across the cell membranes. This database is typical of a very large number of small curated biological databases. For ex- ample, unlike UniProt and the World Factbook, it is not backed by a large organisation: most of the cu- ration effort is supplied by volunteers, and only two people are involved with its direct maintenance.

Wikipedia and other wikis are also curated in that they are the product of direct human effort, and they provide some of the features we believe are desirable for curated databases. Wikis differ from most curated databases in that there is little or no structure imposed on the entries.

Curated databases—whether or not they are supported by relational database technology—are usually designed to be machine readable and thus amenable to data extraction tools, such as query languages that are common for databases. Socially, curated databases differ from wikis in that the curation process is usually more heavily orchestrated in the latter.

How ever, there is much to be gained by trying to combine the best of wiki and database technology and some of the research we describe in later parts is an attempt to do just that. The examples above form only the tip of the iceberg. The number of publicly available curated databases is exploding thanks to today's web technology, which makes it relatively easy to publish new databases on-line. Molecular biology alone, for instance, boasts over 1000 on-line databases, many of which are curated.

Measured by the work that goes into producing them, the cost of curated databases is huge. For example, there are over 150 people listed as working full-time on UniProt. As publications, curated databases provide academic kudos: the 'authors' of databases such as UniProt and OMIM are known primarily for providing comprehensive reference works. Given their importance, good tools to support the creation, maintenance, and evolution of curated databases are required. In this respect, curated databases have some characteristics that may challenge some of our precepts of how a database functions:

SOURCE

The majority of curated data is data that is copied and edited from existing sources, perhaps other curated databases or printed articles. Often, the closest one may get to 'source' data is an opinion of the curator that has been added as an annotation. All the other data has been painstakingly extracted from other databases. Since, the value of curated databases lies in their quality and organisation, knowing the origin of the curated data—its provenance—is particularly important. Manually recording provenance is both tedious and error-prone, thus automatic provenance recording support is desirable.

ANNOTATION

In addition to the core data, curated data-bases also contain annotations that carry additional pieces of information such as provenance, the conjectured function of a gene, etc. For the purpose of easy construction of such annotations, it becomes necessary to propagate annotations made on a user's view of the database back to the actual core data, a non-trivial problem as we shall see.

UPDATE

A common practice is to maintain a working database that is updated by a community of curators and periodically to 'publish' versions of the database by distributing copies of the working database or by converting it to an appropriate format for web publishing.

Given the role of curated databases as publications, it becomes important to be able to cite particular versions of the database, and to be able to retrieve a particular cited version when looking up a reference. In other words, one must make sure that the previous versions of the database are digitally preserved.

Since, human data entry is slow, curated databases do not grow or change rapidly, and specialised archiving techniques can be used to reduce the amount of storage necessary to record the complete history of the database. Archiving techniques should also support temporal queries, which are particularly important for databases like the World Factbook.

For example, one might want to query previous versions to retrieve useful information such as the Internet penetration of Liechtenstein over the past five years, and perhaps correlate it with economic data in this or another archived database.

SCHEMA AND STRUCTURE

Many curated databases are constructed 'on the cheap', starting life with a simple, structured design that allows basic description of the database 'entries' which are usually stored in a text file. Almost inevitably, the structure of the entries evolves over time. UniProt, for example, has always been distributed electronically in a specialised data format, but the format has been evolved to include new fields. As they evolve, curated databases may increase their dependence on database technology, but the design is seldom fully normalised; the fields themselves may contain structured text, and there is often some redundancy.

In other words: database technology is used more to support persistence, concurrent access, and indexing rather than the data model. In order for database technology to succeed in also providing the data model for future curated databases, it is important to gain an understanding of the processes by which the structure of curated databases evolves. There are economic and social factors that are equally important to the long-term usefulness of curated databases. It is therefore worth taking a brief look at these factors because they may also suggest some interesting long-term challenges for database technology.

SUSTAINABILITY

During the nineteenth and twentieth century, thanks to the development of public, university and other institutional libraries, the function of libraries changed from one of ownership of data to one of distribution. A secondary but useful effect of this is that much more was preserved. Nearly all of our knowledge has been preserved by copying it: by an oral tradition, by copying manuscripts, by the printing press, and now by a plethora of digital media and computer networks such as the Internet. Concentrating it in archival institutions such as the libraries of Alexandria, Baghdad, Cotton, and Louvain, which were all destroyed in various ways, was probably counterproductive. Today—by archiving at remote sites—we have reasonable methods for protecting our data from physical destruction, but this is no guarantee against the economic collapse of the organisation that maintains the data. There has been a proliferation of data centers over the past years—many dedicated to the storage of scientific and economic data—but one wonders whether, by analogy with early libraries, we are endangering our data by placing it in such centers.

These depend on continued public funding and there are signs that such centers are no more sustainable than early libraries. A move towards massive systematic distribution of electronic publications is the LOCKSS project in which a large number of university libraries each keep a repository of a set of publications, and a peer-to-peer synchronisation process ensures that the repositories are consistent and cannot be corrupted either by bit-rot or deliberate interference. We have likened curated databases to publications, so could one build a LOCKSS system for databases? In addition to the requirements for files, such a system would have to work on incremental updates and would also have to work well with archiving.

OPEN ACCESS

Another transition that was in part due to the proliferation of university libraries was that, in the second half of the twentieth century, academics and other scholars stopped having to pay to get their research into print and disseminated. Unlike textbooks, research articles are, unfortunately, not a highly saleable commodity.

The fact that we no longer must pay for their distribution is largely due to libraries who purchase our papers on behalf of the communities that they serve. This economic model of distribution is still very much in use for electronic publications, but it is showing signs of collapse. Although there are costs associated with the production of an electronic journal, they are mostly initial costs and should be small compared with paper distribution. The idea of open access is that the initial costs should be paid for by the person responsible for a publication. After this it should be freely available. Curated databases are unlike research papers in that they are constantly updated.

So while many scientific curated databases are open access, it is not clear that this is the right economic model for sup- porting them. It is almost impossible to obtain indefinite funding to support the development of a database, and un- less there is institutional support for a curated database, it is likely to lead a hand-to-mouth existence. Of course, many curated databases—encyclopaedias, dictionaries and other reference works—have evolved from paper publications that were sold, and they continue to charge for their use.

But charging policies vary and are generally ill-defined: we give you small amounts of data for free, but you have to pay for the whole database; or, we give you the old data for free but you have to pay for the current stuff. For scientific data, if we draw an analogy between a curated database and a textbook or reference work, it is not unreasonable to expect the user of the database to pay for access, but how does one charge? Could a system of micro-payments be designed for these databases? The problem is complicated by the fact that curated databases copy one another and if one database charges for access to some piece of data, it might be required that some of payment goes to the sources of that data.

If such a scheme were to be developed, a satisfactory model of provenance is essential. These are just two areas of curated databases in which the right model of data and data communication could be enormously valuable. Open access impinges on copyright and intellectual property issues, which are hugely problematic areas even before databases are considered Organisation.

PROPAGATION OF ANNOTATIONS

In UniProt the fields are classified into core data and annotation. Core data includes information like the protein sequence itself, which is extracted from other databases. An- notation is additional information, like the conjectured function of a gene, that has been entered manually or is machine generated by classification and sequence matching programmes. In UniProt, the process of annotation is carefully controlled and annotations are placed only in designated annotation fields.

By contrast, the *Distributed Annotation Server* (DAS) is a client-server system that conveys annotations that are external to the underlying database between user interfaces. A an arbitrary user may annotate something such as a segment of sequence data that appears in his or her interface the data, and the annotation will appear to another user using a different interface. Each user interface can combine information from a number of annotation servers, each of which acts as an external database for annotations.

Annotation Models

an- notating a view of some data and asking that the annotation be carried backwards to the source data as well as forwards to some other view. Since, we are typically annotating a small piece of data, such as a base data value, this requires us to identify where, in the source, that piece came from–its where-provenance. The importance of being able to connect elements of the output of a query with those in the input was first recognised in in the context of data integration. The process of annotation immediately complicates traditional notions of query equivalence and hence, query optimisation.

Consider the two SQL queries:

- Q1: SELECT R.A, R.B FROM R,S WHERE R.A=S.A AND R.B=50
- Q2: SELECT S.A, 50 AS B FROM R,S WHERE R.A = S.A AND R.B=50

These queries are normally regarded as equivalent, and the simple rewrite of R.B to 50 as B in the select clause is a typical low-level optimisation. If one regards the queries as copying base values from the input to the output, however, the queries behave differently: A-values in the output of Q1 are copied from R, while A-values in the output of Q2 are copied from S. Moreover, B-values in the output of Q2 are apparently created by Q2 itself. It is initially annoying that we need to break the principle of substitution of equals for equals for the purpose of annotation propagation; it calls for a different model of both the underlying data and query evaluation.

The model that is developed in and implicitly used in is to add unique colours to components of the input. These colours may be used to represent annotations or to identify components for provenance tracking. We then formalise how queries operate on coloured tables. In the following example there are instances of R and S in which each base value has been annotated with a distinct colour, b1, b2,...,. The output of the two queries Q1 and Q2 shows how these colours are propagated.

A	B
10^{b1}	49^{b2}
12^{b3}	50^{b4}

R

A	B
11^{b5}	49^{b6}
12^{b7}	50^{b8}

S

A	B
12^{b3}	50^{b4}

Q_1

A	B
12^{b7}	$50^{\perp}$

Q_2

One can consider an alternative representation of these annotated databases in which colours are first-class values by pairing each column with another column of colours. An immediate question is whether the transfer of colours that is implicit in our queries can be represented by another query on the alternative representation that explicitly manipulates colours.

The problem is that in operations such as union and set-theoretic projection, two base values can be 'merged' and the annotation is then a set of colours. For conjunctive queries, it is established in that there is indeed an explicit query that can be used to express the annotation transfer.

The authors also examine the extension of SQL with explicit statements to 'steer' annotations through queries. In addition, they propose the 'DEFAULT ALL' propagation scheme in which any two base values that are explicitly found to be equal in a selection or that are implicitly identified in a union or natural join have their annotations merged. Finally, the authors also investigate the efficiency of computing annotation propagation. Although most work on annotation has considered annotations only on single base values or whole rows, provides a system for attaching annotations to sets of base values occurring in the same tuple.

The authors point out that an annotation on a base value should be regarded as a curator's opinion of the validity of the value and that this is better modelled as an annotation on the relationship between the base value and the key for the tuple containing that value. In addition, they introduce a query language—a 'colour algebra'—for querying annotations. Again an explicit relational representation of such block-coloured databases is introduced and the colour algebra is shown to express exactly all queries that the positive relational algebra can express over the explicit relational representation of block-coloured databases. This result was later extended in to full relational algebra.

Reverse Propagation of Annotations

We noted earlier that there is a need to propagate an- notations from a user's view of the database back to the source data: if an annotation is attached to some base value in the output of a query, to what base value in the input should it be attached? Given the rules proposed in for propagating input colours to the output of a query, one can in principle answer this question by reversing the propagation rules. In the case that the query contains a union or a projection, however, a given colour on an output base value could be produced by more than one possible placing of that colour on an input value.

Moreover in the case of a join, a colour placed on an output base value can only come from a single base value in the source, but that colour when carried forward may 'spread' to other base values. A source annotation that does not have any such side-effects, *i.e.,* that produces precisely the view annotation, is called side-effect free. In the problem of finding a side-effect free annotation is shown to have NP-hard query complexity for queries containing both a projection and join and was later strengthened to DP-hardness in. In all other cases of positive queries, there is a polynomial time solution.

The problem of finding side-effect free annotation placements is related to the view deletion problem: find a minimal set of tuples in the source to cause the deletion of a tuple in the output. It is yet to be seen whether any of these complexity results form a practical barrier to building general systems for the reverse propagation of annotation. In fact shows that these problems become tractable for classes of key-preserving queries. We should note, however, that these results are for the default propagation rules for relational algebra. There appear to be no results for reversing the more complex forms of annotation suggested in.

UPDATES IN CURATED DATABASES

We have discussed annotation for queries and its relation- ship to where—provenance in some detail, but let us return to the larger picture of curated databases. In systems such as DAS, annotations are external to the core database and are superimposed on it. In UniProt, however, an annotation is simply a part of the database that has been entered or modified by a curator. Curated databases are created by copying or abstracting data from other sources and later correcting it.

This is a process that is entirely familiar to anyone who has constructed bibliographies for papers such as this one. When doing so, one typically tries to find a bibtex entry on the web, copies and pastes it into one's own bibliography, and then corrects it in accordance with one's own preferences. If this entry were an entry in a scientific database, where-provenance information would include both the source for the entry and a record of what update was made and who made it. A whimsical account of duration is given in.

It is important to reiterate that curated databases are constructed by updates to an existing structure; they are not views. So while UniProt contains some parts—such as the taxonomic lineage and the citations—that have probably been imported automatically into the database, many of the fields are entered by people making individual updates, and it is this activity that gives value to the data-base. The source of these updates is sometimes information extracted by the curator from a paper; it is also sometimes simply copied from another, possibly curated, database.

It is quite common for this copying to be done by the common copy and paste commands that work in most desktop environments. When data is copied between applications or systems, its annotation, context, and especially where-provenance information is lost.

A Copy-paste Model of Curation

In an attempt to model this process exploits a model in which curated databases are semi-structured trees, and the fundamental operation is to copy a data element—as sub-tree—from one tree to another. This provides a simple model of provenance in which it is possible to ask questions such as when some data value was first created, by what process did that value arrive in a database, when was a sub-tree last modified, etc.

The cost of storing such provenance information appears to be prohibitive if done naively because some trail of information needs to be kept of each node in the tree. However this can be mitigated by two observations: first that provenance information is hereditary: unless a node in the tree has been modified, its provenance is that of its parent node. Second, one can collect a sequence of basic operations into a transaction, and there is a description of the effects of the transaction that is shorter than recording the log of basic operations.

The latter is potentially useful for databases that are published periodically. The major unsolved challenge here is the practical goal of building provenance recording into the tools that a curator normally uses. This is a hard problem involving not only data management, query language design and efficiency issues but also usability and organisational problems. While addressed the problem of recording and storing provenance, the task of formulating queries against the resulting provenance store was left to users. Can we design a query language that provides good high-level support for writing sophisticated queries against curated databases involving provenance, the raw data, and perhaps previous versions? This is challenging, since, reasoning about copy-paste operations on trees is non-trivial. On the organisational side, how can we convince both database, operating system, and other application vendors and independent database curators to adopt common standards for provenance? This is a significant long-term challenge requiring both technical and social development.

In practice, updates to a curated database are performed through the update expressions of SQL. This includes both manual copy-paste operations and bulk loading of data into one database from another. Just as where-provenance has been studied for query languages we may ask how update languages manipulate where-provenance. Figure shows three SQL programmes. Although they all have the same 'result', the way they carry provenance is different.

The first SQL programme is a query and is copying as a provenance-preserving transformation. The second and third programme are SQL updates and are not copying as provenance-preserving transformations: they preserve the colour of a tuple or table while changing one of its components. Updates in this language satisfy a weaker semantic provenance condition than queries, called kind-preservation: if a value appears in the output with a given colour, then the corresponding value in the input must have the same type; furthermore, if the value is an atom, then the corresponding value in the input must be the same atom.

Thus a kind preserving transformation can drop or add fields in tuples, or insert and delete elements of sets, while preserving their provenance. The update language with implicit provenance is shown to be complete with regard to the update language in which colours can be explicitly manipulated under the kind preserving, bounded inventing, and no colour-equality test conditions. It is still not known how these results for the complex object update language transfer to SQL updates on flat relations.

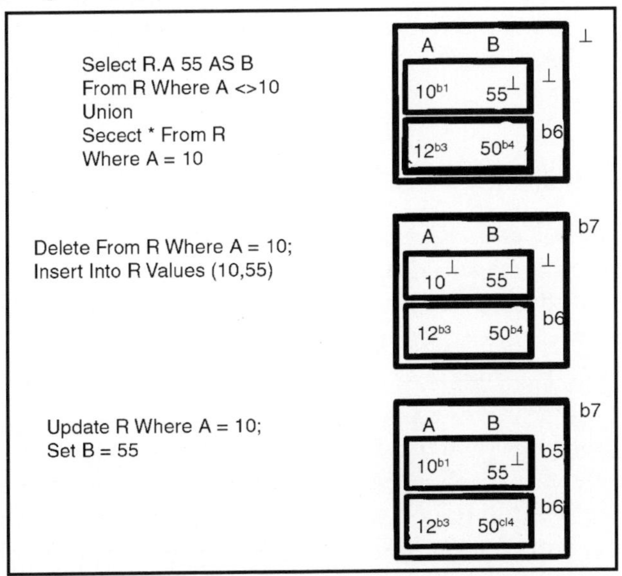

When measured by the transformations between input and output domains that they express, update languages such as the update fragment of SQL do not add anything to query languages; in contrast, provenance mappings provide an alternative method of characterising update languages that highlights differences with queries. But kind- preservation is a very weak condition.

It allows one to empty out a tuple and insert completely different fields into it while preserving provenance. Whether this is a useful knowledge is debatable and reminiscent of Theseus' paradox: suppose we build a ship, and then replace each part of it over its lifetime; is it the same ship? There appear to be other possible models of provenance for update languages, for example one could associate provenance with some form of key preservation. In addition, there has yet to be any work on provenance in update languages for XML and other forms of semi-structured data. Although it appears straightforward to extend the approach of to where-provenance for XQuery-style queries, update languages for XML are still in development. Most of them abandon a key design principle of XQuery by permitting unrestricted side-effecting operations inside queries. Their semantics is sufficiently complex that designing provenance-tracking techniques for them is probably premature.

Why-Provenance and Updates

We have argued earlier in the chapter that updates are essential in curated databases. If where-provenance makes sense for updates, what about why-provenance? A curated database is built through a long sequence of updates. It is likely that only a very small number of those updates had any effect on the data of interest, and that a satisfactory answer is to provide the subsequence of relevant updates and their sources. But what does 'relevant' mean here, and is it sensible to use the same approach as in why-provenance for queries? Our experience with where-provenance suggests that simply translating sequences of updates to 'equivalent' queries may be unsatisfactory from the point of view of provenance.

Provenance and Workflow

No discussion of provenance would be complete without mention of the large amount of work on workflow provenance. Many scientific data sets are derived from raw data by a complex analysis process involving several programmes—a workflow. Scientists need to record the enactment of the workflow for two reasons: first to record precisely how the data set was described and to avoid recomputation; second because it is sometimes cheaper not to keep the derived data, but to recompute it when needed.

The recording of a workflow enactment is also called provenance. Workflow provenance is sufficiently important that there is a workshop largely devoted to this topic; and workflow systems such as Taverna and Kepler have been developed that record this form of provenance.

To date there has been little interaction between workflow and data provenance research. In the workflow setting, the solution to recording interactions with databases is simply to record the state of the database itself and the query. Note that this solution presupposes some form of archiving. Quite recently, the importance of combining the two views of provenance has been recognised.

In there is a proposal for a stream-based model of workflow equipped with a notion of provenance for elements of a stream. In a more sophisticated model is developed based on Petri nets in which the tokens are complex objects and the transitions can perform certain elementary operations on these objects. While this is a rather low-level description of workflows, it may well lead to a general notion of provenance that embraces both data and workflow provenance. Reconciling these two notions is one of the most immediate and interesting challenges of provenance research.

ARCHIVING AND CITATION

Most curated databases ask you to cite them, or provide a link to them, but they differ widely in suggesting how you are to do this. The IUPHAR database, for example, provides links to the whole database or to one of the receptor families. The problem with this is that anyone using this link gets the current version of the database rather than the version that was used when the link was created. Since, the database may be expected to change, the usual principles of citation dictate that one should cite, or link to, the appropriate version of the database.

This requires that all old versions are recoverable even when the database gets constantly updated. There are numerous ways to do this—from simply keeping all older versions of the database and optionally compressing them with tools such as zip, to logging all updates made to a database or keeping differences between versions of the database. Such methods for archiving generally work very well if the objective is simply to ensure that all past versions are recoverable. However, they are not friendly to temporal or longitudinal queries that are common for databases that change. For example, it is frequently the case that temporal queries on demographic and economic data arise when one browses the World Factbook. It would be difficult to answer such queries over the archives constructed with the these methods without at least an attempt to evaluate the query on each version of the database or an analysis of the log or diff files in the archive.

Database Archiving

Commercial relational database systems have started to provide for 'time travel' queries to temporal databases. The traditional method of providing past snapshots of the database have been implemented by undoing the transaction logs, which are a critical component of transaction processing. This technique is problematic because detailed transaction logs are usually not retained permanently.

Since, they can only be used to reconstruct past database states, it is difficult to compare between versions of the database using the transaction log. An alternative, well-known method is to tag each tuple with the interval during which it remained present and unaltered in the database, *i.e.,* its trans- action time. An update to a tuple at time t causes the old tuple to be preserved with t as its end time and a new tuple to be generated with t as its start time. Past states of the database are recovered by selecting the subset of tuples that were active at a given time.

An alternative strategy for archiving hierarchical data essentially keeps all database versions intact in a compact database archive. By viewing hierarchical data as a tree, each node is associated with a time interval that captures the time during which the node exists in the database if it is different from the time interval of its parent node.

This is a generalisation of the fat node method in 'persistent' data structures described in. The main technical difficulty in is how to merge a cur- rent version of the database with the database archive. The solution in leverages hierarchical key constraints that naturally arise in well-organised curated databases such as UniProt. In the presence of hierarchical key constraints, it becomes possible to identify a node in a tree in a way that is invariant to updates that are performed on the tree. An archive is incrementally created by merging a node in the database version with its identical node in the archive, if present. Otherwise, a new node is created in the data-base archive.

This method has been shown to work well for databases in which updates are mostly additions and when a node tends to persist through many versions of the database. Curated databases such as UniProt possess these two properties and it has been shown that this archiving technique is a space-efficient method for recording all past versions.

Since, the archive is effectively another database, this archiving technique is also a promising solution for answering a range of temporal queries over hierarchical data by, essentially, executing them directly on the archive. Temporal queries for XML are starting to attract some interest. An open question is whether one could create an archive directly from the transaction log. For hierarchical databases that are actually stored in a native XML store, it may also be possible to use the archive itself as the database.

Citation

For electronic documents, it is not yet clear whether citations are needed when one has reliable hyper linking. This is a big 'if': it assumes that the hyper linking mechanism–such as a URL or digital object identifier—is stable and that the target of the hyperlink, the cited document, continues to exist. An electronic citation often carries a hyperlink, but it is more than a hyperlink in that it carries a small amount of extra information such as title and author which may help the reader recognise the cited work and avoid the need to dereference the link.

If we assume that citations will continue to be used in electronic documents, then they will also be needed for curated databases, but the citation system needs to be more flexible. It is appropriate to cite the authorship of an entry in the IUPHAR database in a citation, since, the authorship is recorded in the database, and the authors want to be cited. This is not the case for other curated databases, but some alternative information might be appropriate instead. Initial proposals on how to generate such citations automatically from the database and how to organise the database so that it is cite able have been reported in. We should emphasise that proper archiving is needed both for accurate citation and hyperlinking.

EVOLUTION OF STRUCTURE

The design of a database is almost impossible to get right on the first try. The best one can hope for is to build some- thing that is workable and that can be extended without too much disruption to the applications that were written for the initial design.

For example, adding columns to a table in a relational database seldom interferes with existing applications. Evolution of structure is particularly problematic for curated databases. *First,* curated databases are often constructed 'on the cheap', starting from a design that is not well-informed by database design principles. *Second,* once the database becomes widely used, it is often useful to extend it with additional data imported from other databases. *Third,* with the advance of scientific theories, the 'world model' e may change over time. Finally, the data model itself may not initially be precise.

This is especially true of curated databases that evolve from semi-structured or text format into a more structured description. Curated databases almost invariably consist of a sequence of entries, each of some hierarchical form. That biologists needed a flexible method of building databases was first recognised in the development of AceDB, based on a simple edge-labelled tree model of data.

Like the first proposals for semi-structured data, an AceDB database could be created without a schema, and a schema could, if needed, be retro-fitted to the data. By encoding lists as binary trees and by allowing pointers to top-level entries, a range of data types could be simulated in AceDB.

The fact that it is still in use today and has found applications outside of biology indicates the need for a schema-less, semi-structured approach to database construction, at least in the early stages of data-base construction. Since, eventually one will want to retro-fit a schema to the data, it also points to the need of automatic schema inference for semi-structured data, a topic that has been investigated for web pages as well as XML, and ad-hoc semi-structured data.

The evolution of the schema of the UniProt entry in figure is interesting. Originally, this schema consisted of a simple, line-oriented format which could not be extended because it would break existing parsing tools. As a work-around, extra fields such as FUNCTION, SUBUNIT, and SIMILARITY were embedded in the comment field, something that has been retained in the XML representation of UniProt entries. So here, an extension that is easy for relational representations is complicated by the fact that we are using a serial data format. The World Factbook shows a different kind of evolution. It appears from past versions that the top-levels of the hierarchical description of each country are reasonably stable, but that there is great variation in the sub-properties.

One of the problems here is that for categories such as 'government' there is no easy way of describing all possible governmental structures by a uniform list of properties and sub-properties. For example, Government/Elections was a property unique to Iceland that has been deprecated in recent versions of the World Factbook. Only in the past year or so has a schema been explicitly published; before that the schema was implicit in the data.

XML and the Evolution of Structure

The hierarchical structure of curated data naturally suggests using XML. The conventional wisdom in the research community is that DTDs or XML Schemas are the most appropriate method for specifying the structure of these databases. We believe this is debatable, if for no other reason than that DTDs or XML Schemas seem to be used rarely in practice, and when they are, only a few of their features are actually used. We believe that one reason for this is that DTDs do not lend themselves to even simple forms of schema evolution. In relational databases, adding a column is one of the most harmless operations: it is a reasonable bet that existing applications will continue to work correctly after such a modification.

This is an example of record sub typing in programming languages, where we can always use a record with fields A,B,C anywhere one with fields A,B is expected. Suppose, however that we want to do the same with an XML transformation specified against a DTD. For example, suppose we want to insert a new symbol a into a regular expression. One possibility is to add a at the end of r, thereby obtaining. Essentially all work on type checking and sub typing for XML programming and query languages is based on language inclusion.

Thus, a transformation that expects an element of *r* may break if we provide an element, since, the language *ra* is not a subtype of *r*. Therefore, it appears worthwhile to investigate alternative definitions of subtyping that provide more flexibility when the schema changes. For example, consider a form of width subtyping: *r* is a subtype of *r2* if every element of *r2* is a prefix of some element of *r*. This would suffice for the simple example above, but it might not be ideal either, because XML's ordered data model forces some arbitrary choices. For example, suppose we add *b* to the end of *ra* get subtype *rab*, and have a query *q* that uses *r* and *b* but not *a*. If we later remove *a,* then this form of subtyping would provide no guarantee that *q* would still work on *rb*.

A possible refinement that avoids this order-dependence is to base subtyping on interleaving. If we define *r1#r2* to be the set of all strings constructed by interleaving some string in *r1* with some string in *r2* we can express both record sub- typing and the order constraints imposed by regular expressions. Complexity issues associated with such an operator have been studied in. In particular, removing interleaving can lead to an exponential increase in the size of the regular expression, as is apparent from *a# b# c#*.... It is not at all clear that either of these approaches is satisfactory; however, until a good solution is found, XML processing languages that are based on regular expression types and inclusion subtyping will continue to have problems with the kinds of extensibility to which we are accustomed in database work. XML Schema tries to address this problem simply by including both unordered record and regular expression types, but it forbids their mixture.

In the face of this complexity one is forced to ask why we are using DTDs to describe the structure of a curated database in the first place? Perhaps we are confusing three things: the underlying data model, the format by which the data is commonly displayed, and the transmission format. A simple complex-object model in which records, sets, and lists can be freely combined, with record subtyping rather than inclusion subtyping, is often adequate as an underlying data model for the curated databases we have encountered. Style-sheets for presentation based on such a model are easy to construct, as is an appropriate variant of XPath.

Note that most XPath expressions are insensitive to the addition of new tags, so we would expect them to have the same kinds of guarantees about extensibility as we do for relational databases and SQL. Thus, perhaps the problems involving the evolution of structure are better addressed on the complex-object level, and XML should be used only for presentation and data transmission. If we focus on these better-motivated aspects of XML, and not on using it to store or manage data within a database, a number of interesting questions arise in connection with optimality. Suppose one wants to move a substantial quantity of data from one database to another.

What is the best XML serialisation format? Even if the databases' schemas and contents are identical, this may be nontrivial–for ex- ample, suppose we have two tables with the same schemas and the same constraints, but the tables are clustered on different keys. There is an immediate problem of constructing the best serial format to optimise some combination of extracting and loading costs; there appears to be little work on this topic.

Object Fission and Fusion

There is a form of evolution that is problematic for curated databases in which data entries split or have to be merged. Splitting is a phenomenon one would expect in the World Factbook over its existence. Merging also occurs in genetic databases when it is discovered, for example, that two entries refer to the same gene. Fusion has been studied in the context of data integration but fusion in curated databases is qualitatively different because it is a temporal phenomenon. The problem is acute in connection with archiving and temporal queries over the history of a database. To deal with this phenomenon, UniProt introduces and 'retires' object identifiers, but records the retired identifiers along with the new, primary, identifier. This provides some partial evidence of how entries were split and merged, but it is far from complete. Given that fission and fusion are so fundamental to the evolution of databases, they deserve better treatment in data models, which should support, at least, provenance queries of the general form: 'What happened to X?' or 'How did Y come about?'.

Ontologies

A number of curated databases are now called 'ontologies' rather than 'databases'. There appear to be two, almost orthogonal, issues at play here. The first is that ontologies involve hierarchical classification or taxonomies. The Gene Ontology has three such hierarchies erected over an underlying database of entries. From a database perspective, the most interesting challenge is the representation and re-cursive querying of hierarchical data–a challenge that has been largely solved, but has not been realised in practical systems. The second point is that useful tools have been built for the construction of knowledge representation in the style of KL-One. One of the attractions of these systems is that one can, as with semi-structured data, create data- bases without having first constructed a schema; although a better description of such an ontology would be that it does not distinguish between the construction of schema and data. As we have noted, in the early stages of construction of a curated database, it is an advantage to be unconstrained by a fixed schema; and this may be the reason for the growing popularity of these tools in curated databases. As far as we are aware the study of many of the topics described in this chapter are as much in their infancy for ontologies as they are for databases.

OTHER STANDARDS RELATED TO BIBLIOGRAPHIC DATABASE

Z39.50 Retrieval protocol

Z39.50 refers to the International Standard, ISO 23950: "Information

Retrieval (Z39.50): Application Service Definition and Protocol Specification", and to ANSI/NISO Z39.50. The standard specifies a client/serverbased protocol for searching and retrieving information from remote databases.

OAI (Open Archive Initiative)

The Open Archive Initiative (OAI) for metadata harvesting is a new protocol dedicated to solving problems of digital library interoperability by defining simple protocols, most recently for the exchange of metadata. Although, Z39.50 Information Retrieval Protocol is also one of the harvesting protocols. Some digital library systems are using for retrieving and searching the records for example Maxwell System. It is crucial to explain, discuss, and disambiguate the concepts and terminology used among OAI implementers to harvesting approach to interoperability. The harvesting protocol defined by the OAI is a request / response protocol with 6 request types, *viz., Identity, ListMetadataFormats, ListSets, GetRecords ListRecord, and ListIdentifiers.* It has defined in such a way to support a common set of principles and a technical framework to achieve interoperability. Although, both the standards are not being used with the INFLIBNET database right now, but being explored to implement it in near future.

PURPOSE OF THE BIBLIOGRAPHIC STANDARDS

Mostly, purpose of using these standards for creating bibliographic databases or suggesting using it at libraries of India, has following reasons behind it:

- Pursuing Universal Bibliographic Control
- Exchange of information among union databases for the purpose of global resource sharing
- Cooperation at the local level, transferring data from one system to another

IMPORTANCE OF THE BIBLIOGRAPHIC STANDARDS

Following bibliographic standards for creating the databases produces following importance:

- It makes uniformity in records
- It provides better resource sharing between different resource centres
- It helps in exchanging of records and facilitates it without data loss
- It helps in creating national / International bibliographic union database
- It helps to adopt any system and provides platform interoperability

THE WEB AS THE WORLD'S BIGGEST RELATIONAL DATABASE

The way that an RDBMS references rows from multiple tables can be compared to Web links. A Web page is, in some ways, much like an RDBMS "view" of disparate data. From a user perspective, the content is brought together based on a predefined logic and a series of "keys" or "pointers" that identify relevant material. A dynamically generated Web page comes even closer to the conceptual model of an RDBMS, particularly if much of the content of the page is based on remote network resources retrieved through URLs. For example, a search of a library catalogue on the Web typically involves a cgi-bin program that dynamically displays results using HTML.

Each result record is usually linked to a fuller display via a URL that specifies from where the information is to be retrieved. The linking mechanisms of the Web have recently been leveraged to support the OpenURL framework. The OpenURL framework has been proposed as an architecture for retrieving references to scholarly works by enabling third parties to provide links for a referenced item. Although OpenURLs have typically been deployed to provide links to the full text of scholarly works, the framework can also be utilized to identify a catalogued item in an ILS. Ex Libris' ALEPH500 System, for example, directly supports OpenURL, and exploratory work has been carried out to generalize the OpenURL framework beyond reference linking scholarly environments. If the Web can be thought of as an ever-growing RDBMS, and OpenURLs can be utilized to provide "RDBMS-like" standard and precise links between specific items in information systems, then there are possibilities for providing extensive distributed search and retrieval functions in Web-based library services. For example, a remote database consisting of Library of Congress names and subject headings could be searched within a browser environment, and the results could provide links to items in the local catalogue.

Web-based union catalogues support standardized indexing and searching at a central location. With OpenURLs, links can be made to point to holdings and other localized information within the member library's Integrated Library System. All of this fits within the RDBMS notion of creating and maintaining data with as little duplication as possible, and linking it together to provide a logical view of the content itself. XML plays a role by greatly enhancing the linking mechanisms of the Web. XML technologies such as Xinclude, Xpath, and Xlink, provide sophisticated methods for drawing on network resources. Xinclude allows the contents of a separate XML resource to be inserted into an XML document based on a link . Xpath will be familiar to anyone who has worked with XSTL and other XML stylesheet tools. It allows the creation of expressions for specifying every visual and interface portion of a document.

Xlink is the XML linking language and offers much more sophisticated types of linking than currently offered by the familiar HREF and NAME elements found in HTML. Xlink's extended element can name one or more linked resources. The arc element in this example tells an application about the behaviour expected when moving through the linked resources. The role and title attributes are used to describe the function of the linked resource in the context of the local resource. Role is meant to be descriptive to the application and title is meant to be descriptive to the user. In this case, the roles are meant to identify an author's works and biographies. The *acutate* element describes how the resources should appear. The value "onRequest" specifies that the resource should appear when the link is selected, and the value "embed" for the *show* attribute tells the application to insert the specified resource inline within the current document. Finally, an *item* element is used to represent where this particular resource can be found in physical form in the library. If an XML representation of an RDBMS-based library catalogue or other library database is made available, the library can make use of XML linking technologies and other XML tools for manipulating database contents. OpenURL lays the groundwork for using links as virtual keys to content that goes far beyond individual tables, and the content can be as broad as the diversity of the Web itself.

STANDARDS FOR CREATING BIBLIOGRAPHIC DATABASES

The concept of "standard" in the field of library and information science is interpreted as codes of cataloguing rules, classification schemes, subject headings and various other documents contained recommendations for good library practice, all of which are subject to varying interpretation. But, for another professionals, standards are extremely precise technical specifications for communication between software and machines in an automated information-processing environment. For example, Operating Systems, TCP/IP etc. Standards are documented agreements containing technical specifications or other precise criteria to be used consistently as rules, guidelines, or definitions of characteristics, to ensure that materials, products, processes and services are fit for their purpose Field of bibliographic standards are not limited to the rules only but spread up to the authority files such as person names, corporate names, subject headings, classification schemes, series names, institution names, software and standardization form and format etc.

In beginning, during the initiation of automation to library professionals, there was not much focus on bibliographic standards and were creating databases in any formats. That affected to the automation of their libraries, which forced them to think over the issue. Now, gradually, the libraries and information centres are realizing the importance of bibliographic standards. Centres like Information and Library Network (INFLIBNET), Ahmedabad is playing important role in bringing all libraries together to work on a single platform of standards with linking under one huge national network i.e. UGC-Infonet. INFLIBNET Centre is an Inter-University Centre of University Grants Commission (UGC), working on Academic library system in India. In 1990, UGC launched it as a programme for five years on pilot basis. On June 1996, the programme was recognized as a full-fledged Centre. UGC-Infonet is a project of UGC being implemented by INFLIBNET Centre in collaboration with ERNET (Education and Research Network), New Delhi. It is an Intra-Network of Indian universities and colleges across the country based on the Open IP platform, employing state-of-the-art technologies like IP or TV, enabling online response to queries. The network facilitates Intranet and Internet access to its users on high data rates.

STANDARDS FOR BIBLIOGRAPHIC DATABASE

Well-known simple definition of database is a set of records and record is a set of fields, where, field is a combination of different pieces of information. Bibliographic database is a database of resources available at libraries in print format. With the revolution of information technology in the field of libraries, bibliographic catalogue has come up into the form of bibliographic database. For making compatible with these changes, there, many library institutions have come up with different standards and formats such as CCF, AUSMARC, CANMARC, UKMARC, USMARC, UNIMARC, MARC21, AACR2, ISBD, LCSH, MeSH etc. Some of the Internationally recognized standards and formats being used by many libraries of different countries for creating databases. As per the INFLIBNET's guidelines following standards are recommended for use:

Standardized Bibliographic Formats

During the inception of the Programme, The Task Group on "Union Catalogue, Data Capturing and Standardization" was constituted by UGC. The Task Group was assisted by a Sub-Committee on implementation of Common Communication Format (CCF) for data capturing and data exchange. Later on, the Sub-Committee formalized some fields based on CCF and named it as "Guidelines for Data Capturing: a user manual". During the initial stage of automation, Micro CDS/ISIS software (developed by Unesco) were suggested to use for creating bibliographic databases based on the format recommended by the Centre.

Simultaneously, other DBMS such as DBase, FoxPro, FoxBase etc. were also being used by different libraries for creating the databases. In addition, the Centre had also the library house keeping software called "ILMS – Integrated Library Management System" developed on COBOL language on Unix platform, and was distributed freely to the member libraries of the Centre. Later in February 2000, Centre developed another library house keeping software called "SOUL – Software for University Libraries" on Power Builder language on Windows platform by using the client-server architecture to keep in mind the shortcomings being faced in ILMS software. The software is developed based on the format formalized by Sub-Committee of the Task Force.

Later, early 2001, The Ministry of Human Resource Development (MHRD), Govt. of India visualizes building up a national database of library holdings in the country based on the MARC21 format. Further, after approval the committee directed INFLIBNET Centre to implement the MARC21 format in all libraries of the country. In this regards, the Centre formed the MARC21

Core Group during December 2001, which formalized the fields for implementing it with the SOUL library house keeping software. The main reason for preferring MARC21 over CCF and other formats was that most of the countries in the world use MARC and it is comprehensive having number of fields. Also there is constant development taking place in MARC21 and is updated regularly whereas CCF has become stagnant.

STANDARD FOR RENDERING INFORMATION/ BIBLIOGRAPHIC DESCRIPTIONS

AACR2R, ISBD and CCC are standards for bibliographic descriptions. But, INFLIBNET Centre suggests their participating libraries to follow the Anglo American Cataloging Rules-II (AACRII) Revised version for rendering bibliographic information.

STANDARDIZED SUBJECT HEADINGS

Different subject headings list are available, developed by different institutions such as LCSH, Sear's List of Subject Headings, MeSH, Thesaurus etc. But INFLIBNET suggests to its member library to use LCSH (for generalized subject headings) and Engineering Index, MeSH and thesaurus (for specialized Subject Headings).

STANDARD FOR CLASSIFICATION SCHEMES

There are various classification schemes have been developed by different organizations for classifying the books on different subjects. Functionally, most of the libraries are using the Dewey Decimal Classification (DDC) for assigning the Classification Number to the documents. But, under INFLIBNET umbrella, all the libraries are free to use any classification scheme for classifying the document, as it is very difficult for any library to reclassify the entire collection based on any new scheme. As per the library practice any classification scheme can be used as MARC21 has capability to adopt any kind of classification schemes.

ISO–2709 INFORMATION EXCHANGE FORMAT

This standard specifies the requirements for generalized interchange format that will accommodate data describing all forms of material. It describes a generalized structure designed specifically for exchange of data between processing systems and not necessarily for use as a processing format within systems. The format may be used for the interchange of records using various communication media. INFLIBNET Centre recommends to follow this Exchange Format for contributing records to the Centre. The exchange format has implemented too with the in-house developed software SOUL for exchanging records.

Physical Structure

General Structure of the Record:

Leader

Each record begins with a leader of fixed length of 24 character positions and is the first instance of the ISO 2709 format of a record. It contains:

- Record length (5 characters): The length of the record includes the leader, directory, data fields and record separator.
- Record Status Code (1 character): Always '0' for output files, ignored on input files.
- Implementation Codes (4 characters): These codes are defined for each specific implementation of the ISO 2709 format. Second character position represents Bibliographic level codes (*i.e.,* s- serials, m- single volume monographs, c- multivolume monographs, a-component part) and rest of the character positioned not used. Here, Bibliographic level is defined here as per the INFLIBNET's use. For the MARC21 based records, it follows the description defined for bibliographic level in MARC21 bibliographic format.
- Indicator length (1 character): This is always '0', because here at INFLIBNET database indicator is not being used. But the value is '2', when we export records from SOUL to MARC21 in ISO 2709 format.
- Subfield identifier length (1 character): '2' The subfield identifier length. This shows the number of characters being used for the subfield identifier.
- Base address of data (5 characters): A decimal number indicating the number of control characters (length of leader plus directory and field separator) which precede the variable data fields. This number, when added to the starting address of the record, gives the address of the first character of the variable fields.
- For user systems (3 characters): These character positions are not used. Always '000' in output files.
- Length of "Length of Datafield" field (1 character): '4' the length of "Length of Datafield" in the directory. (Use of 4 characters permits datafields as long as 9,999 characters)
- Length of "Starting character" position (1 character): '5' the length is "Starting character position" in the directory.
- Rest (2 characters): These character positions are not used. Always sets on '00'.

Directory

A directory entry in this bibliographic record is made up of a tag, length-of-field, and field starting position. It is of variable length and consists of a series of fixed fields, referred to as "entries". One directory entry is associated with each datafield present in the record. Each directory entry is 12 characters in length and is divided into three parts:

- Tag: A three numeric ASCII character code identifying the datafield, which corresponds to the directory entry. In software, names of the fields are being used in alphabetical name, but during the export in ISO 2709 format and display on screen, it converts in three-numeric digit ASCII character code.
- Length of datafield: A four digit number showing how many characters are occupied by the datafield, including datafield separator but excluding the record separator code if the datafield is the last field in the record.
- Starting character position: A five-digit number giving the position of the first character of the datafield relative to the base address of data, *i.e.,* the first character of the first of the datafields.

Datafields

A datafield consists of subfield and datafield separator:

- Subflield : A subfield consists of a subfield identifier followed by a data string, which is terminated by either another subfield identifier or a field separator. A subfield identifier consists of a subfield identifier flag *i.e.,* cap (^) sign followed by one another character, that can be alphabet a to z (small or capital) and numeric 1 to 9, INFLIBNET Centre uses here small alphabets. For MARC21 based records "$" graphical sign is used as a subfield identifier.
- Datafield Separator : The datafield separator *i.e.,* hash (#) sign constitutes the final character of every datafield. ASCII value 30 (character 1/14 of ISO 646) is being used as a field separator in MARC21 based data.

A datafield, which has a single subfield, will be organised as follows:

Record Terminator / Separator

The record terminator is the final character of the record *i.e.,* hash (#) sign. It follows the field separator of the final datafield of the record. ASCII 29 (character 1/13 of ISO 646) is being used as record separator in MARC21 based data.

3

Changes in Library and Information Management

INTRODUCTION

Due to fast-paced technological change and new skill requirements, information professionals are increasingly required to renew their skills and practice in order to gain an awareness of technological advances. As a result, the profession itself exists in a state of flux alongside these emerging technologies, with traditional roles being increasingly subsumed by new skills and working environments, and, therefore, job descriptions. Thus, information professionals are now expected to be aware of and capable of using and demonstrating emerging ICTs. There is a need for additional training to augment the traditional skill and knowledge base with a competency in ICT use. Information professionals must be flexible, and adopt traditional skills to incorporate the requirements of technological advances.

Given the current situation, wherein ICTs are being continuously updated or introduced and traditional formats are being replaced or supplemented by digital formats, it seems likely that there will continue to be a need for regular training for information professionals. There is also an increased focus on communication skills, with more people involved in the electronic information environment. Information professionals are being called upon to work closely with ICT users and providers - including IT staff - and to work in collaboration with others in the profession. Some groups of users lack the necessary IT skills to obtain quality information and information professionals will therefore be called upon to act as both educators and intermediaries.

Given these circumstances, information professionals are required to have additional teaching and communication skills. Thus, it is vital for those in management positions to recognise the imperative of *continuing professional development* (CPD) and ensure that the staff is proactive in maintaining up-to-date levels of expertise. The significance of CPD in this milieu has been acknowledged by both the United Kingdom's *Chartered Institute of Library and Information Professionals* (CILIP) and the United States' *American Library Association* (ALA).

Certain active roles are necessary for change management to:

- *Establish the quality goals of the library:* Library and Information Centres (LICs) should aim to establish the quality goals for qualitative service to its user community.
- *Provide the resources to their library:* LICs should provide all necessary resources suitable in the ICT era to manage the LICs in a better way.
- *Provide the quality-oriented training to the library staff:* New generation library staff are almost trained with ICT applications to LICs but old staff and others who are novices in such applications need quality training because without quality training library staff are unable to provide automated services.
- *Stimulate quality improvement in the day to day activities of library:* This is the age of competition. Like other organisations, to survive the LICs, top management should stimulate the staff for quality improvement in the day to day activities of LICs.
- *Review progress of the library activities:* Higher management should review the progress of library activities to maintain the quality and quantity of assigned job to the staff.
- *Give recognition to library staff:* Top level management should recognise the operational level library staff for quality performance, without which they will be demoralised to perform the job in a better way.

With the change in environment the objectives need to be revised to face the challenges of future. Over a period of time, due to the impact of technological advances, research and development, economic, social and political factors, the objectives also tend to change. To adopt these changes, it is essential to state objectives and functions of information system in changing context. For this purpose the following steps should be followed.

Structure Related Changes

The structure related changes in libraries and information centres may include:

- *Change in the work design:* The work design of a traditional library is not similar to modern automated library, so a change in the work design is compulsory for the success of automated library.
- *Change in the basis of departmentalisation:* There are various departments in university and research libraries. In case of automated library, book acquisition, classification and cataloguing, circulation, serial control assignments are being done through computer with specific software instead of doing manually. Besides these

departments, modern library has other departments like barcoding, RFID tagging, OPAC/web-OPAC, e-journals, e-books, CD-ROM, digital library, touch screen kiosk, server maintenance etc.

- *Change in the number of operation levels to perform various activities, routine work of library staff:* As there is a major change in the processing and service departments a change in the number of staff in the lower level or operational level management has become essential.
- *Change in the plans, programmes, policies and procedures to and improving integration among various sections:* Due to changse in the pattern of service; plans, programmes, policies and procedures and integration within various departments it is very essential to cater to the service in a better way.
- *Change in the span of management and levels of management for effective co-ordination mechanism and flow of task:* Since the nature of job of modern automated library is more complex than traditional library, it is very difficult to manage large number of operational level staff under one middle level manager. In view of this span of management should be narrow and levels of management should be changed because top and middle level management have to be directly linked with every department to perform each department's functions in a better way as well as for effective co-ordination mechanism with every department.
- *Change in line-staff and functional authority, work group relations between people and functions to improve their ability:* Line positions are responsible for accomplishing the organisation's primary objectives; they have final authority to make decisions. Staff positions, on the other hand, provide suggestions and advice for the line positions but cannot, theoretically make decisions for the line positions. An organisation seeks to keep authority for decision making in the positions accountable for results and to preserve a clear chain of command from the top to the bottom of the organisation. But in the automated library system there should be no hurdle between line and staff position because anyone who is aware about a particular system can give his advice. It helps to improve the work group relation as well as the ability of the all levels of management.

Structural changes affect relationships among the organisational positions and in the interactions among internal departments, the reporting mechanism, interactions of all sections in the library and the functional relationships.

Changes for Technological Advancement

The technology refers to the sum total of human knowledge providing ways to do the things in a better way with the help of techniques. It may include inventions and techniques affecting the ways of doing things.

Thus, technology related changes may include:

- *Use of new machines and equipments for developing new services or modifying existing services:* Many new machines and equipments, *e.g.*, computer, server, barcoding equipments, RFID tools are necessary for developing new services or modifying existing manual services. So the awareness about the use of new machines, equipments and tools is very essential.
- *The procedure of doing things which may result in change of work process:* The methods and procedures of doing new tasks should be changed in context of old library system. So that the work process is not disrupted.
- *Introduction of technological devices like computers and computer related technologies:* Introduction of technological devices like computers and computer related technologies is necessary for automated library. Without computers and related technologies, we are unable to cater to services in automated library system.
- *Change in the existing techniques for making or doing the things in effective way or adoption of new techniques for creative work:* Automated library is ICT oriented and some technique is involved in every work. So existing techniques of traditional library management should be changed and adoption of new techniques is very essential to carry out every task and service in automated library environment.
- *Change in the methods of using new tools equipments and products:* In the traditional library system, there are only a few equipments like fumigation chamber, catalogue cabinet, book rack, cardex, journal display rack, etc. But now computer terminals, server, barcoding equipments, RFID tools, etc., equipments and products are being used, so it is very natural to change the methods of using new tools, equipments and products.

The change in the technology affects the nature of work and activities, organisational structure, the processes and the people's behaviour.

Task-related Changes

Technology related changes determine the ways to complete the task effectively and efficiently. Task related changes helps to achieve major gains in terms of cost, service and time.

Task related changes may include:

- *Identifying the steps involved in performing tasks:* It is very necessary to organise meeting with library staff at all levels to identify the steps to perform the tasks effectively.
- *Task identification:* Every task should be identified to depute the staff who is efficient in that work. So, proper task identification is the key

factor to perform the task properly and to serve the user community in a better way.

- *Significance of task related changes in attaining the organisational and institutional objectives:* As the nature of library has been changed so it is very significant to change the task which is relevant in changed atmosphere to attain the organisational and institutional objectives.
- *Identifying the skills and abilities required for the changed task:* It is very natural to identify the skills and abilities required for the changed task and to assign the specific job to the specific staff that is suitable for that particular job.
- *Improving both quality and quantity of work/ service:* For the satisfaction of our customer we should improve our quality as well as quantum of day to day work/service.
- *Bringing cost-effective solutions through maximum use of available resources:* Cost-effectiveness is concerned with the value. It asks, "This is what the service costs. Is it worth it?" So effectiveness of the resources is the key to maximum use of available resources.
- *Improving the work performance:* Quality training of staff is very essential to aware the task of each and every personnel effectively which improves the work performance.

People-related Changes

Change in any factor has an impact on human resources and human behaviour.

In the context of Library and Information Science, the people-related categories include:

- *The library staff:* In case of library staff, it requires the corresponding changes to be made in the skills, abilities and the performance of the employees.
- *New investment in training and development activities so that employees acquire new skills and activities:* New skills and activities are required in automated library system so new investment in training and development is essential. Library can get the fund from UGC for this purpose by making a systematic and comprehensive proposal
- *Socialising employees into the organisational structure so that they learn the new routines on which organisational performance depends....':* Top management should meet with middle and operational level management to become aware about the every bit of work with theory and practical and to assign the job to every personnel as well as time required for this purpose. Through socialising the employees organisational efficiency can also be increased.

Accordingly the change may also include –

- *Change in skill levels of the workforce:* Skill levels of each and every employee should be changed to cope up with new task.
- *Change in the training programmes to improve performance levels:* Training programme should be organised in a scientific way to sensitise the employee about every practical aspect of work and service. So change in training programmes is essential to improve performance levels of the staff.
- *Change in attitude and values:* Change in attitude and values is a must for better performance in work and service in the changed library environment.
- *Change in behaviour and interaction pattern:* As the library scenario has changed from traditional to automated one, behavioural and interaction pattern regarding work and service should also be changed.
- *Change in technology requires different skills of the operator:* Presently, library is technology controlled. To cope up with this change, the library personnel requires different skills to carry out their own task because it is very difficult to work properly for a unskilled staff.
- *Change in the structure requires change in their position, their authority, responsibility, etc.:* Due to shift from traditional to automated library, structural change is required. For this purpose positional, authoritative and responsibility change is necessary for better performance.
- *The readers:* Readers/users/customers are our prime focus. To serve the right user to the right information at the right time, we have to organise our resources systematically through which they can collect their information himself/herself. Such a systematic arrangement helps us to work and serve the users with less human resources.

Any change in the processes demands that it should be communicated to the readers to enable them to adjust to these changes. Readers are ultimately getting the benefits of all the technological advances, procedures, services, activities as well as other resources for their satisfaction in the libraries and information centres.

Changes in Library Policies

Change in the objectives and functions of the library and information system by the planning body would directly impact the existing plans and policies of the library. Accordingly, change in plans and policies become essential. The developmental plans and policies should be in conformity with the objectives and functions of library and information system as well as the institution it serves.

Changes in Objectives and Functions of Information System

The information system in the changed environment shall aim at:

- *Ensuring maximum use of all available resources:* Top management should ensure maximum use of all available resources through cost-effective solutions.
- *Promotion and development of all units in the library:* In the automated library, to cater the service to the users in a right way, it is very essential to develop all units in a proper way.
- *Better communication of ideas to achieve the objectives in an ever changing environment:* To communicate every new ideas to all levels of management is essential to achieve the objectives in constantly changing environment of library work and service.
- *Minimising the time, cost and efforts involved in all the activities, processes and functions:* Top level management should plan with with staff at middle and operational level for proper coordination of every function with minimum time, cost and efforts because duplicity of activities, processes and functions increases the time, cost and efforts.

In order to achieve the newly stated objectives as per the requirement of changing circumstances, certain functions are to be carried out. These functions may relate to adoption of latest technologies, use of modern tools and techniques, updating professional skill, ability and knowledge through education and training, future prospects of change in goals, objectives and functions, etc.

Librarians will need to be ready for competition and prepared to find new ways to make their skills and services distinct from those offered by the competition from media companies, publishers, internet companies, intermediary service providers and also from technologists parking on traditional library territory with technical names for old fashioned library ideas.

INFORMATION RETRIEVAL IN LIBRARY

In the early and mid-1950s, a critical mass of scientists, engineers, librarians, and entrepreneurs started working enthusiastically on the problem and solution defined by Bush. By 1960s this became a large and relatively well-funded effort and organized activity. Often, there were heated arguments and controversies about the “best” solution, technique, or system.

These arguments brought on the tradition of evaluation, a major staple of IR research and development. What is now TREC started with Cranfield evaluations in the late 1950s and early 1960s. Remarkably, the basic evaluation principles developed then are still the underpinning of TREC today. Calvin Mooers, an active and highly visible pioneer of information science, coined the term *information retrieval* in 1951. The term took hold, and today is a part of the English language.

At that time, Mooers not only coined the term, but also defined the problems to be addressed:

> “Information retrieval embraces the intellectual aspects of the description of information and its specification for search, and also

whatever systems, techniques or machines that are employed to carry out the operation.

Today, we would add that IR also and particularly involves interaction in all of these, with all the contextual-cognitive, affective, situational—aspects that interaction embraces. An expanded Mooers' conception is still valid. As it advanced, IR produced a number of theoretical, empirical, and pragmatic concepts and constructs. Numerous IR systems were developed and successfully deployed.

A great many historical examples can be given to illustrate the remarkable evolution of IR systems and techniques, adapting the ever-evolving information technology, from punch cards in the midcentury to the Internet at its close. Based on IR, an online information industry emerged in the 1970s, and grew through its own version of information explosion, as chronicled by Hahn. IR is one of the most widely spread applications of any information system worldwide. It has a proud history. Surely, information science is more than IR, but many of the problems raised by IR or derived from objects and phenomena involved in IR, are at its core.

Approaches and Paradigm Split

The approach taken by Mooers was to concentrate on the building of systems. This systems emphasis which was formulated early in the 1950s, was the sole approach to IR for some decades. It still predominates in a good part of IR research to this day.

Consequently, most of the IR research and practice concentrated on retrieval systems and processes. However, starting in the late 1970s and gaining steam in the 1980s, a different line of reasoning and research evolved-one that concentrates on the cognitive, interactive, and contextual end of the process. It addressed users, use, situations, context, and interaction with systems, rather than IR systems alone as a primary focus.

The retrieval cluster started splitting into subclusters, as noted by White and McCain, and before by others such as Saracevic and Harter. We now have two distinct communities and approaches to research in the retrieval cluster. They became commonly known as *systems-centred* and *user-centred.* Both address retrieval, but from very different ends and perspectives. The split is not only conceptual, looking very differently at the same process, but also organizational. The systemscentered side is now mostly concentrated in the *Special Interest Group on Information Retrieval* (SIGIR) of the *Association for Computing Machinery* (ACM), while the user-centered cluster congregates around the *American Society for Information Science* (ASIS).

Each has its own communication outlets-journals, proceedings, and conferences. There is less and less overlap of authors and works between the two outlets. We have two camps, two islands, with, unfortunately, relatively little traffic in-between. The systems-centered approach is exemplified by work on algorithms and evaluation based on the traditional IR model, a model that does not consider the users or interaction. The massive research that evaluates a variety of IR algorithms and approaches within TREC is a culmination of this approach.

In contrast, cognitive, situational, and interactive studies and models, involving the use of retrieval systems exemplify the human-centered approach. Following that approach, interactive models, differing significantly from the traditional IR model, started to emerge. Even in TREC, a group of researchers started an interaction track, but so far have a hard time conceptually and methodologically, thus demonstrating the difficulty in merging the traditional and interactive models and approaches. Let me characterize, in a simplified way, the relationship between the two approaches or subclusters addressing different sides of retrieval.

On the one hand, the human-centred side was often highly critical of the systems side for ignoring users and use, and tried valiantly to establish humans as the proper center of IR work. The mantra of human-centred research is that the results have implications for systems design and practice. Unfortunately, in most human-centred research, beyond suggestions, concrete design solutions were not delivered. On the other hand, the systems side, by and large, ignores the human side and user studies, and is even often completely ignorant of them. As to design, the stance is "tell us what to do and as suggested, do it." But nobody is really telling, or if telling, nobody is listening.

As a rule, in systems-oriented projects, people and users are absent. Thus, there are not many interactions between the two camps. Let me provide some examples. A rough analysis of the 1997 SIGIR proceedings found only 3 papers of some 34 that dealt in some way with people and users; in the ACM's Digital Libraries 1997 conference proceedings, of 25 papers only 3 mentioned people and users. If one reads authors such as Dervin and Nilan, and many of their successors, who champion the human centered approach, one gets the impression that there is a real conflict between the two sides and approaches, and that there is an alternative way to the "dreadful" systems approach.

In a way, this stance is a backlash caused by the excesses, failures, and blind spots of systems-centered approaches not only in IR, but also in great many other technological applica-tions. Unfortunately, sometimes the backlash is justified. All of us who work on the humancentered side are not that dismissive of the systems side. But the issue is not whether we should have systems-*or* humancentered approaches. The issue is even less of human*versus* systems-centered. *The issue is how to make human*and *systems-centered approaches work together.* In this sense, a number of works have addressed integrating usercentered and systems-centered approaches in IR, but this has been discussed mostly by researchers from the usercentered side.

Examples are works by:

- Bates,
- Belkin,
- Cool,
- Stein,
- Thiel,
- Fidel
- Efthimidiadis,
- Robertson and
- Beaulieu.

To reiterate, it is not one camp against the other but how can we incorporate the best features of both approaches and make them work jointly. The issue is how to deliver and incorporate the desired design features that will improve systems orientations towards users, integrate them with systems features, and use advantages provided by both, humans and technology. In other words, the issue is *putting the human in the loop* to build better algorithms and to exploit computational advantages. Real progress in information science, and by extension in IR, will come when we achieve this. Lately, the NSF has championed human-centered design involving an interdisciplinary approach to information systems. Hopefully, this will go beyond rhetoric. It is not easy to do. But, that is what research is for—to address difficult, not only easy problems.

Proprietary IR

By the 1980s, the commercial information industry based on IR became successful and profitable. Out of academe, grants, and government, IR became a money-making propo-sition. This, of course, is another and important sign of success. Not surprisingly, a number of former IR researchers, practitioners, and graduates of IR programmes ventured out to become IR entrepreneurs.

Sure enough, throughout information science history there were many entrepreneurs, and they were highly significant in development of the field. But this generation of entrepre-neurs was different. They ventured to develop and market a variety of IR procedures based on algorithms, applicable and scalable to large files, multiple applications, and/or various advanced technologies. It was knowledge industry at its purest. But, as in all commercial knowledge industries, the product was proprietary. While it was not that hard to guess the base of these various proprietary algorithms and how they worked—after all they were derived from publicly available knowledge and experiences, such as those that came from SMART experi-ments—they remain unpublished and "secret."

A new kind of IR evolved, separate from the rest, not communicating as to intellectual advances with the rest. None of these ventures became a high commercial success, as measured by Silicon Valley standards. But the World Wide Web, emerging in the first half of the 1990s, changed all this. The acceleration of the growth of the Web is an information explosion of the like never before seen in history. Not surprisingly then, the Web is a mess. No wonder that everybody is interested in some form of IR as a solution to fix it.

A number of academic-based efforts were initiated to develop mechanisms, search engines, "intelligent" agents, crawlers, and so forth, to help control the Web. Some of these were IR scaled, and adapted to the problem; others were a variety of extensions of IR. Many had few, if any original, developments, besides new packaging or labeling; and a good number were just the usual hype. The wheel was reinvented a number of times. But out of this, and fast, came commercial ventures, such as the pioneering Yahoo!, whose basic objective is to provide search mechanisms for finding something of relevance for users on demand.

And to make a lot of money. These enterprises pride themselves on having proprietary methods by which they are accomplishing the retrieval tasks. The connection to the information science community is tenuous, and almost non-existent. The flow of knowledge, if any, is onesided, from IR research results into proprietary engines. The reverse contribution to public knowledge is zero. A number of evaluations of these search engines have been undertaken simply by comparing some results between them or comparing of their retrieval against some benchmarks.

Some evaluations were done within, others outside of information science. Results were not complimentary. The Web-based proprietary IR is expanding and flourishing outside of the field. It is addressing a vexing problem, the like we have not seen before. But as yet, the success is elusive and questionable.

RELEVANCE

As information science pioneers developed IR processes and systems in the 1950s, they defined as the main objective retrieval of *relevant* information. Effectiveness was expressed in terms of relevance. From then to now, IR is explicitly geared not towards any old kind of information, but towards *relevant information*. Various IR approaches, algorithms, and practices were, and still are, evaluated in relation to relevance. Thus, relevance became a key notion in information science. It is also a complex phenomenon with a long and turbulent history in information science transcending IR, going back to early 1950s. Of course, there was a choice.

Relevance did not have to emerge as the key notion. Uncertainty was one choice suggested by a number of theorists to be the base of IR, and thus to reflect effectiveness. But it did not take. In contrast, uncertainty is the basic notion underlying expert systems. If the pioneers had not embraced relevance, but instead, let's say, uncertainty, as the base for IR, we would have today a very different IR, and probably not that successful. In general, relevance, according to *Webster*, means having significant bearing on matter at hand. As with many other concepts, relevance assumes related but more specific meaning in more specific contexts and applications.

In the context of information science, relevance is the attribute or criterion reflecting the effectiveness of exchange of information between people and IR systems in communi-cation contacts based on valuation by people. With relevance as the criterion, and human judgments of relevance of retrieved objects as the measuring instrument, the measures of precision and recall are widely used in evaluation of IR systems. The strength of these measures is that they involve people—users—as judges of effectiveness of performance. The weakness is the same: it involves judgement by people, with all the perils of subjectivity and variability. Relevance indicates a relation. For relevance, many relations have been investigated.

An consensus has emerged in information science that we can distinguish between several differing relations that account for different manifestations or types of relevance:

- *System or Algorithmic Relevance:* Relation between a query and information objects in the file of a system as retrieved, or as failed to be retrieved, by a given procedure or algorithm. Comparative effectiveness in inferring relevance is the criterion for system relevance.
- *Topical or Subject Relevance:* Relation between the subject or topic expressed in a query and topic or subject covered by retrieved texts, or, more broadly, by texts in the system file, or even in existence. Aboutness is the criterion by which topicality is inferred.
- *Cognitive Relevance or Pertinence:* Relation between the state of knowledge and cognitive information need of a user and texts retrieved, or in the file of a system, or even in existence. Cognitive correspondence, infor-mativeness, novelty, information quality, and the like are criteria by which cognitive relevance is inferred.
- *Situational Relevance or Utility:* Relation between the situation, task or problem at hand and texts retrieved by a system, or in the file of a system, or even in existence. Usefulness in decision making, appropriateness of information in resolution of a problem, reduction of uncertainty, and the like are criteria by which situational relevance is inferred.
- *Motivational or Affective Relevance:* Relation between the intents, goals, and motivations of a user and texts retrieved by a system, or in the file of a system, or even in existence. Satisfaction, success, accomplish-ment, and the like are the criteria for inferring motivational relevance.

Practically, IR systems assess systems relevance only-that is, they respond to queries-hoping that the objects retrieved may also be of cognitive relevance, and even more so of utility. However, a user may judge an object by any or all types of relevance-for a user they may interact dynamically. Difficulties arise when an object is of system relevance but not of cognitive relevance or utility, or conversely.

If items are of cognitive relevance or utility, but were not reflected in the query, they are not and cannot be retrieved. At the bottom of IR research is a quest to align systems with other types of relevance. People all over have a strong intuitive understanding of relevance, thus, they intuitively understand, without manuals, what IR is all about. This makes IR systems generally understandable and acceptable-a critical attribute in their widespread application.

DISCIPLINARY RELATIONS

Two things introduced interdisciplinarity in information science. First and foremost, the problems addressed cannot be resolved with approaches and constructs from any single discipline-thus, intedisciplinarity is predetermined, as it is in many modern fields. Second, interdisciplinarity in information science was introduced and is being perpetuated to the present by the very differences in backgrounds of people addressing the described problems. Differences in background are many; they make for richness of the field and difficulties in communication and education. Clearly not every discipline in the background of people working on the problem made an equally relevant contri-bution, but the assortment was responsible for sustaining a strong interdisciplinary characteristic of information science. I will concentrate on interdisciplinary relations with two fields: librarianship and computer science. Obviously, other fields, most notably cognitive science and communication, have also interdisciplinary relations, but these are the most significant and developed ones.

Librarianship

Librarianship has a long and proud history devoted to organization, preservation, and use of graphic records and records in other media. This is done through libraries not only as a particular organization or type of information system, but even more so as an indispensable social, cultural, and educational institution whose value has been proven manifold throughout human history, and across all geographic and cultural boundaries.

Researcher defines the library as:

- . . .Contributing to the total communication system in society. . . Though the library is an instrumentality created to maximize the utility of graphic records for the benefits of society, it achieves that goal by working with the individual and through the individual it reaches society.

The common ground between library science and information science, which is a strong one, is in sharing of their social role and in their general concern with effective utilization of graphic and other records, particularly by individuals.

But there are also very significant differences in several critical respects, among them:

- *Selection of Problems Addressed and the Way they were Defined*: A majority of the problems were not and are not addressed in library science;
- *Theoretical Questions Asked and Frameworks Established*: The theories and conceptual frameworks in librarian-ship have no counterpart in information science, and *vice versa*;
- *The Nature and Degree of Experimentation and Empirical Development and the Resulting Practical Knowledge and Competencies Dderived*: There is very little overlap in experimentation and development between the two, and professional requirements differ as well to a significant degree;
- *Tools and Approaches Used:* A most telling example is the very different approach undertaken in relation to utilization of technology in IR and in library automation; and
- *The Nature and Strength of Interdisciplinary Relations Established and the Dependence of Progress on Inter-disciplinary Approaches*: Librarianship is much more selfcontained.

All of these differences warrant a conclusion that librarian-ship and information science are two different fields in strong interdisciplinary relations, rather than one and the same field, or one being a special case of the other. This is not a matter of turf battles, or of one being better or worse than the other. Such arguments, while common between many fields, matter little to progress of either field. But differences in selection and/or definition of problems addressed, agenda, paradigms, theoretical base, and practical solutions *do* matter. Thus the conclusion that librarianship and information science, while related, are different fields. The differences are most pronounced in the research agenda and directions.

Interestingly, research on OPACs, now that they are incorporating more and more IR features, is bringing the two fields in closer relation. Probably, so will the research in digital libraries, but at this time, it is too early to tell. The conclusion is not without heated controversy.

Among other authors, Vakkari contends on information science and librarianship being one and the same field, with the now commonly used name of "library and information science." Does it matter? Administratively yes, very much so, particularly in universities and professional societies. Otherwise, no. The issue is, and always will be, in the problems addressed and solutions undertaken. I contend that they differ significantly.

Computer Science

The basis of relation between information science and computer science lies in the application of computers and computing in IR, and the associated products, services, and networks. In the last few years, this relation also involves research on the evolving digital libraries, with their strong technological base.

To illustrate the connection, we use a definition by Denning:

> "The discipline of computing is the systematic study of algorithmic processes that describe and transfer information: their theory, analysis, design, efficiency, implementation, and application. The fundamental question underlying all of the computing is: "What can be automated?"

Computer science is about algorithms related to infor-mation interpreted in the first, whereas information science is about the very nature of information and its use by humans, interpreted in the third or broadest sense. Computer science is about symbol manipulation, whereas information science is about content manipulation, where symbol manipulation is the indispensable infrastructure. The two concerns are not in competition, they are complementary—they lead to different basic and applied agendas. Computer science is also many times larger than information science.

A number of computer scientists have been involved in research and development on information and its many spin-offs, to the point of being recognized leaders in information science. Gerard Salton is a prime example. In addition, there are several streams of research and development in computer science that had no connection with the early evolution of information science, but have addressed information problems similar to those in information science. Among others, these include works on expert systems, knowledge bases, hypertext, and human-computer interaction.

More recently, this involves research and development on digital libraries, a "hot", financially heavily supported area by a host of government agencies in the U.S. and many other countries. Bolstered by heavy support, interest in digital library research exploded on the scene in 1990s, attracting the attention of computer scientists from a wide variety of streams, as well as people from many other disciplines. These areas have a significant informational component that is associated with information representation, its intellectual organization, and linkages; meta-information, information seeking, searching, retrieving, and filtering; use, quality, value, and impact of information; evaluation of information systems from user and use perspective; and the like-all traditionally addressed in information science.

Conversely, these streams of computer science research and development provide a different outlook, framework, and approach, and even a different paradigm, not only for information science research and development, but also for its academic and continuing education. Again, as with librarianship, the issue is not about turf. It is about paradigms, theoretical foundations, and pragmatic solutions; and ultimately, it is about their appropriateness to human information problems.

EDUCATION

That education is critical for any field is a truism that hardly needs to be stated. In particular, research lives by education, it cannot be better than the education that researchers receive and then extend and plow back into education. Unfortunately, education in information science has not received the attention that it deserves. This may explain the many difficulties in the field that I have discussed. Educational models that evolved differed to a degree or even substantially from country to country. I am concentrating here on the U.S. models only. In the United States, two educational models evolved over time. I call them the Shera and Salton models, after those that pioneered them. Both have strengths and weaknesses. Jesse H. Shera was a legendary library school dean from the 1950s until the 1970s at Western Reserve University. Among others, he was instrumental in starting the Center for Documentation and Communication Research in 1955. Shortly thereafter, the library school curriculum started to include courses such as "Machine Literature Searching" and several other more advanced courses and laboratories on the topics of research in the Centre.

The basic approach was to append those courses, mostly as electives, to the existing library school curriculum, without modifications of the curriculum as a whole, and particularly not the required core courses. Information science became one of the specialty areas of library science. The base or core courses that students were taking rested in the traditional library curriculum. Information science education was an appendage to library science. A few attempts to spin off information science as an independent degree and curriculum were not followed widely. But Shera's model was. Library schools in the U.S. and in many other countries imitated Shera's model.

They used the same approach and started incorporating information science courses in their existing curriculum as a specialty. Out of this was borne the current designation "library and information science." Shera's model is still the prevalent approach in schools of library and information science. The strength of the Shera model is that it posits education within a service framework, connects the education to professional practice and to a broader and user-oriented frame of a number of other information services, and relates it to a great diversity of information resources.

The weakness is a lack of a broader theoretical frame-work and a total lack of teaching of any formalism related to systems, such as development and understanding of algori-thms. The majority of researchers in the human-centered side, as I described earlier, came from or are associated with this educa-tional environment. Gerard Salton was first and foremost a scientist, a computer scientist, and the father of modern IR.

As such, he pioneered the incorporation into IR research a whole array of formal and experimental methods from science, as modified for algorithmic and other approaches used so successfully in computer science. His primary orientation was research. For education, he took the time-honoured approach of a close involvement with research. Salton's model was a laboratory and research approach to education.

As Shera's model resulted in information science educa-tion being an appendage to library science education, Salton's model of IR education resulted in it being a specialty of and an appendage to computer science education. Computer science students that were already well-grounded in the discipline, got involved in SMART and other projects directed by Salton, worked and did research in the laboratory, completed their theses in areas related to IR, and participated in the legendary IR seminars.

They also published widely with Salton and with each other, and participated with high visibility in national and international conferences. From Harvard and Cornell, his students went to a number of computer science departments where they replicated Salton's model. Many other computer science departments in the U.S. and abroad took the same approach.

The strength of Salton's model is that it:

"Starts from a base of a firm grounding in formal mathematical and other methods, and in algorithms, and

- Relates directly to research.

The weakness is in that it:

- Ignores the broader aspects of information science, as well as any other disciplines and approaches dealing with the human aspects that have great relevance to both the outcomes of IR research and the research itself, and
- Does not incorporate professional practice where these systems are realised and used. It loses users.

Consequently, this is a successful, but narrowly concen-trated education in IR as a specialty of computer science, rather then in information science. Not surprisingly, the researchers in the systems-centred approach came out of this tradition. The two educational approaches are completely independent of each other. Neither is connected to the other. Neither reflects fully what is going on in the field. While in each model there is an increase in cognizance of the other, there is no educational integration of the systems-and usercentered approaches.

The evident strengths that are provided by Shera and Salton model are not put together. Their weaknesses are perpetuated. It is high time for communities from each model to try to integrate education for information science. It is an open question whether the human-and systems-centered approaches can fruitfully work together as urged in all those calls for human-centered design until an educational inte-gration occurs.

While library education receives formal attention from the *American Library Association* (ALA), and education for computer science from ACM, no such formal attention is paid by any professional/scientific society to education for information science, or for IR in particular. Neither ASIS nor SIGIR, as primary homes for information science, have been involved to any great extent in educational matters, such as setting of standards or devising model curricula. Clearly, there is a need and an opportunity for more substantive involvement by both organizations in educational issues.

INFORMATION MANAGEMENT IN DIGITAL LIBRARIES

The Self-Organising Map (SOM) has been proposed as an alternative interface for exploring Digital Libraries (DL), in addition to conventional search and browsing. With advanced visualisations assisting the user in understanding the contents of the map and its structure, as well as advanced interaction modes as zooming, panning and area selection, the SOM becomes a feasible alternative to classical search and browse interfaces.

Several applications show the SOMs utility for this task. However, there are still shortcomings in helping the user understanding the map there are insufficient methods developed for describing the map to support the user in the analysis of the map contents.

In this paper, we give an overview of existing techniques and applications of SOMs in Digital Libraries, and present recent work in assisting the user in exploring the map by automatically describing maps using advanced labelling and summarisation of map regions. Therewith, the SOM becomes an attractive tool for Information Management.

The Self-Organising Map (SOM):

- Is a popular unsupervised neural network model that provides a mapping from a high-dimensional input space (for example text documents described in a vector space model) to a low, often two-dimensional, output space. The mapping of the SOM is topology preserving – elements close in the input space will also be close in the output space. Due to its interesting properties, the SOM has been used in several applications to automatically organise documents in a Digital Library by their content. Examples are text, as in the SOMLib Digital Library system.
- Or in a map of news texts.
- Or music in the SOMeJB system.
- As a recent example also the Digital Library Management System (DLMS) developed by the DELOS Network of Excellence.
- Reckons the possibilities of using the SOM as an interface to a Digital Library's content, as it offers the user support in analysing and exploring the content. With advanced visualisations and interaction possibilities, the user can exploit the full potential of the SOM.

However, we still lack techniques to adequately help the user in analysing the contents of the map. For large maps, containing several tens of thousands documents describing various different topics, it becomes increasingly difficult to quickly analyse the map.

In this paper, we give an overview of existing applications of the Self-Organising Map in Digital Libraries and techniques to explore and interact with the map.

Furthermore, we present recent work in making the SOM more usable for Information Management by automatically describing regions in the map through adding semantic labels to the SOM, using clustering methods to identify topical areas and selecting representative labels for those regions. Moreover, we present work on automatically summarising the content of those regions on the SOM.

The remainder of this paper is organised as follows: Section II gives a brief overview of the Self-Organising Map and its application in the context of Digital Libraries. Section III describes our work in labelling and summarising regions, while Section IV presents the experiments conducted. Section V presents conclusions and future work.

SELF-ORGANISING MAP

The Self-Organising Map (SOM) has been successfully used for clustering various kinds of data. It provides a mapping from a high-dimensional input space to a lower-dimensional output space.

In the context of Digital Libraries, the input space is mostly a vector-space model representation of the documents the Digital Library holds, may it be text, images, audio, video, or any other media that can be represented in vectorial form.

Although many different architectures exist, the output space is in many applications organised as a two-dimensional rectangular grid of units, a representation that is easily understandable for users due to its analogy to 2-D maps. Each of the units on the map is assigned a weight vector, which is of the same dimensionality as the vectors in the input space.

During the training process, vectors from the input space are presented to the Self-Organising Map, and the unit with the most similar weight vector to this input vector is determined.

The weight vector of this unit, and, to a lesser extent, of the neighbouring units, are adapted towards the input vector, *i.e.,* their distance in the input space is reduced.

At the end of the training process, the output space will be arranged in a way to represent the input space as closely as possible.

For more details on the SOM training process, please refer *e.g.,* to. An important property of the SOM is that the mapping is topology preserving – elements which are located close to each other in the input space will also be closely located in the output space, while dissimilar patterns will be mapped on opposite regions of the map.

The SOM therefore provides a sort of clustering of the data, however, without explicitly assigning data items to clusters. It neither identifies cluster boundaries as opposed to, e.g, the k-Means method.

The generated map can help the user in getting a quick overview of the patterns in the input space. With fitting visualisations highlighting boundaries, it also allows an easier interpretation of the cluster structures and correlations in the content.

A. Self-Organising Maps in Digital Libraries

The Self-Organising Map as an interface to digital document collections has already been proposed in the WEBSOM project., where the contents of a newsgroup collection containing a million of articles was clustered on the map. The application provides the user with a map of the document collection which she can zoom into by pre-defined levels and navigate in.

- On the most detailed zooming level, a list of the documents mapped onto that region of the map is provided. The map itself, and the exact position of the documents on the map, is not available anymore. To add semantic meaning, the map gets automatically labelled by the names of the most dominant corresponding newsgroups, which is a feasible approach when some kind of categorisation is available for the documents. The labels are however not determined by topical clusters, but rather on a unit basis. The SOM as an interface to Digital Libraries has further been demonstrated in the SOMLib Digital Library System
- The SOMLib system utilises the SOM and other techniques to support the user by employing as many concepts as possible which she already knows from a conventional library. Similar to a map of a conventional library, depicting the arrangement of the shelves where books on certain topics are located, the SOM gives the overview over the contents of the Digital Library. Similar to finding related books in the same shelf, once the user has found a specific document of interest, she can find documents that are related in content in the neighbourhood of that document. A symbolic visualisation of bookshelves using the LIBViewer method further supports this metaphor. The SOMLib system utilises a labelling algorithm to automatically add semantic descriptors to the single map units, without having the need for any category information being available.
- The SOM is used to create a web-based knowledge map of news articles. The application supports hierarchical zooming into the map in pre-defined levels of zoom. However, the map layout changes on

different levels of zooming. Besides the map, also a hierarchical list of topics is displayed as an alternative for users who prefer a onedimensional visualisation. uses clustering on the map to apply labels to regions, which are generated based on term and document frequencies, using a tf × idf-based approach.

The focus in this work is on the visualisation, which tries to resemble geographical maps as closely as possible. This is achieved using a separate GIS software system.

The interaction possibilities for the user are limitedzooming is in predefined levels, the labels cannot be changed interactively, and only one type of visualisation is available. Based on the concept of the SOMLib system, a sophisticated desktop client software has been developed, which allows for various ways of user interaction with the Digital Library content.. With zooming and panning functionalities, the user can analyse the content at any desired detail level, from viewing the whole map at once down to viewing single documents.

Tools for selecting rectangular regions or units along a path allow the user to select several documents at once, and open them for example in a text viewer or in an audio application for playlist generation. One important aspect of SOMs as interfaces to Digital Libraries is that they should not be meant to replace traditional query and retrieval techniques, but rather be complementary to it. This approach is presented in., where a Self-Organising Map is integrated into the popular open-source system Greenstone as a new service, based on the existing query services such as search or list browsing.

That way, the user can still use all the basic functionalities provided by Greenstone, but she will also be able to use the wealth of additional information the SOM mapping provides about the documents matching the query results and the whole collection itself.

A screenshot of the system is depicted in Figure, where the left side figures the traditional Greenstone search interface, the lower part the document result listing, and the right part holds the map. The map can be used in two different ways. First, results of the Greenstone search will be highlighted on the map by markers.

The user can immediately see which documents have a topical similarity, as these documents will usually all be located close to each other and form a cluster on the map. This way, distinguishing between different topics found on an ambiguous word as *e.g.,* 'jaguar' becomes easily – the documents referring to the sports car will be clearly separated from those talking about the animal because they appear in a different context together with other words.

Additionally, outliers found via the search become visible as isolated spots on the map. Secondly, the user can explore the map – she can select nodes, upon which the documents lying on that nodes will be added to the result list of the Greenstone search.

This allows the user to retrieve potentially relevant documents for a specific information need, even if they were not initially retrieved by the (usually rather short) query issued. Documents that have been matched both by the map selection and the search result will be marked especially, as they may be of higher importance.

The user can get additional information on the content of the collection by mouse-over popups displaying terms that best describe the documents on a certain node. A small user study suggested that this interface is suitable for Digital Libraries once the user has become a bit familiar with the map.

The SOM has also been used for other types of media besides text. In the SOMeJB project, the concept of the SOMLib system has been extended to audio and music documents. Similar to the SOMLib system, the SOMeJB arranges musical pieces, described by a set of feature vectors extracted solely from the audio content, into topical clusters by the sound characteristics, as the user is familiar with from a traditional record store. In the PicSOM project., the SOM has been used for Information Retrieval in image databases, incorporating methods of relevance feedback.

III. DESCRIBING THE SELF-ORGANISING MAP REGIONS

In this section we present our work on identifying and describing regions in the mapping generated by the Self- Organising Map. As the SOM does not generate a partition of the map into separate clusters, we utilise another clustering algorithm on the weight vectors of the units to identify the regions.

Applying the LabelSOM method, we create semantic labels for those regions that assist the user in getting a first glance overview of the contents of the map. To further support the analysis phase, we additionally provide summarisation of documents of the regions using Automatic Text Summarisation methods.

Clustering

Clustering is an unsupervised process of finding natural groupings amongst unlabelled objects. The members of a cluster are similar in some way, and are dissimilar to members of other clusters.

To identify topical regions, we are clustering the units of a SOM applying an agglomerative, hierarchical clustering algorithm on the units' weight vectors.

In the beginning of an agglomerative clustering process, every unit lies in its own cluster. In each subsequent step, the two nearest clusters are merged, until finally only one cluster remains. Specifically, we use Ward's linkage (also known as minimum variance clustering) as one of the most performant within the linkage clustering families.

In this algorithm, the distance of each pair of clusters is defined by the increase in the "error sum of squares" (ESS) if the two clusters are to be combined. The ESS of a cluster X of $|X|$ values is defined as:

$$ESS(X) = \sum_{i=1}^{|X|} \left| x_i - \frac{1}{|X|} \sum_{j=1}^{|X|} x_j \right|^2$$

and the distance D between two clucters X and Y is defind by

$$D(X,Y) = ESS(X,Y) - [ESS(X) + ESS(Y)]$$

where XY is the union of clusters X and Y. The result of the Ward's algorithm is a hierarchy of clusters which the user can browse through. Increasing the number of displayed clusters means splitting existing clusters into two new ones, while reducing the number of clusters is achieved by merging two clusters into one.

This is advantageous over a non-hierarchical clustering algorithm, where changing the number of clusters might completely change the layout of clusters, which obviously is not a desired behaviour when we want to allow the user to interactively analyse the map contents by changing the number of clusters.

Moreover, hierarchical clustering allows us to at the same time display multiple layers with a different number of clusters. In contrast to other clustering algorithms, the clusters of a layer with more clusters can never be cut by clusters of a layer with less clusters.

Labelling Units with LabelSOM

To assist the user in interpreting the regions of the SOM, we automatically generate labels for the clusters we identified previously.

The cluster labels are based on the units labels generated by the LabelSOM method, which assigns labels to the units of the SOM describing the features of the data points mapped onto the respective unit.

This is done by utilising the quantisation error qik of the vector elements, which is the sum of the distances for a feature between the unit's weight vector mi and all the input vectors xj 2 Ci, *i.e.,* the vectors mapped onto the unit i.

$$q_{i_k} = \sum_{x_j \in C_i} \sqrt{\left(m_{i_k} - x_{j_k}\right)^2} \quad k = 1 \ldots n$$

This means that a low quantisation error characterises a feature that is similar in all input vectors to the weight vector. Thus the assumption is made that this feature describes the unit well.

If the input vector however contains features which are non-existent and therefore have the value of 0, those attributes often also have a quantisation error of almost 0 for a unit.

Such features are in most cases not appropriate for labelling the unit, since this would describe what the unit does not contain. Therefore, we require a feature to also have a minimum average value, calculated from all the input vectors mapped to the unit.

Labelling Regions

To choose a label for a region, we consider only the unit labels present in that cluster, as the unit labels are already a selection of features describing the contents of each unit. This method is faster in computation than checking all possible features. Depending on the data, it is preferable to choose the region label based upon a low average quantisation error, a high mean value, or a combination of both.

Therefore we offer the user the possibility to interactively assign priority weights for those two measures, to achieve more meaningful labels.

Making use of the properties of the hierarchical clustering as described in Section III-A, we can also display two or more different levels of labels, some being more global, some being more local. In the visualisation of the SOM, the labels are placed in the centroid of the cluster, which may result in some overlapping labels.

To achieve a clear arrangement, the labels can be manually moved on the map, or adjusted in their size and rotation. For some labels, it might also be useful to edit their text, for example if the label text is only a word stem as in our experiment described later in this paper.

Region Summarisation

Even though labelling the map regions assists the user in quickly getting a coarse overview of the topics, labels can still be ambiguous or not conveying enough information. Therefore, we also employ methods from the Automatic Text Summarisation field.

Based on the regions identified from the clustering process, we automatically provide a short summary of the contents of the documents mapped onto those regions, allowing the user to get a deeper insight into the contents.

Automatic Text Summarisation tries to automatically generate a summary of one or more texts to present the main ideas of the contents in a short and compact form. It can in principle be divided into two areas: single and multidocument summarisation.

Single document summarisation deals with providing a summary of a single document, may it be by extraction of the most relevant sentences, or the more sophisticated approach of generating an abstract of the text. Multi-Document summarisation, on the other hand, deals with generating summaries of a whole collection of documents. Simple approaches would just treat each single document separately, generate the summary of it, and then present all the summaries to the user.

This approach of course does not consider redundancy in the extracted sentences. More advanced techniques would treat the whole document collection at once, and extract the sentences which are most important concerning all documents. Redundant sentences are eliminated first by applying a measure for overlapping words, and remove sentences with too high similarity.

Although we also provide summaries of single documents in our application, the main focus is to assist the user in analysing the contents of the Digital Library by providing summaries of the previously identified regions using multidocument summarisation. The application allows the user to select whole regions, or manually any other rectangular shape or units a long a path.

For the chosen documents, the user can choose from several different summarisation algorithms using different weighting schemes to determine the importance of sentences for the summaries, and can also specify the desired length of the summary, measured in per cent of the original sentences.

EXPERIMENTS

The following experiments were performed using the 20 newsgroups data set1, a big benchmark corpus which has become very popular for text experiments in the field of machine learning. The data set consists of newsgroup postings from the 20 newsgroups listed in Table.

Each newsgroup contains 1,000 articles from the year 1993; each text consists of the message body and in addition the 'Subject' and the 'From' header lines.

Table. The 20 Newsgroups Data Set.

alt.atheism	rec.motorcycles	soc.religion.christian	comp.graphics
rec.sport.baseball	talk.politics.guns	comp.os.ms-	rec.sport.hockey
talk.politics.mideast			
windows.misc			
comp.sys.ibm. pc.hardware	sci.crypt	talk.politics.misc	
comp.sys.mac. hardware	sci.electronics	talk.religion.misc	
comp. windows.x	misc.forsale	sci.med	
rec.autos	sci.space		

In our experiments we used a standard bag-of-words indexing approach. Porter's stemming algorithm was applied to remove prefixes and suffixes to obtain word stems. From the remaining word stems, the features for the input vectors were selected according to their document frequency, and the weights are computed using a standard tf $\times$ idf weighting scheme.

This resulted in a 3151 dimensional feature vector for each document, from which the maps were trained. The specific map we will use in the remainder of this paper to illustrate our results is of 75 $\times$ 55 units in size.

Cluster Hierarchy Browsing and Labelling Regions

In our application it is possible to explore the clustered SOM interactively: to view the different levels of clustering and to zoom into the map to view the single postings. The user can browse the clustering levels either viewing only the cluster borders, or also highlighting each cluster in a different colour.

The former is shown in Figure, illustrating the steps from one to eight clusters. There is a special cluster in the lower right-hand corner with the a label also used on other clusters – 'god' in the fourth step, and 'gun' in the steps five to seven.

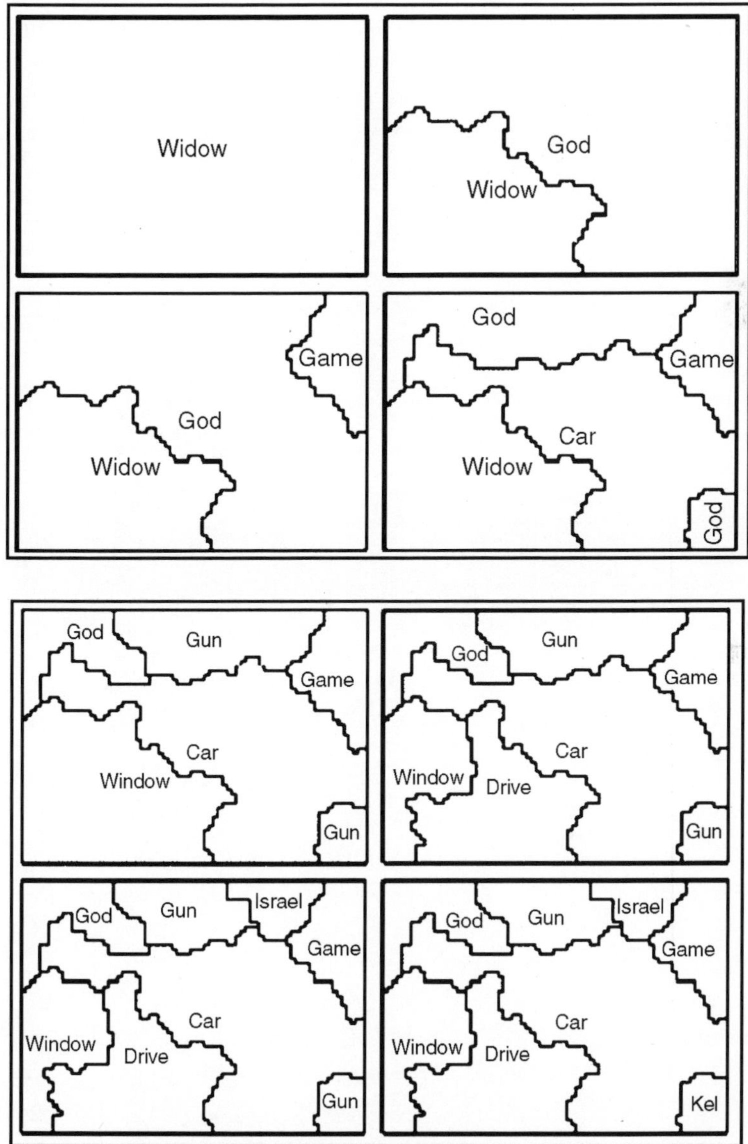

Fig. Clusters With Labels.

This cluster is, however, not a separate one when viewing the clustering with colours, it becomes apparent that this area is part of the disjoint clusters 'god' and 'gun', respectively, in the upper part of the map. With this interactive exploration of the clusters, the user can gain valuable information about the structure of the documents in the collection.

The upper image in Figure shows nine clusters with larger labels, and in addition 67 clusters with smaller labels.

The two clusters labelled 'david' are in fact one disjointed cluster. As a result of the stemming algorithm, words ending with an y now end with an i, for example the labels 'kei' (containing most of sci.crypt) or 'batteri' (various postings *e.g.,* from sci.electronics or rec.motorcycles). There are also some labels where obviously the suffixes of the original words have been removed, as in the labels 'imag' or 'insur'.

The labels were not edited to show the terms based on which the map has been created. In the top right-hand corner is a large cluster labelled 'game' containing most postings from the two sports related newsgroups.

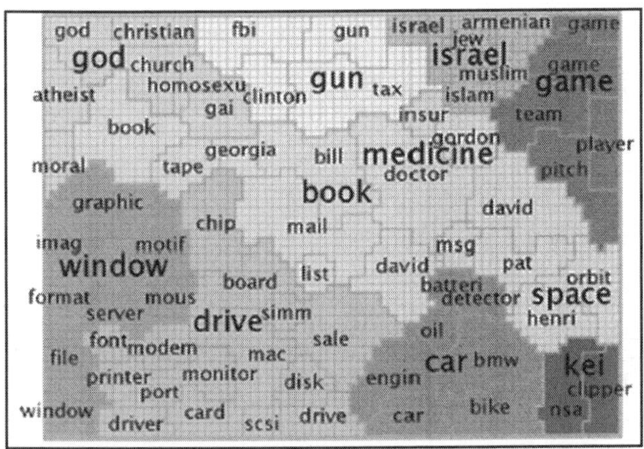

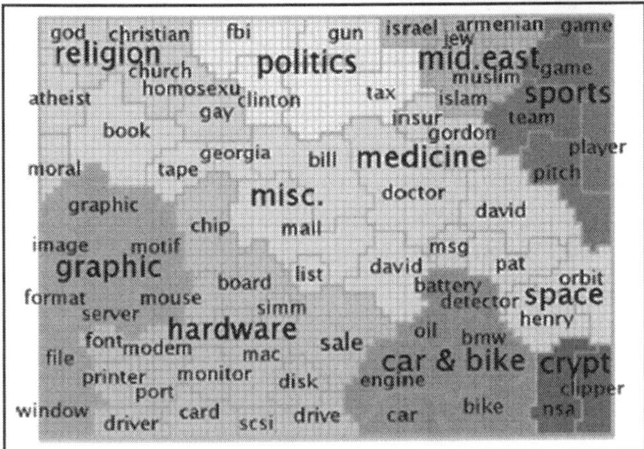

Fig. Nine Coloured and Labelled Clusters and 67 Smaller Clusters with Labels.

The large cluster next to it labelled 'israel' contains mainly postings from talk.politics.mideast. In the upper left-hand corner there is a cluster labelled 'god' containing all the newsgroups dealing with religion, *i.e.,* alt.atheism, soc.religion.christian and talk.religion.misc. It is interesting to note, that in contrast to the newsgroup hierarchy, where these groups lie in three different top level hierarchies, they are combined into one cluster here. The large cluster in the middle labelled 'book' contains many of small clusters of which only a few have meaningful labels.

The small clusters labelled 'insur' and 'doctor' suggest that they contain postings from the sci.med newsgroup and the cluster label 'orbit' relates to the newsgroup sci.space. The labels containing names such as 'gordon', 'david' or 'bill' do not help in identifying the underlying topics in those areas of the map.

However, names cannot be easily automatically removed, as some common names as Mark or Bill are also a verb or noun respectively. Furthermore names can sometimes be useful labels, for example if they refer to a famous person. The small cluster labelled 'drive' lies in the cluster with the hardware topics but also directly next to the cluster labelled 'car'.

It imples that in this area lies an transition of the word drive being used in the meaning of hard disk drive or in the meaning of to drive a car. To enhance the comprehensibility of the map some labels are manually edited, which is shown in the lower image of Figure: word endings have been added and the labels of the larger areas have been edited to better suit the diverse topics.

For example the cluster automatically labelled 'car' is extended to 'car and bike' to point out both newsgroups contained in this cluster.

The cluster previously labelled 'gun' containing the newsgroups talk.politics.guns and parts of talk.politics.misc and talk.politics.mideast is adapted to 'politics'. The large cluster in the middle is manually described with three labels to point out the various topics inside.

The map thus created can now be used to interactively present the contained information of the Digital Library in an intuitive way.

In this paper we presented the usage of the Self-Organising Map as an interface to Digital Libraries. On top of this well-known approach, we presented recent work on methods to assist the user in interacting with the map. We employ clustering of the SOM to reveal hierarchical structures which can be explored by the user to get a rough overview of the structure of the data on the map.

The clustering identifies regions, which we describe on the one hand very concisely by single descriptive words extracted from the document contents, and secondly by applying automatic text summarisation techniques to generate executive summaries of the contents. All methods are integrated into a single application, that provides additional features such as visualisations and advanced interaction via zooming and panning, and selection of arbitrary regions of the map.

With these tools available, the user can be greatly assisted in analysing the SOM generated from the contents of the Digital Library, and therefore getting a quick overview of the contents of the Digital Library itself, and the structure and relationship of the documents it contains, even if the number of documents is huge and their topics diverse.

Therewith, the SOM becomes an attractive tool to support Information Management. Future work will focus on user studies on the region identification, labelling and summarisation, and the interaction possibilities with the map.

MANAGEMENT INFORMATION SYSTEMS

Researcher has defined a Management Information System as:

- the process and structure used by an organisation to identify, collect, evaluate, transfer, and utilise information in order to fulfil its objectives. It is a system that provides management with information to make decisions, evaluate alternatives, measure performance, and detect situations requiring corrective action.

The implementation of performance assessment in academic libraries is an essential part of good management practice. Although she had reservations about the current Management Information Systems in university libraries because, for example, few academic libraries had produced a statement of their objectives, she still believed that Management Information Systems could contribute to effective management of library activities.

The four main objectives for Management Information systems have been defined as:

1. To facilitate the decision making process in the library by providing the managers with accurate, timely, and selective information that assists them in determining a specific course of action.
2. To provide for the objective performance measurement and assessment of selected relevant areas of the library. The areas are to be determined during strategic planning.
3. To provide pertinent information about the library's internal and external environments.
4. To provide information on alternative strategies and contingency plans.

The purposes can only be implemented if people look upon Management Information Systems as an integral part of the framework of management in the academic library and not as a peripheral system which has been installed for the benefit of an individual or a single department.

- There may be subsystems within the larger system, which may be branch libraries, or departmental divisions such as cataloguing, acquisitions or circulation, but they must still be seen as integrated parts of the whole, and must function as such. In the systems approach, however, the library organisation must be seen as an organic whole, with information as its lifeblood and in which each part of the system is integrated by the flow of information throughout.

An integrated Management Information System is very important because it can be used to provide supporting information to determine:

- *Efficiency*: is the library doing things right.
- *Effectiveness*: is the library doing the right things.
- *Competitiveness*: is the library heading in a direction which is consistent with the environment.

Any discussion of the Management Information System must lead to consideration of the inputs data, processing data and the outputs data. Inputs to the management information system consist of both internally and externally generated library data. External information covers factors such as legislation, politics, trends in society, changes in technology, user demand, and comparative statistics for other, similar institutions. Internal data is that derived from administrative routines and transactional information. Administrative routines include those related to personnel, finance, acquisition, cataloguing, processing of materials, binding, building services, maintenance services, etc.

Output measures will include data of circulation, general user satisfaction, etc. All service points will need to be monitored so that internal performance comparisons can be made and the contribution of each service point are the overall objectives of the organisation assessed. In term of library managers' needs, a variety of inputs is evidently needed. It may be necessary to process information in different ways for different levels of decision-making needs, and different types of output reports will be needed to meet those different needs.

Selection of appropriate data elements for inclusion in a Management Information System assumes that:

- Clear goals and measurable objectives have been developed for the library,
- For each data element there is rationale for how it will be used or in what combinations with other data elements it can be used to determine success towards the accomplishment of objectives, overall library effectiveness, or performance measures for specific library services/operations, and
- The library can, in fact, collect reliable and valid data for a particular data element.'

The data in a management information system also needs to be processed to turn it into meaningful information for library management. For this reason, management information systems require an appropriate data processing system. Data processing is the capture, storage and processing of data for the purpose of transforming it into information useful for decision making.

In recent years, data processing for management information systems in business and industry has increasingly been undertaken by computers:

- A modem MIS will always rely to some extent on computer technology, although a computer is not a requirement. The reality of the 1980's would indicate that a computer is a necessity for the most sophisticated systems.

In libraries, in contrast, the development of the use of computer has been:

- Modular, in the sense that it is based on a single library operation such as acquisitions, serials, control or cataloguing. The more general applications of management information lay hidden, as it is often seen only as a departmental resource.

This need not necessarily have been so. An early prediction of the advantages of information produced by computers was made in 1979 by Tague, who suggested that computers should produce information for control at both macro and micro level in libraries.

However, in 1986, Brophy, having analysed eight large computer systems used in British libraries, noted that:

- Automated library systems seem to be primarily about control at the micro level. Moreover, they produced management information which was relatively crude, highly structured and very much a system by-product.

The needs of individual managers tended to be overlooked, especially when the design of MIS was in the hands of computer personnel.

- Too often, management information has been produced as an afterthought following computerisation. Most computerised issue systems, for example, were never designed to produce management information although librarians have often struggled over the data generated by these systems in an attempt to derive some meaningful information about issue patterns.

Technological changes have helped to ease this problem. As opposed to the use of mainframe and mini-computers, 'the advent of the microcomputer now provides an alternative to the dependence on large-scale centralised computer systems. Computer power can now be deployed cheaply to different parts of an organisation to allow for local processing of data.'

Computers should be easily able to provide four types of report: periodic reports, exception reports, on demand reports, and predictive reports. Periodic reports provide routine, statistical information in detailed or summarised form. Exception reports highlight areas requiring managerial attention and would focus on those that have been overlooked. On demand reports provide a response to a particular non-standard question. Predictive reports give forecasts and provide comparisons based on statistical manipulation of data.

The principal requirement of the outputs of academic library management information systems is that they should be of interest to:

- The relevant committee - the members wish to know how the library service is performing and whether the institution, is getting value for money.

- The chief financial officer - his role is primarily custodial, and he wants to be assured that there is no overspending and that money is used for the purpose intended.
- The chief librarian - who wants to know how services under his control are performing in accordance with plans, targets and budgets.
- The managers of individual sections or services—who want to have data on the operations and performance with plans, targets and budgets.
- Outside organisations requesting library perfor-mance data on a regular basis.

In these ways, the outputs of management information systems become information for decision making.

In general, management information is:

- 'The right information in the right form at the right time, so enabling the manager effectively and effici-ently to do his/her job.'

The value or quality of management information is determined by three factors. They are:

1. The content of information: Information is the substance of communication, but to be information rather than data or noise, it must be meaningful, relevant and new to the receiver.
2. The form or presentation of the information: Information should be presented in a style and format readily understandable by the manager. This means that the producer of information must be aware of the recipient's knowledge of technical terms, numeracy/literacy levels, his individual characteristics, the characteristics of the group with which he works and so on. These and other factors help the information producer to form an idea of the perception level of the manager and increase the likelihood of producing understandable information capable of being used which, it will be recalled, is the only way information can create value.
3. The timing of its presentation: Information which is produced must be communicated to the manager in time to be used. Delays in data gathering, processing or communication can transform potentially vital information into worthless waste paper.

In the planning process, information should support the decision making process. Since one of the major problems facing academic libraries is the impact of changes in available financial support, the Colleges of Further and Higher Education Group (CoFHE) of the Library Association has been considering the categories of management information required for making decisions concerning the budget.

They concluded that these are:

- Information about the institutional identity of the library.
- Information about the target group.

- Information about the collection resources.
- Information about the financial resources.
- Information about library personnel.
- Information about facilities and equipment.
- Information about various programmes and functions.

CoFHE also considered the requirements for collecting management information, and suggested the following guidelines:

- The information sought must be worth the costs of collecting it - direct and indirect.
- Consider sources of information already available within the institution before setting up mechanisms to collect it.
- Keep the collection of information relevant, *i.e.,* remember the purpose - 'to support the budget request.'
- Remember to consider qualitative and quantitative data as both can be relevant.

DIGITAL INFORMATION PRESERVATION

In this Chapter we discuss long-term digital preservation from an information perspective, rather than the predominant approaches; the Archival and the Technocratic Approach. Our standpoint is that information is at the core of long-term digital preservation. This means that information is the object of preservation in the long term. Information lives longer than people, organizations and tools (software).

The Information Continuum Model provides support for this standpoint. However, we find that there exists no concept to support practical action in preservation from the information perspective. Existing concepts as information object, digital object, preservation object, electronic record, information package and significant properties are context dependent and focus on the object to be preserved, rather than preservation of information.

Consequently, they are not suitable for realizing the information perspective in long-term digital preservation. The concept of Digital Information Preservation Object is therefore introduced and a tentative definition of the concept is presented.

We believe that Gladney is worth to be quoted to begin this paper. He stated, "If all that information is worth creating in the first place, surely some of it is worth saving!" During the last years, the development of digital technologies has been very fast and for the most unpredictable. Consequently, the amount of information created in electronic form is growing exponentially. Records like scholarly studies, multi-media recordings, business, scientific, government and personal records convey information critical to democratic institutions and to human well-being.

Every citizen depends on some information, partly portions unique to him, for practical as well as cultural reasons. According to Runardotter et al., digital information has to be available for the future society by legal, historical and democratic reasons. For instance, archivists have as their mission the preservation of records and its continuing value and the providing access to those records.

At the same time, the development of technologies has created unforeseen problems, such as the obsolescence of hardware and software. There is no information system capable to retain and make the information accessible for more than 30 years.

Constant upgrading of operative systems and software applications in one hand and new storage technologies on other hand are leading to the very difficult access to information.

File formats are experiencing the same problem because what today is standard for some applications or platform shifts or disappears within a decade. The solutions that are today for preservations and foremost to make digital material accessible on long time are insufficient.

Archival inquiry "Archives for Everyone – Now and in the Future", called attention to these great shortcomings and argued that models, methods and platform-independent software for preservation of the digital material are omitted largely.

On one hand, the "problem" with digital preservation is the lack of proven methods to ensure that the digital information will continue to exist On the other hand, the software currently available does not include good tools for saving digital recorded information in the face of rapid hardware and software obsolescence.

It states that digital preservation is suddenly urgent because the needed technology and infrastructure are not in place. The challenges that needed to be addressed include legal, educational, and technical aspects.

Among these challenges only one difficult technical problem impeded digital archiving until recently – how to preserve information through technology changes. Within the practice of preservation, archives are still using methods developed since 1970-1980. These methods cause losing of functionalities of the records when archiving.

Archival science has not developed as rapid as information technology. Information in the digital era demands several kinds of tools for its processing. Nevertheless, there is a lowest common denominator: digital processing.

However, such processing tools are viewed as mediator for digitally recorded information. Digital material that is produced on a certain platform, with a certain application, a certain version and in a certain format, needs to be converted to other platforms, applications and/or formats in order to gain access to information over time.

Another way of retrieving stored information is to emulate the original software (and platform) in which digital material has been produced. In either way, information might be lost and the information retrieved might not be fully reliable.

According to Runardotter et al., the concepts that are fundamental in archival science, such as record, document or archival record, has not the same dignity in systems science. In information systems sciences there are not methods that in the same degree as in archival science deals with long-term, "forever" perspectives.

This has not been detected as an issue in systems science until recently. The transition between paper based mediums to digital media was not preceded by a strategy for long-term digital preservation.

This phenomenon explained in terms of lack of knowledge and experience when handling digital material. Besides, no one could foresee the speed and complexity of the evolution of computers and software.. Information and long-term digital preservation is one of the acutest questions for all kinds of preservation institutions like archives, libraries, local authorities and for society as a whole.

Society and information curators must face the challenge of finding some sustainable solutions to ensure that digital recorded information of today become accessible and understandable in the future. Otherwise, digital material and likewise one part of society's future cultural heritage and history are in danger of disappearing forever. Consequently, legal and democratic demands cannot be fulfilled.

According to Gladney it was stated, that technology has influence in almost every aspect of long-term digital preservation and it is not widely believed these solutions can be achieved solely through technological means.

To find solutions to the problem much research was limited to technical aspects of preservation but our research has taken another view on long-term digital preservation, which puts information in focus. This paper therefore discusses the concept of information as central for long-term digital preservation.

FACING LONG-TERM DIGITAL PRESERVATION

The authors of this paper are connected to the Long-term Digital Preservation Centre (LDP Centre) in Sweden. The major activities of the LDP Centre concern research and systems development within the field of long-term digital preservation.

The LDP Centre has adopted, at this stage, migration as method for preservation. The starting point for digital preservation was the OAIS Reference Model. In this work, the LDP Centre has developed a model for structure for Information Package.

This structure was (and is) intended to be used by archive creating organizations, in order to later deliver digitally recorded information to long-term digital preservation archives. Conceptually, this model consists of a base structure, and other elements. The base structure consists of different sets of metadata according to well-established international metadata standards used in archiving.

These standards are Metadata Encoding and Transmission Standard (METS, covering technical and provenience metadata), Encoded Archival Context (EAC, covering archival metadata about the creator of the information), Encoded Archival Description (EAD, covering structural metadata) and PREservation Metadata Implementation Strategies (PREMIS, covering technical and process metadata).

We found out that the existing models for structuring information about the object to be preserved, produces problems in implementation. As we can realise from the descriptions above, these structures are used as "wrappers" carrying metadata sometimes overlapping one another.

Consequently, dealing with all these structures causes both intellectual complications and technical implementation difficulties. We, at the LDP Centre, have experienced that all these structures have some kind of inherent philosophy which focuses on special features or attributes of digital material. Here we did three significant observations.

- The used structures do not focus specifically on information.
- Using several structures sometimes causes an intelle-ctual "mess" due to their inherent philosophies (such as ontological confusion).
- The used structures are inherited from the archival world and, as we see, they support legislative (or authority) records more than digitally recorded information in general.

We also found out that putting a lot of efforts on these structures, made us loss focus on that we believe is important to preserve, to be precise information. It is obvious that technical or other aspects of the digital material to be preserved are Ó÷üëéï: kika i boken! indeed important to deal with, but those are just means of preserving information while the digital "technology is a live".

We do not know how long this technology and its tools are going to be a part of our society. Perhaps in just some years from now a new informational paradigm will occur. Another issue concerns the fact it was archival institutions that early experienced the need of digital preservation, it was obvious that the first efforts on preservation started from archival work practices.

Consequently (archival) metadata standards were developed in order to support digital preservation. The archival inheritance spokes for the principle of provenience as one of the stone corners in long-term digital preservation, because this principle supports authenticity and trustworth-iness of any kind of digitally recorded information.

Consequently today's "solutions", based on the Archival and/or the Technocratic Approach, supports preservation only in a (relatively) short-term.

To approach a solution concerning the question about how to preserve information through technology changes and surpassing the archival inheritance, the LDP Centre's research activities has taken a new view on long-term digital preservation, which puts information in focus.

This includes the development of a detached *Digital Information Preservation Object* that is independent of technology and deals with the question of provenience in a new way. Such preservation object might be transferred between different technologies.

This is viewed as the main key to a viable solution for long-term digital preservation. Such view demands a higher level perspective of information and its continuing value without neglecting the constant changing technical aspects of digital preservation.

Developing the Information Approach

This paper is a result of two research activities, literature review and interaction in the developing R&D team at the LDP Centre. The literature review was carried out with the purpose of developing a definition of Digital Information Preservation Object and the interaction helped to gather data about the developed structure through seminars, (informal) "interviews" and systems development meetings.

There is a large quantity of literature about the concept of information. But in comparison, the amount of literature in the field of long-term digital preservation is relatively small.

The process of critical selection of relevant literature was based upon parameters such as "well known writers", "established perspectives and/or schools", in order to address the key sources, key theories and definitions of the topic. Since our intention was to provide a broad view on the subject, the initial literature review made it clear that several research projects have shown its own approaches to what we call Digital Information Preservation Object.

The development of the base structure, were a joint task of the entire LDP Centre. Everyone (at some extent) was involved in its development and several research observations were made during these activities.

The resemblance with Action Research as research method is purely unintentional. Nevertheless, adopting Action Research as a research method in this work will underpin the scientific value of the paper. Some words about Action Research are then necessary.

Action Research, as research method, is suitable in order to describe the origins of the gathered data (the structure developed by the LDP Centre). Further, some of the parts of the named structure were and still are being developed in joint seminars between system developers and researchers at the LDP Centre. This implies that a social context is set up.

This team interacts together in order to find improvements to already existing drafts. Together, the team define problems, co-generate relevant knowledge, learn and take actions. This "socio-technical" unit, is relatively small (nine persons) self-managing and "posses the skills and authority to control the operation of their technology" and appropriate to carry out Action Research a low-system level. In our work, we tackle questions like: what are the elements of the Information

Approach? what properties/characteristics constitute a definition of the notion Digital Information Preservation Object? Since the LDP Centre intends to develop a general preservation model in which Digital Information Preservation Object is the mediator for preservation, this paper will have influence for further research as well as for what methods, models and techniques that will be developed and used. Furthermore, our result will influence the development of the information systems intended to serve long-term digital preservation.

About Information

The term information is used with different meanings by different groups and in different contexts and there is no well-defined definition of the terms "data" and "information". A common and short definition is that information is interpreted data. Hence, data is signs used to represent information, or signs which carries with them the possibility to compose and/or decompose the text, photo, music etc. from which it is derived.

Thus, retrieving the source provides access to information and we can start reading/viewing/listening but also interpreting and analysing the information existing in the source.

This results in the creation of knowledge, that is, we learn from information. The central idea is that data become information by a process of interpretation. The infological equation states that I = i (D, S, t) where *I* represent the information we can get through the interpretation process *i*, which is operating on data *D*, together with our pre-knowledge *S*, during a certain time *t*. Langefors [ibid.] states that "One of the central insights from infology is that data or texts do not "contain" information (knowledge) but will only, at best, represent the information to those who have the requisite 'pre-knowledge'" and he also means that the infological equation is a representation of this.

Dealing with information systems require a broad view of information, since using a computer implicitly involves information services of some kind, that is, we get service by being informed by data. According to Langefors it is necessary to define information as knowledge, since "information is knowledge and not physical signs".

He regards information as knowledge structured in such a way that it is communicated. Because of this it can also be stored, which leads to information being stored knowledge. Checkland and Holwell provides the view that information is a service that supports decision making within organizations. Data are facts and a starting point for mental processes.

They introduce the concept of "capta", which is the result of selection of certain data (we pay attention to, create some new category or get surprised by the data). In other words, data that catches our interest transforms to capta, a consciousness of something.

This signifies that turning data into information is done through a mental process and during that process the data changes shape, and will ultimately lead to knowledge. Once we have selected, paid attention to or created some data, or turned it into capta, we relate it to other things or put it in a context, we attribute meaning to it, and by this we once again convert it, this time to information.

This can be done individually or collectively and this process, selection and conversion of data into meaningful information can lead to larger structures of related information, or what we call knowledge. The interpretation process emphasizes is implicit in this reasoning.

This is line with our claim – that information is not equated with knowledge. Just like data must be interpreted in order to become information, so must information be interpreted and analysed in order to be knowledge. Information is never the knowledge itself, the knowledge is within the knower.

We agree with Langefors with his notion that in order to understand information people must have pre-knowledge. This we see as knowledge that consists of the ability to assimilate the information, but also to have an understanding of the information content, or the subject in focus.

If these abilities are found, new knowledge is created the moment someone (individually or in a group) thinks of an issue. When people's ideas, or knowledge, are being shaped and transferred to a media they are made available for others to share. Hence, the knowledge has now once again become information and exists physically (or digitally), available for people who need it in order to learn and increase their knowledge of something, for example within an organization.

Information Continuum Perspective

Runardotter et al., put information in a long-term digital preservation context that is a new circular view of the information life cycle. Information lives longer than people, organizations and tools. The authors manifested that information is a living concept and is in progress during constant ongoing process.

The fact is that people, organizations and tools are replaced over time. Further, they observed the phenomenon that information never dies provided that it is preserved and used. The statement is based on that information is constantly shaped and reshaped, evolving through time, picking up further information or losing some parts and in that way information is all the time under reconstruction.

To keep information alive demands a set of ongoing activities, both organizational and technical. The idea of living spiral is also supported by the Records Continuum Model and Information Continuum Model. According these models information and records continues to evolve in space/time and therefore are no end products..

The Records Continuum Model is widely known about and discussed in the archival profession, unlike the Information Continuum Model discussion of which is only just beginning to be opened up. The named models are founded on Giddens' structuration theory.

This theory of time/space distanciation has been translated into a "rhythm" for information processing derived from the processes of creating information, capturing it as recorded information, organising it and bringing it together within the plural domains of competition.

Each item of information once created, may or may not be recorded, stored and managed in ways that can benefit individuals, groups, communities, and can push that information out into the plural domains of the further reaches of space/time.

The continua (the dimesions of the model) in the Information Continuum Model are collectively meant to focus analytical attention on the nature of recorded information as an allocative resource, something to be shared and to be used within our activities.

The continua in the Records Continuum Model collectively are meant to focus analytical attention on the nature of recorded information as an authoritative resource, something to be relied upon not because of its content but because of the way, it has been created and maintained with some continuing contact to the original specificities of its occurrence.

According to Upward, information (and its reconstituted products) outwardly spiral from the original act of creation of a document. This idea is also derived from Giddens' theory of structuration. In the Information Continuum Model, information is derived from a principle source (for example, an information object such as an interview), and becomes transformed through the agency of people and technologies for different purposes.

Information Objects are both embedded in the "context of the action in which they are part, and are recursively involved". Information artefacts, as records and outcomes of action, become disembedded and reused in other contexts, for example, a research interview is "unitised" and its parts are reconstituted via different technologies or processes as evidence for particular research and theoretical constructions in academic production.

The interview, or any data, is therefore moved space/time, and is reconstituted, reused, re-embedded according to particular human or machine agency (human speech is transformed by agency of speech recognition software into text), or human agency makes particular interpretive decisions about how ambiguous sounds should be transcribed in transcription.

The interview data (or its constituent parts) become pluralized with the production of different knowledge artefacts: theory, the application of theory and the development of scholarly and practical publications. Its pluralisation can also lead to it being used in other forms of action, such as social action, lobbying, or policymaking.

The incorporation of the time/space dimension is also important for several reasons. First, it recognises that information object have a changing historical life, and in addition, the reconstruction of time and space through modernity, and particularly through the agency of ICTs, gives information objects new potentiality.

We could use Giddens own "words" and transform these to our vocabulary of Information Continuum. Giddens "structure" equals to rules and resources organized as properties of systems.

Systems equal to reproduced relations between actors or collectivities organized as social practices. Finally structuration equals to the continuity or transformation of structures, and therefore the reproduction of systems.

The dynamic of structuration is crucial in our view. "Social practices evolve over time and space and must replicate even to stay the same" (the essence of long-term digital preservation). The term of continuity (*i.e.,* continuum) promotes the reproduction of systems (*i.e.,* memory traces, organized social practices) by means of digitally recorded information and its continuing value. Information is seen as an (allocative) resource, something to be shared and to be used within our activities.

In the long-term gaining access to digitally recorded information (through longterm digital preservation activities) will tell us what sorts of things were out there in the world. We could summarize our view in simple words as "Digital preservation will ensure, through the continuing value of information, that social systems will be reproduced as memory tracks of human activities".

Predominant Approaches in Long-term Digital Preservation

In our research we could observe that there are two predominant approaches trying to define the object of preservation. The first is closely related to Archival (including Records Management) and the second is a technical (or merely a technocratic) perspective. We could also observe the lack of an approach based on Information (and/or Information Continuum) perspective.

The Object of Preservation in the Archival Approach

A definition of Preservation Object is given by Dollar as "Preservation Objects are those to be archived. These objects are physically compound by set of files in maybe different formats. The objects logically are compound by data – the content for instance birth date of a person, and metadata – that should describe the context when the birth date of a particular person was used".

The Records concept opens another view on the object of preservation. Preservation is a key characteristic for records, which is followed by their creation purpose to be re-used. The preservation also makes the record a vital component in the memory of organizations, individuals and in some cases of society. A record is more than just information, it suppose to be trustworthy *i.e.,* being able to serve as evidence, and support accountability. The time for preservation could vary from days or months up to hundreds of years. The International Standards Organization definition of records is: "Information created, received, and maintained as evidence and information by an organizations or person, in pursuance of legal obligations or in transaction of business."

In the Guide for Managing Electronic Records of the International Council on Archives, from an archival perspective, a similar definition of record is given as "recorded information produced or received in the initiation, conduct or completion of an institutional or individual activity and that comprises content, context and structure sufficient to provide evidence of the activity."

Records can occur in different forms and representations.

They are usually represented as logically delimited information objects, for example, as distinct documents. But increasingly we find records in the form of distributed objects, such as relational databases and compound documents.

According to Thomassen a record has four characteristics, which make the record unique in relation to other types of information:

- Records serve as evidence over actions and transactions
- Records support accountability
- Records are related to processes, *i.e.,* information that is generated by and linked to some work processes
- Records are going to be preserved, some even for eternity.

Cox stated that the evidential value of a record can only exist if the content, structure and context are preserved. The context is the link between different records that belongs together, and also to the process where the record was created. According to Dollar the electronic record is more of a logical entity, where integral parts can be managed at different places within an information system, or even in different information systems.

The question "What is a record" has been one of the fundamental issues in debates and discussions in archiving and digital preservation over the past twenty years. Attempts to arrive at general definition of an *electronic record* were made in the last decade by several research projects and have by now being replaced by more constructive approach to define properties and functionalities of electronic records that need to be preserved in a given context.

An electronic record can be understood as a package or a set of technical properties and possibilities, and of administrative context where some of these technical possibilities were put to use. In contrast, one approach in Digital Libraries that might have a significant difference is proposed by Nichols.

In this approach the concept of "artifact" is central an defined as "a physical object produced at some time in the past, and attesting to a given set of practices, thinking, and ways of viewing the world, but whose importance will be defined by present and foreseeable future needs and use. The value of the artifact is strongly influenced, but not completely determined by, the document/object's features that are unique". An artifact is then an object with a set of values such as Evidential, aesthetic,

Associational, Market and Exhibition value. An artifact is of value to the extent that it testifies to the information being original, faithful, fixed, or stable. Although, this approach do not mention the term record but "artefact", we interpret this approach to be similar to the Archival Approach.

The definitions of records are to some extent usable in our perspective. Nevertheless the usage of terms as "legal obligations" or "accountability" or "evidential" are strongly connected to Records Management and Archiving. Information is important but not central. We perceive the evidentiallity of records as the major focus of Archiving and Records Management and less focus is given to records as informational source. Thomassen gives emphasis in the need of preservation of records in order to be reused as memory traces.

This encompasses our Continuum perspective which is beyond of just records. The "big difference" is that our perspective is turning the precedence of information in relation to Archiving. Another difference is that our perspective deals with any kind of digitally recorded information as evidence of human activities not just with records as legal evidence.

The Object of Preservation in the Technocratic Approach

A definition of Digital Object is given by Blanchi and Petrone as "a unique identified data abstraction that encapsulates content and access policies while providing a high-level, self-describing, type definition. Digital Objects are described trough the use of an abstract typing mechanism that we refer to as content type".

The concept of Information Package of the OAIS Reference Model states that data is interpreted using its Representation Information (described in metadata), which produces information, that an information object consists of not only data content, but also the information necessary to interpret that content. In order to successfully preserve such a generic Information Object, it is critical for an Open

Archival Information System (OAIS) to clearly identify and understand the Data Object and its associated Representation Information, which together forms what, is called an Information Package.

The PREMIS data model describes intellectual entities, objects, rights, agents and events. Objects, according to PREMIS, can be bitstreams, files or representations (digital objects "instantiation or embodying an intellectual entity") Further, in scientific material the notion Preservation Object can be compared to the approach of Persistent Object articulated by the US National Archives (NARA) in cooperation with the San Diego Supercomputing Centre (SDSC).

The persistent object method presumes that all records can be represented as objects with their specific characteristics and behaviour.

The concept of Significant Properties, proposed by the National Library of Australia (NLA), are functions or characteristics of an object that are essential to its meaning. Preservation of digital objects, in this approach, in some cases will necessitate changes in look, feel, functionality or content if the object is to remain usable at all. Although significant properties may be seen as individual and specific to a given object, most digital archives try to create classes of objects based on common properties.

In the Cedars project, Significant Properties were associated with the Underlying Abstract Form (UAF) of an object. Therefore, objects with the same UAF have the same significant properties. Conversely, if significant properties varied, than objects that were otherwise similar could have different UAFs.

The PREMIS working group, following on the work of OAIS, Cedars and NLA, defined Significant Properties as those "characteristics of a particular object subjectively determined to be important to maintain through preservation actions", noting that "Significant properties may be objective technical characteristics subjectively considered to be particularly important, or subjectively determined characteristics".

Further, the FEDORA architecture describes a content container abstraction, the Digital Object, and the nature of Repositories that provide access to these containers.

They conceptualize a Digital Object as having:

- A structural kernel, which encapsulates content as opaque byte stream packages
- An interface, or behaviour, layer that gives contextual meaning to the data in the Digital Object.

One useful metaphor for a Digital Object is that of a cell. A similar approach is given by Saidis et al. as Digital Object Prototypes (DOPs) which provides the Digital Library (DL) designer with the ability to model diverse types of digital objects in a uniform manner while offering digital object type conformance.

They described a Digital Object that has constituent components, that is to say files, metadata, behaviours and relationships. The derived digital object typing information – that is, which components constitute each different type of object and how each object behaves – is not realized in a manner suitable for effective use by higher level Digital Library application logic including DL modules and services.

A DOP is a digital object type definition that provides a detailed specification of its constituent parts and behaviours. Digital objects are conceived as instances of their respective prototypes.

The approach to Digital Libraries proposed by Arms et al. described the "digital object" in a slightly different manner. The main building blocks in this approach are: "digital objects", which are used to manage digital material in a networked environment; "handles", which identify digital objects and other network resources; and "repositories", in which digital objects are stored.

From a computing view, the digital library is built up from simple components, notably digital objects. A digital object is a way of structuring information in digital form, some of which may be metadata, and includes a unique identifier, called a handle. First lets have a look to the terms and concepts used by this approach.

Very common are the terms of "data abstraction", "data", "bitstreams", "files", "instantiation", "characteristics and behaviour", "functions", "functionality", "objective technical characteristics", "structural kernel", "encapsulates opaque byte stream packages", "interface", "metadata", "behaviours and relationships", "manage digital material in a networked environment", "stored". Looking to the ontology of this approach is quite obvious that the terms utilized comes from computer science in general and at some extent from Object Oriented terminology.

This spokes for data management through information systems making data central. The term object is also important being conceptualization of data (such as files, bitstreams, etc.) having some behaviour (its functionality or implemented functions in as information system). No emphasis is made on information neither on its contents as traces of human activities.

Towards a Definition of Digital Information Preservation Object

Every other approach to define a the object of preservation has focused from different perspectives of preservation and from different characteristics of the digital object using its own ontology. Furthermore, we found that a) there is no existing or established definition of Digital Information Preservation Object, b) existing concepts are context dependent and focuses specifically on object to be preserved. After our study we came to conclusions that research carried out so far do not handle

Digital Information Preservation Object from Information Continuum perspective and do not contribute with any definition of the notion Digital Information Preservation Object. However, the studied research results merely focus on the structure and physical nature of the digital object. Their described abstractions are conceptualizations of the underlying physical level. Nevertheless, although these approaches support our activities to some extent, the definitions provided by these approaches are not suitable for our view, hence; we experienced the emergence of an own definition of Digital Information Preservation Object that specifically focuses on information.

However, this study gave us insights to take another perspective. To define the notion of Digital Information Preservation Object it is needed to take a standpoint. We cannot begin the definition from structure of the object; nonetheless, we will begin definition from a global view. If we start from the structure, we are viewing an object as a delimited entity at structural level, since our focus is on information, not the object itself.

We want to distinguish the conventional view to the object that is a construction, a container or a carrier to hold together the elements (depending on level of conceptualization) from the view that is to see an object from continuum perspective. An object there is a piece or pieces of information that reflects human action in a social context in the continuum.

There is an important remark before we provide our tentative definition of Digital Information Preservation Object (DIPO). We need to state that any for any object is to say that its analysis is made depending on the level of abstraction adopted and due a set of variables at that specific level.

The Structure developed at the LDP Centre and the descriptions in section are (technical) conceptualizations of "digital (physical) objects"; they concentrate their efforts in describing or defining (at a very low level) the object to preserve regardless of its continuing information value. Our intention (or level of abstraction) lay merely in the general level or, so to say, we try to define DIPO at an "ethereal" level; we want to define the "thing" DIPO.

We take stand in the philosophy of Dooyeweerd who stated that Meaning rather than Existence is the primary property in created reality. In our perspective, this view encompasses the Information Continuum

Model perspective in which put the continuing value of information (*i.e.*, its reconstruction of human social actions) as the meaning (*raison d'être*) of the DIPO. The DIPO is a recorded result of human's action in form of information pieces. This information is categorized in an information type from social context. These information pieces can have relationships to other information pieces either within its own physical carrier or towards other objects.

The vital characteristic of the information object from continuum perspective is that new object can be created through the combination of information pieces that can be a piece of other objects. In that way, the information will be reused in another context and reproducing human social actions. It means that information can be related to processes (that is generated by, and linked to work processes). Furthermore, the information in the object must serve as evidence over actions and transactions as well.

The natural question that arises, should be what is this definition good for? Having a definition of DIPO and a clear perspective of the continuum, long-term digital preservation issues might be easier to tackle. Something we observe is that there is a need of a uniform "aspectual abstraction" of the Digital Information Preservation Object.

This level should be based in deep philosophical foundations that should cover several aspects of the object (*i.e.,* its attributes, characteristics or properties), such as physical aspects: decay of materials, biotic: pests eating it the storage material, lingual: language changes over long term, social: social and cultural connotations and meanings change over long-term, juridical: legal matters of *e.g.,* long-term ownership, for instance after someone has died, pistic: the religious or faith, moral ethical, normative contexts that can change, probably slowly (over centuries), so this might provide a better degree of harmony over the preservation period than earlier aspects.

4

Research Areas in Digital Library Infrastructure

This section describes each of the major research areas of the Cornell Digital Library Research Group.

DIGITAL LIBRARY INFRASTRUCTURE

Historically and conceptually the core work of the CDLRG lies in the formulation and investigation of infrastructure to facilitate component-based digital libraries.

Work on infrastructure within the CDLRG began with the CS-TR (Computer Science Technical Reports) Project, a DARPA (U.S. Defence Advanced Research Projects Agency) funded effort to examine tools for electronic publication of Computer Science Technical Reports.

This early digital library project was a collaboration of the "top five" computer science institutions in the United States: Berkeley, Carnegie-Mellon, Cornell, MIT, and Stanford.

Cornell contributed the mechanism for interoperability in the project, a system called Dienst (Distributed Interactive Extensible Network Server for Techreports). (Dienst, pronounced dçnst, is also the Dutch word for "service".)

In the context of our research, the word "Dienst" refers to a number of things:

- A conceptual architecture for distributed digital libraries.
- A protocol for service communication in that architecture.
- A software system that serves as a reference implementation of the protocol and architecture.

Broadly speaking, Dienst is a system for configuring a set of individual *services* running on distributed *servers* to cooperate in providing the services of a digital library.

The *open architecture* of the Dienst system exposure of the functionality through a defined protocol makes it possible to combine Dienst services in flexible ways and augment the existing services with other *mediator services*, which build on the functionality of the existing services.

A complete description of Dienst is outside the scope of this paper, but a brief listing of the features of the architecture is as follows:

- A document model that incorporates unique naming, multiple versions, logical structuring, and multiple content-type disseminations. This document model is fully exposed through the protocol, allowing multiple *disseminations* objects stored in Dienst repositories.
- A set of individually defined services that expose their operational semantics through an open protocol.. The interaction between a set of core Dienst services User Interface, Query Mediator (QM), Name Server (NS), Index, and Repository is illustrated in Figure.
- A mechanism for combining services and content into multiple collections.
- A mechanism for distributing collections among regions to facilitate global distribution.

Over the past several years, Dienst has provided fertile ground for both practical deployment and as a testbed for research into distributed digital libraries.

The most notable deployment of Dienst is as the technical infrastructure for NCSTRL (Networked Computer Science Technical Reference Library), a globally distributed digital library that incorporates content from over 100 institutions. Dienst also provides technology for a number of other collections including CoRR (the Computing Research Repository) and ETRDL (ERCIM Technical Reference Digital Library).

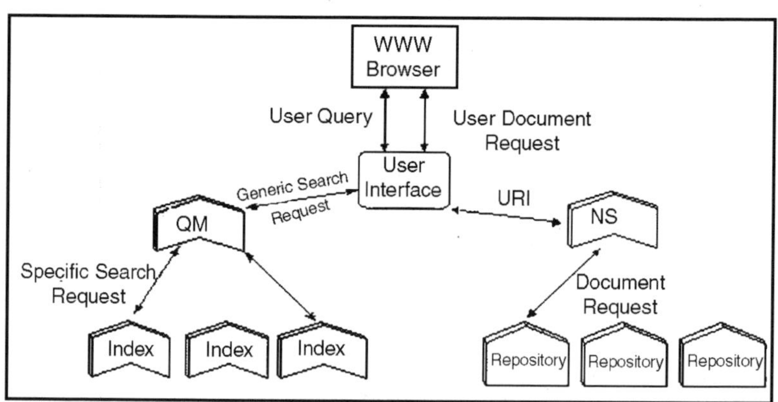

Fig. Dienst Service Interaction.

Within the CDLRG, we have exploited the Dienst system and implementation for a number of research investigations. One particular area is distributed searching; mechanisms for determining query routing among distributed search engines. Another research area is the mechanism for creating collections in globally-distributed digital librarie. Work on the Dienst architecture, protocol, and impleme-ntation is ongoing. We are, at the time of writing of this paper, in the final stages of producing a new software release that supports a new version of the Dienst protocol.

These new versions considerably enhance the functionality of the Dienst system (*e.g.*, a more powerful document model for structured documents, increased metadata functionality) and improve the modularity of the system. This not only facilitates administration of a Dienst server, but makes the system more amenable for research experimentation (by making it easy to improve and replace service modules).

THE CHALLENGES OF DIGITAL PRESERVATION

The purpose of preservation is to ensure protection of information of enduring value for access by present and future generations (Conway, 1990: 206). Libraries and archives have served as the central institutional focus for preservation, and both types of institutions include preservation as one of their core functions. In recent decades, many major libraries and archives have established formal preservation programmes for traditional materials which include regular allocation of resources for preservation, preventive measures to arrest deterioration of materials, remedial measures to restore the usability of selected materials, and the incorporation of preservation needs and requirements into overall programme planning.

Preservationists within the library and archival community have been instrumental in developing an array of tools and methodologies to reduce the decay of traditional materials and to restore books and documents that have deteriorated to such an extent that their longevity and usability are threatened. Provisions for fire protection and adequate environmental controls frequently are incorporated into new library and archival facilities. Rehousing of acid-based paper materials is a common task in many repositories and microfilming is used extensively and cost effectively to preserve endangered materials.

Undertakings such as the brittle books initiative, the American Newspapers Project, and the NEH-funded microfilming programme have saved millions of unique and imperiled items (Preserving the Intellectual Heritage). Many libraries and archives have curbed their voracious appetites for acquisition and collecting in an effort to balance the breadth and depth of their holdings against long-term stewardship responsibilities. The change over from acid to alkaline paper in publishing and much desktop printing counts as a significant victory for preservation. Much remains to be done to preserve cultural, intellectual, and scholarly resources in traditional formats that form the foundation for humanities research and teaching.

An estimated 80 million embrittled books reside in American libraries, 10 million of which are unique; and countless journals, newspapers, photographs, and documents require preservation treatment to survive well into the next century. Thousands of repositories lack the means for disaster prevention or adequate environmental controls to avoid catastrophic loss of their holdings.

The success stories and regular use of established preservation methods are found almost exclusively in developed countries, and within developed countries in preservation of print materials in major institutions (Preservation of Archival Materials).

Digital preservation raises challenges of a fundamentally different nature which are added to the problems of preserving traditional format materials. By digital preservation, I mean the planning, resource allocation, and application of preservation methods and technologies necessary to ensure that digital information of continuing value remains accessible and usable. I intentionally use the term "continuing" rather than "permanent" value to avoid both the absolutism and the idealism that the term "permanent" implies (O'Toole). My concept of digital preservation encompasses material that begins its life in digital form as well as material that is converted from traditional to digital formats.

Recording media for digital materials are vulnerable to deterioration and catastrophic loss, and even under ideal conditions they are short lived relative to traditional format materials. Although archivists have been battling acid-based papers, thermo-fax, nitrate film, and other fragile media for decades, the threat posed by magnetic and optical media is qualitatively different. They are the first reusable media and they can deteriorate rapidly, making the time frame for decisions and actions to prevent loss is a matter of years, not decades.

More insidious and challenging than media deterioration is the problem of obsolescence in retrieval and playback technologies. Innovation in the computer hardware, storage, and software industries continues at a rapid pace, usually yielding greater storage and processing capacities at lower cost. Devices, processes, and software for recording and storing information are being replaced with new products and methods on a regular three-to five-year cycle, driven primarily by market forces. Records created in digital form in the first instance and those converted retrospectively from paper or microfilm to digital form are equally vulnerable to technological obsolescence. Another challenge is the absence of established standards, protocols, and proven methods for preserving digital information.

With few exceptions, digital library research has focussed on architectures and systems for information organization and retrieval, presentation and visualization, and administration of intellectual property rights (Levy and Marshall). The critical role of digital libraries and archives in ensuring the future accessibility of information with enduring value has taken a back seat to enhancing access to current and actively used materials. As a consequence, digital preservation remains largely experimental and replete with the risks associated with untested methods; and digital preservation requirements have not been factored into the architecture, resource allocation, or planning for digital libraries.

My assigned topic "mass storage and long-term preservation" offers fertile ground for discussing conceptual and methodological challenges facing digital libraries and archives. The two terms "mass storage" and "long-term preservation" embrace a contradiction in the current state of affairs of digital library development, representing a time bomb that threatens the long-term viability of this new type of library. New technologies for mass storage of digital information abound, yet the technologies and methods for long-term preservation of the vast and growing store of digital information lag far behind.

Strategies, methods, and technologies for long-term preservation of digital information that already exist or are being discussed, designed, and developed today have yet to demonstrate the technological or economic feasibility of operating on a mass scale. Our ability to create, amass and store digital materials far exceeds our current capacity to preserve even that small amount with continuing value.

Digital Preservation Requirements

In order to preserve digital materials on a scale commensurate with mass storage capabilities and in formats that are accessible and usable, it is necessary to articulate some basic requirements. There are two ways to examine digital preservation requirements: from the perspective of users of digital materials and from the view of libraries, archives, and other custodians who assume responsibility for their maintenance, preservation, and distribution. Libraries and archives will not accomplish their preservation missions if they do not satisfy the requirements of their users by preserving materials in formats that enable the types of analyses that users wish to perform.

At the same time, libraries and archives are unlikely to be able to satisfy all requirements of all potential users primarily due to resource constraints. By making explicit preservation requirements from both the users' and custodians' perspectives, libraries and archives will be better able to integrate digital preservation into overall planning and resource allocation.

The potential uses of digital materials are varied, unpredictable, and almost endless (Gould). Any generalizations, even if restricted to one community of users such as humanities scholars, run the risk of overlooking and understating potential user needs. Precise requirements for presentation and analytical tools vary among disciplines, yet some basic requirements are likely to transcend fields and disciplines. The ability to establish the authenticity and integrity of a source is critical to users, whether it is generated by an individual, created in the conduct of institutional business, or produced through a formal publication process (Lynch). Mechanisms that will enable users to establish authenticity require archives and libraries to store much more than the content of digital documents. Attributes such as formal document structures, metadata that document the maintenance and use history of the document, time and date stamps, and a series of references among documents are essential for determining authenticity and for understanding the provenance of sources and placing them in a larger context (Graham).

Michelson and Rothenberg (1992) argue that networking and access to digital sources will change all dimensions the scholarly work process, including identifying sources, communicating with colleagues, interpreting and analyzing data, disseminating research findings, and teaching. If their projections are correct, digital preservation programmes must support a high degree of integration of source material into analytical processes by coupling research sources with the tools necessary to analyze them; by maintaining linkages between research results and the sources on which they are based; and by providing a means to incorporate primary sources into teaching. Users will seek documents that are easily retrieved and manipulated, transmittable, and transportable from a repository to the sites of research, presentation, and teaching. It seems safe to assume that humanities scholars will need the capability to search through and select relevant sources from large bodies of heterogenous materials, to compare sources to each other, and to view specific documents at high levels of granularity.

Digital preservation will add little value to the research process if it serves only as an alternative form of storage from which analog replicas are produced for use with conventional analytical methods. Preserving digital materials in formats that are reliable and usable, however, will require long-term maintenance of structural characteristics, descriptive metadata, and display, computational, and analytical capabilities that are very demanding of both mass storage and software for retrieval and interpretation.

Digital preservation requirements may be expressed differently by archives, libraries, and other types of repositories that are struggling to meet escalating user expectations with limited financial and technical resources. Storage systems should be capable of handling digital information in a wide variety of formats, including text, data, graphics, video, and sound. Digital storage is not only an alternative means for storing print formats because many types of digital objects do not have print equivalents and cannot be preserved in non-digital formats.

Ideally, storage media will have a long life expectancy, a high degree of disaster resistance, sufficient durability to withstand regular use, and very large storage capacities. Conversion from analog to digital formats and migration to new generations of technology will be rapid, accurate, and inexpensive enough to permit very large scale transfers of heterogeneous materials. Storage space requirements will be minimal and not demand highly sensitive environmental controls. To make digital preservation affordable to the widest possible range of organizations and individuals, equipment, media, and maintenance costs must be modest.

Current Preservation Strategies and Their Limitations

Most librarians and archivists have accepted the basic wisdom—for now at least—that digital preservation depends upon copying, not on the survival of the physical media (Lesk). But copying, also referred to as "refreshing" or "migration" is more complex than simply transferring a stream of bits from old to new media or from one generation of systems to the next. Complex and expensive transformations of digital objects often are necessary to preserve digital materials so that they remain authentic representations of the original versions and useful sources for analysis and research (Task Force on Archiving of Digital Information).

Current methods for preserving digital materials do not fully support achieving these objectives. When faced with the responsibility for preserving digital materials, archives and libraries face a series of complex and difficult choices based on the format of the original materials, the anticipated uses for it, and the technical and financial resources available to invest in preservation initiatives. I will review some current preservation strategies beginning with the most elementary and established methods and ending with proposals that have not yet been tested.

Probably the most commonly used preservation strategy is to transfer digital information from less stable magnetic and optical media by printing page images on paper or microfilm. It seems ironic that just as libraries and archives are discovering digital conversion as a cost-effective preservation method for certain deteriorating materials, much information that begins its life in electronic form is printed on paper or microfilm for safe, secure long-term storage. Yet, high-quality acid neutral paper can last a century or longer while archival quality microfilm is projected to last 300 years or more. Paper and microfilm have the additional advantage of requiring no special hardware or software for retrieval or viewing. Perhaps this explains why in many digital conversion projects, the digital images serve as a complement to rather than a replacement for the original hard copy materials (Conway, 1994).

Another strategy for digital preservation is to preserve digital information in the simplest possible digital formats in order to minimize the requirements for sophisticated retrieval software. Digital information can be transferred across successive generations of technology in a "software-independent" format as ASCII text files or as flat files with simple, uniform structures. Several data archives hold large collections of numerical data that were captured on punch cards in the 1950s or 1960s, migrated to two or three different magnetic tape formats, and now reside on optical media. As new media and storage formats were introduced, the data were migrated without any significant change in their logical structure.

This approach has the distinct advantage of being universal and easy to implement. It is a cost-effective strategy for preserving digital information in those cases where retaining the content is paramount, but display, indexing, and computational characteristics are not critical. As long as the preservation community lacks more robust and cost-effective migration strategies, printing to paper or film and preserving flat files will remain the methods of last resort for many institutions and for certain formats of digital information.

Libraries and archives with large, complex, and diverse collections of digital materials are only beginning to test strategies that normalize various types of holdings by converting digital records from the great multiplicity of formats into a smaller, more manageable number of standard formats (University of the State of New York). A repository might accept textual documents only in one or a few commonly available commercial word processing formats or require that documents conform to standards like SGML (ISO 8879). Databases might be stored in one or a few common formats or converted to a SQL (Structured Query Language) compliant format, while image files might conform to the tagged image file format (TIFF) with standard compression algorithms.

This approach has the advantage of preserving more of the display, dissemination, and computational characteristics of the original materials, while reducing the large variety of customized transformations that would otherwise be necessary to migrate material to future generations of technology. The strategy rests on the assumption that software products which are either compliant with widely adopted standards or are widely dispersed in the marketplace are less volatile than the software market as a whole. Most common commercial products today provide utilities for backward compatibility and for swapping documents, databases, and more complex objects between software systems. Although this strategy simplifies migration and may lower digital preservation costs by reducing the amount of customized reformatting needed as technology changes, it does not eliminate the need for regular migration of digital materials. Software and standards both continue to evolve and even repositories with structurally homogeneous holdings can expect to be required to migrate their digital materials periodically.

Current methods fall far short of what is required to preserve digital materials. All current preservation methods involve trade-offs between what is desirable from the standpoint of functionality, dependability, and cost and what is possible and affordable with current technologies and methods. Consequently, most repositories are coping by employing interim and less than desirable strategies, if they are addressing digital preservation issues at all. For example, the simplicity and universality of printing to paper or microfilm come at the expense of great losses in the functionality of digital information. Migration strategies that involve reformatting of digital materials to a simple standard format usually eliminate the structure of documents and relationships imbedded in databases. Computation capabilities, graphic display, indexing, and other features often are lost, thus limiting future analytical potential. Normalization to standard formats is not always technically feasible and it usually is quite costly.

Archives and libraries must also contend with entirely new forms of electronically-enabled discourse and new forms of artistic and cultural expression that do not have predecessors in the analog world. No current preservation method is adequate for preserving dynamic data objects from complex systems. There are no established conceptual models or technical processes for preserving multi-media works, interactive hyper-media, on-line dialogues, or many of the new electronic forms being created today. The archival requirements to preserve content, context, and structure and to maintain the capability to display, link, and manipulate digital objects only heighten their software dependency.

The preservation community is only beginning to explore possible alternatives to storing digital information in "software-independent" form. Rothenberg (1995) proposed an approach for maintaining the content of digital materials intact without losing the ability to retrieve meaning-rich sources. He recommended retaining the original document in its original format encapsulated in a virtual "envelope" that contains software instructions for retrieval, display, and processing of the message in the envelope. The envelopes would contain contextual information and the transformational history of each object. Execution of the instructions would rely on an archive of hardware and software emulators or on instructions in the envelope with specifications to construct emulators. Important research is underway to define standards for data interchange that can support electronic commerce and satisfy business requirements in a variety of environments.

A major research project at the University of Pittsburgh is defining metadata requirements for evidence that will support the need for integrity, authenticity, reliability, and archiving through standards for "metadata encapsulated objects" (Bearman and Sochats). Archives, libraries, and other institutions with preservation responsibilities will benefit if systems are built to implement such metadata standards. Wide scale adoption of data and communication standards by the originators of digital information to support current business needs will also facilitate long-term preservation. Rapid implementation of electronic commerce depends on widespread development and adoption of standards for EDI (electronic data interchange) transaction sets under auspices of the ANSI X.12 committee, and many organizations are adopting standards for format and definitions to enable exchange, reuse, and sale of digital information and to reduce conversion and maintenance costs.

Standards initiatives that address business needs for the secure and reliable exchange of digital information among the current generation of systems will impose standardization and normalization of data that ultimately will facilitate migrations to new generations of technology. Yet to benefit fully from the synergy between business needs and preservation requirements we have to move beyond simply paying lip service to cultural heritage concerns and recognize that equally critical social goals, such as long-term genetic research, monitoring global environmental change, locating nuclear waste sites, and establishing property rights are also dependent on long-term access to reliable, electronic evidence.

Much remains to be done in research, development, and implementation before we can assume that even a small portion of our digital heritage will survive more than a few years. It is fair to say that the state of development in digital preservation remains largely experimental. Only a few libraries, archives, and other institutions have established digital preservation programmes, while most research and innovation comes from pilot projects and prototypes. Tested methods that have proven effective on a small scale in a limited number of repositories are not feasible for preservation of many of the types of digital materials that archives and libraries will confront in their preservation endeavours.

Areas for Research and Development

The current state of digital preservation suggests several fruitful areas for research and development. I will discuss four areas: storage media, migration, conversion, and management tools. These four domains are often mutually dependent and ultimately must to be integrated into an infrastructure for digital preservation. Yet better solutions are necessary in all four areas before such integration can occur. Finally, I will share some observations about the issues of scale and cost that must be considered if we are going to achieve any degree of systematic preservation.

Storage Media

The limited life of magnetic and optical media pose a significant problem, although this is not the primary limiting factor for digital preservation. Recent research on the longevity of magnetic media indicate a useful life span of 10 to 30 years if they are handled and stored properly. Some optical disk technologies promise life spans of up to 100 years. Most authorities argue that enhanced media longevity is of little value because current media outlast the software and devices needed to retrieve recorded information.

Nevertheless, improvements in the stability, capacity, and longevity of the base storage media are needed to drastically reduce the vulnerability of digital materials to loss and alteration and to lower storage costs. Ample research and experience provide evidence of what can go wrong with magnetic media as a result of binder degradation, magnetic particle instabilities, and substrate deformation (Van Bogart). Optical media are susceptible to damage from high humidity, rapid and extreme temperature fluctuations, and contamination from airborne particulate matter (U.S. National Archives and Records Administration).

To prevent these problems, it is imperative to store magnetic and optical media under strict environmental controls that are not always available, affordable, or convenient. Even modest improvements which produce storage media with larger per unit storage capacities and greater tolerance to variations in temperature and humidity will lower preservation costs by lessening the need for strict environmental controls, reducing the frequency with which digital media must be "refreshed" through recopying, and decreasing the number of storage units that must be handled.

This raises the question, however, of whether research on incremental improvements in current storage technologies will benefit preservation in the long run or whether we should seek alternative approaches to digital storage that more adequately meet archival requirements. As a frame of reference it is worth remembering that microfilm, which is considered the only acceptable archival storage medium, lasts at least 300 years with minimal maintenance if stored properly. Last June, the Los Alamos National Laboratory announced the invention of a High-Density Read-Only Memory (HD-ROM) technology that uses an ion beam to inscribe information on pins of stainless steel, iridium, or other materials.

The HD-ROM is capable of storing 180 times more information than current CD-ROM technology at roughly one-half percent of CD-ROM costs. According to the release about this technology, the HD-ROM is impervious to material degradation and it requires no bit stream interpreter because the technology can describe in human-readable form all of the instructions needed to interpret the data (LANL Ion Beam Storage). Such an approach illustrates the potential for solutions built on entirely new storage technologies.

Migration

Better methods for migration of digital materials to new generations of hardware and software are much needed for digital preservation regardless of breakthroughs in mass storage technologies. Planning for migration is difficult because there is limited experience with the types of migrations needed to maintain access to complex digital objects over extended periods of time. When a custodian assumes responsibility for preserving a digital object it may be difficult to predict when migration will be necessary, how much reformatting will be needed, and how much migration will cost. There are no reliable or comprehensive data on costs associated with migrations, either for specific technologies and formats or for particular collections, and little research underway on methodologies that would reduce the costs and burdens of migration.

The preservation community as a whole would benefit tremendously from the development of backward compatibility paths that would be included as a standard feature of all software. Backward compatibility or migration paths would enable a new generation of software to "read" data from older systems without substantial reformatting and without loss of retrieval, display and computational capabilities. Although backward compatibility is increasingly common within software product lines, migration paths are not commonly provided between competing software products or for products that fail in the marketplace.

Stewards of digital material have a range of options for preserving digital information. One might preserve an exact replica of a digital record with complete display, retrieval, and computational functionality, or a representation of the record with only partial computation capabilities, or a surrogate for the record such as an abstract, summary, or aggregation. Detail or background noise might be dropped out intentionally through successive generations of migration, and custodians might change the format or storage media. Enhancements are technologically possible through clean-up, mark-up, and linkage, or by adding indexing and other features. These technological possibilities in turn impose serious new responsibilities to present digital materials to users in a way that allows them to determine the authenticity of the information and its relationship to the original record. Methods to document changes in digital objects during their life span need to be incorporated as an integral part of improved migration methods.

There are few well developed methods for preserving and migrating software so that it might be used to recreate digital documents that have the "look and feel" of the original sources. Maintaining repositories of obsolete hardware and software has been discussed periodically, but usually dismissed out of hand as too expensive and not demonstrably feasible. This approach deserves more serious consideration as a strategy for maintaining continuing access to certain types of digital materials. Feasibility studies and cost/benefit analyses should be conducted to determine the technological, economic, and commercial feasibility of maintaining selected legacy software systems and performing specialized migrations or, alternatively, of building and maintaining software emulators. Such an approach would support replay of original sources and contribute to the preservation of software as a significant cultural and intellectual resource in its own right.

Conversion

Faster, cheaper, and higher resolution conversion technologies are another critical element needed to make digital preservation feasible on a large scale. Most archivists and librarians accept the fact that we live in a hybrid environment where paper, microfilm, video, and magnetic and optical media need to interoperate in a more integrated and transparent manner. The vast majority of primary sources today still reside on paper and/or microfilm with little chance that we will see the mass conversion of existing archival and library holdings to digital formats. Research and planning for digital preservation must recognize that we will be dealing with conversion for a long time and that investments in improving capture rates, accuracy, resolution, and verification will have long-term benefits.

Moreover, improvements in conversion technologies may support hybrid solutions to preservation and access problems by permitting repositories to store certain formats of digital material on stable media, such as microfilm, with on demand conversion to digital form for analysis and reuse. Efforts to capture and store descriptive mark-up on film for subsequent conversion are hampered by unacceptable error rates in OCR technology and cumbersome conversion processes (Giguere).

Management Tools

A fourth area for research is in the development of management tools for digital libraries and archives that integrate descriptive control and maintenance with storage technologies. Dynamic digital objects, such as those found in hypertext systems, pose special management problems for both current and future retrieval and reuse. The boundaries of hypertext sources, like those found on the World Wide Web today, are difficult to ascertain because no single party or institution controls changes in the nodes and links that make hypertext objects live and highly responsive information resources.

A high degree of volatility accompanies these objects because the contents of nodes change, the sites where information resources are stored change, and the links between nodes change, move, and vanish. Some recent tools, such as the MOMspider (Multi-Owner Maintenance Spider) and Web:Lookout are capable of traversing a portion of the Web and noting maintenance problems such as broken links, moved documents, modified documents, and objects that have exceeded their expiration dates (Ackerman and Fielding). While tools such as these are useful for current maintenance, they do not address long-term preservation concerns. If further developed to address preservation problems, tools such as these have the potential to serve as filters, identify similar or identical objects, and monitor for maintenance problems.

Research and development of tools that would imbed more intelligence about the preservation status of digital material into the objects themselves would make monitoring and maintenance of large digital collections more automatic. Current methods for monitoring the physical status of digital materials are labour intensive, unreliable, and potentially damaging to the materials themselves. Recommended procedures for monitoring physical deterioration of magnetic tape, for example, involve reading a small sample of tapes periodically to determine whether any data losses have occurred (Eaton). The potential exists to build monitoring and reporting mechanisms into digital objects, storage systems, and network architectures that could support self-reporting of physical status and initiate automatic maintenance procedures.

Despite differences, some lessons from traditional preservation are transferable to the digital environment. In order to avoid commitments that far exceed available resources and costly rescue and restoration efforts, preservation must become an integral part of the planning, design, and resource allocation for digital libraries and archives. Integration of preservation requirements and methods with access and maintenance systems is essential to fully and efficiently support the processes of migration, regeneration, and documentation of the life of digital objects.

Planning for preservation must become an integral part of the design and management of digital libraries and archives. If left as an afterthought, there is little reason to believe that long-term preservation of digital information will be any more affordable than preservation of conventional formats has been.

Some Concluding Comments

In closing, I would like to mention three issues that I discussed only in passing. One concern is the question of scale and scalability. The preservation community has at its disposal a variety of tactics for digital preservation that appear to work effectively for certain types of materials in certain restricted environments, but we have not yet developed solutions that are scalable to the general problem of digital preservation. This is not to suggest that there is or should be a single solution to digital preservation. The methods used will vary depending upon the complexity of the original data objects, the extent to which the functionality for computation, display, indexing, and authentication must be maintained, and the requirements of current or anticipated users. But any solution must be scalable from the laboratory, prototype, or pilot project to the wide range of individuals and institutions who have a need to make digital materials last longer than the current generation of technology permits.

Another closely related issue is the question of affordability. Regardless of how the responsibility for digital preservation is distributed, societies only allocate a small and finite amount of resources to preserving scholarly and cultural resources. And in the digital environment it seems likely that more preservation responsibilities will be distributed to individual creators, rights holders, distributors, small institutions, and other players in the production and dissemination process. Therefore, it seems imperative that digital preservation technologies become affordable and accessible to the wide range of individuals and institutions that will attempt to preserve digital materials.

Finally, it would be beneficial to both the preservation community and to those conducting research on issues of longevity, migration, and conversion if there were more venues for exchange of ideas, requirements, and recent developments. Without a continuing dialogue between humanists, preservationists, and the scientific community it is difficult to include preservation requirements in scientific research endeavours, and it is challenging for those of us outside the scientific community to keep up with and evaluate new products. I hope that the discussion we are beginning at this conference will lead to more regular and formal processes for linking the needs of scholars and preservationists with the research agendas and projects of scientists.

DIGITAL OBJECT ARCHITECTURE

Digital libraries have the potential to represent new types of content and deliver them in innovative ways. Existing digital library research projects and deployed systems give a glimpse of this potential by providing access to digital content in a variety of forms including text, images, video, audio, maps, datasets, and software.

The utility of these single medium digital resources is indisputable. However, the rich potential of digital libraries is fully demonstrated by multimedia content that aggregates multiple single medium content streams that are inter-related semantically, structurally, and temporally. The result is digital content that is more informative and more accurately represents physical reality. Across this diversity of content there is the need for a layer of *uniformity* among digital resources; a *digital object* model that provides common high level functionality among all resources regardless of their content. This common functionality includes *deposit* in and *access* from repositories, *discovery* by users and agents, *dissemination* or *presentation* of content, and *access control* for protection of intellectual property.

Such high-level operational uniformity allows multiple objects, each with their own idiosyncratic composition and content, to be combined in distributed digital library collections.

While generic uniformity of digital objects is essential to the (inter) operation of digital libraries, there is also the need for functionality that exposes and exploits object *specificity*. For example, at the most generic level, dissemination from a digital object is simply the output of a stream of bits.

At the object specific level, however, disseminations take on unlimited forms unique to the semantics of the specific digital object; for example, the output of a frame from a "video" digital object, a page from a "book" digital object, or a subroutine from a "programme" digital object.

In the FEDORA (Flexible and Extensible Digital Object and Repository Architecture) project, the CDLRG is investigating a general digital object model and repository architecture for encapsulating and securing digital library content of all forms and genre.

Mechanisms for extensibility are built in to the architecture, thereby allowing individual communities to develop new content types and rights management schemes, yet interoperate in a broad digital library framework.

The key challenges we are addressing in FEDORA include:

- The creation of complex objects that aggregate heterogeneous types of data, which may be distri-buted in location,
- The ability to endow these objects with sets of behaviours that pertain to any global or domain-specific notion of content (such as a book, a journal, an article, a movie, or others), irrespective of the object's underlying structure,

- Client access to multiple views, or *disseminations,* of the object's data through the transparent activation of external mechanisms that execute these *content type* behaviours,
- Association of external rights management schemes with any dissemination of an object's contents.
- Extensibility for content types and rights manage-ment schemes.

FEDORA defines a container abstraction known as the DigitalObject that encapsulates multimedia content in typed byte stream packages called DataStreams. The actual byte stream in a DataStream may be local (or internal) to the DigitalObject, or it may be a reference to data external to the DigitalObject (*e.g.,* a result of a GET transaction from an HTTP server). This allows a DigitalObject to be act as a value-added surrogate for other content; a capability which is exploited in our policy enforcement work.

All DigitalObjects have a set of generic behaviours (the PrimitiveDisseminator methods) to create and access DataStreams and to manipulate the structure of the Digital object. The Digital object also has an extensible interface layer that provides views, or *disseminations*, of encapsulated data in a contextually meaningful manner.

A dissemination can be a direct transcription of stored data (e.g. a page of a book), any computable derivation of stored content, an interactive object (*e.g.,* a book viewing applet), or any mixture of these. A Disseminator is a FEDORA component that associates an extended set of service requests with a DigitalObject to produce disseminations.

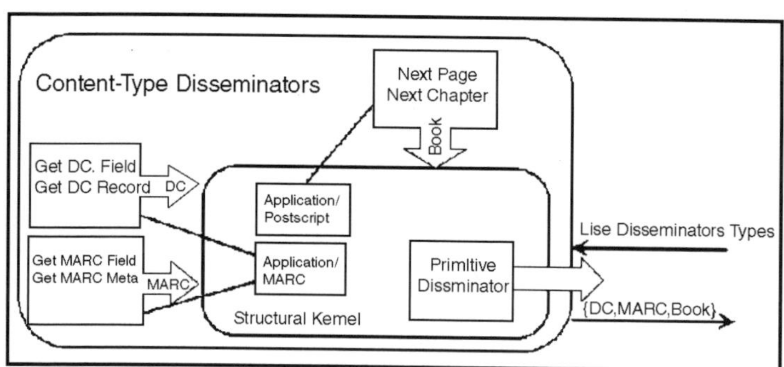

Fig. FEDORA Digital Object.

The architectural segregation of structure, extensible interfaces, and mechanisms for executing extensible behaviours is key to the FEDORA DigitalObject model. Many types of Disseminators can be associated with a DigitalObject to extend its behaviour beyond the generic methods.

For example, a DigitalObject can have a Disseminator that endows it with a set book-like behaviours, allowing a client to interact with the DigitalObject through a set of requests such as "get next page" or "get next chapter." Each Disseminator references a Signature which is a formal definition of the set of methods that pertain to a particular Disseminator Type. It also references a Servlet which is a mechanism (a programme) that executes the methods defined by the referenced Signature. Both Signatures and Servlets can be stored in DigitalObjects and registered with a global naming service (*e.g.,* the Handle System).

This creates a de facto registry of Disseminator Types Signatures and Servlets become "known" when their names (*e.g.,* URNs of their DigitalObject containers) are registered with a global naming service. A FEDORA Repository provides an environment for activating and running Servlets.

A simple FEDORA DigitalObject is depicted in Figure. It contains a *structural kernel* with two DataStreams (a Postscript stream and MARC metadata) and the Primitive Disseminator, which is the set of *generic* service requests. There are also three Disseminators (BOOK, MARC, and DublinCore). Clients can obtain various disseminations of the DigitalObject by invoking the methods of each Disseminator.

For example, a client can obtain a Dublin Core record by invoking the getDCRecord() request. Although there is no Dublin Core data inside this object, the DC Disseminator activates an external mechanism that derives Dublin Core from MARC data. This is one simple example of how the underlying structure of a DigitalObject is distinct from the disseminations it can produce.

Over the past year, the CDLRG has been developing and experimenting with a prototype implementation of the FEDORA architecture. This prototype is implemented in Java and uses the CORBA distributed object model. In our research, the prototype has been used for a range of interoperability experiments with colleagues at CNRI (Corporation for National Research Initiatives).

FEDORA will also be used as the basis for experiments with policy enforcement. In addition, a research packaging of FEDORA is available for other researchers who wish to use the implementation for digital library experimentation.

Policy Enforcement

This paper began with a definition of digital libraries that contains the notion of *management* layered on top of *infrastructure*. In particular: a digital library *infrastructure* provides the service definitions, protocols, and digital object model; digital library *instances* exploit this infrastructure by selecting services and content and administering policies on those selections.

It is illustrative to compare these digital library instances to the current notion of a portal on the Web, for example Lycos, Yahoo, and AltaVista. These portals offer access to distributed content and provide some services over this content (*e.g.,* searching). Yet, there is little argument that these current portals do not provide the level of curatorial responsibility undertaken by existing libraries.

The model of a digital library instance proposed here can be thought of as a *hybrid portal*. It not only expands the traditional portal concept with enhanced services and content, but recognizes the need for *integrity maintenance* (curatorial responsibility) ranging from casual (a distributed e-print archive) to strict and broad ranging (a research library).

The effect then is that content and mechanisms may be shared among multiple digital libraries, but the policies applied to that content and services are tailored to the requirements of the organization administering the digital library instance.

Digital library integrity requirements for security, preservation, or otherwise – can be expressed through formal statements called *policies*. The issue of policy formulation and enforcement for digital libraries is a major focus of the research of the CDLRG.

Policy enforcement mechanisms need to be constructed that permit enforcement regardless of the level of control the digital library (the policy formulator and enforc-ement agent) has over the distributed objects and services. In this context, we are examining the implementation of a *policy layer* through which each digital library can enforce its policies on the range of content and services and range of control over that content and services.

Libraries, digital or otherwise, formulate and enforce a number of policies. In our research we have chosen to focus on two:

1) *security*, management of access to content,

2) *preservation*, the long-term archiving of content. Research in preservation is addressed.

The many forms of content in digital libraries offer new challenges for the formulation of security and preservation policies.

Two examples from the security domain are illustrative:

- Raw databases are likely candidates for inclusion in a digital library, so consider an electronic document that encapsulates an opinion survey (database) with software to access the data. The document's publisher-to protect its investment-might stipulate that the database, though readable in its entirety, never be copied; the survey participants—to protect their privacy—may have stipulated that only certain (personally uncompromising) sets of queries against the database be allowed.
- The provider of an image database might wish to make low-resolution renderings of database images generally available and higher-resolution renderings accessible only under certain conditions.

In order to understand the effect of these many forms of content in digital libraries, one thrust of our research will be a thorough analysis of security and preservation requirements in the digital library context.

This analysis will take into account the diversity of stakeholders that need to be served – for example, traditional and non-traditional publishers, authors, and the established research library community. It will also consider the impact of the portal model, in which content is distributed and therefore lies outside the *control zone* of organizations trying to formulate and enforce policies.

In addition to the formulation of security and preservation policies for these new genres of content, there remains the problem of enforcing the policies in a digital library. The mechanisms for policy enforcement in existing computer applications for example the read, write, and execute access to files and Programmes that most operating systems implement are some distance from those required to enforce the complex policies we envisage in digital libraries.

The prudent course in designing a digital library architecture is to provide support for an extremely wide variety of security policies. Our intention, therefore, is to take *enforceability* as the only hard constraint on what policies are allowed, and build mechanisms based on a formal notion of enforceability.

We base our research in this area on a formal definition of *enforceability* for a class *EM* (for *Execution Monitoring*) of policies that can be enforced using mechanisms that work by monitoring (any aspect of) system execution. The execution steps monitored may range from fine-grained actions (such as memory access) to higher-level operations (such as method calls) to operations that change the state of an object and thus restrict subsequent execution.

The formal definition of *EM* is outside the scope of this paper. As a substitute, a few examples will suffice. All known hardware and operating system-based mechanisms, such as those alluded to earlier that restrict access to files, are in *EM*.

The policies discussed above for the survey database are instances of such *EM*-enforceable access control policies. Rights management policies discussed in connection with electronic documents also fall into this class.

A few examples outside the scope of *EM* are also illustrative. Policy enforcement mechanisms that use more information than becomes available only from observing the steps of a target's execution are, by definition, excluded from EM. Information provided to an EM mechanism is thus insufficient for predicting future steps the target might take, alternative possible executions, or all possible target executions.

Given this notion of enforceability, our research is then proceeding on two tracks:

- Developing notations for expressing security and preservation policies and developing methods and tools for formulating as policies the requirements of authors, publishers, and library customers.
- Developing practical enforcement mechanisms for those policies.

In addressing the two issues, we will exploit on-going work at Cornell in new policy enforcement mechanisms. All *EM*-enforcement mechanisms can be viewed as implementing an automaton that makes a transition each time the target system does and that causes the target system to halt if ever an action is being attempted that does not comply with the policy being enforced. Practical realizations of this abstraction are thus based on three mechanisms:

- There must be a way to identify the transitions in the target system. A transition may correspond to accessing a memory location, to executing a machine language instruction, to executing only certain specific machine language instructions (*e.g.,* supervisor or kernel calls), or to executing certain procedures, functions, or methods. The level of granularity of transitions depends on what events are being constrained by the policy.
- There must be a way to keep track of the enforce-ment-automaton's current state and for the automaton to change state in response to transitions made by the target system.
- There must be a way for the enforcement mechanism to trigger events in the target system (*e.g.,* when the security policy is about to be violated access to a digital object should be terminated).

We are currently experimenting with these policy enforcement mechanisms in the context of our FEDORA digital object model. The assumption is that we can build digital library specific "policy enforcement layers" by creating digital object surrogates for distributed resources.

As described earlier, the DataStreams "contained" in a DigitalObject may, in fact, be remote data disseminated by other digital objects or, in fact, from any other protocol transaction (*e.g.,* HTTP).

Thus, it is possible to, in a sense, "impose" policies on external objects. For example, we can build a surrogate digital object that serves as a *preservation monitor* (that implements some preservation policy) for some external content and that triggers notification events in defined cases (*e.g.,* when conversion of an object is necessary due to a new software version).

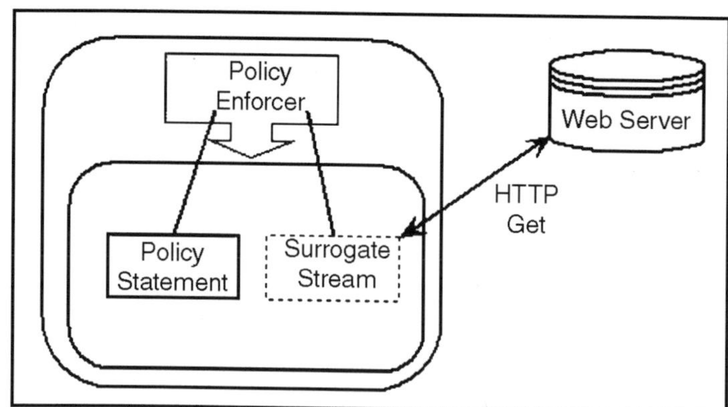

Fig. Policy Carrying Object.

FEDORA digital objects then become *policy carrying* containers, in addition to *content* and *behaviour* carrying containers. This concept is illustrated in

Figure, which shows a simple digital object containing a policy statement and reference content available through an HTTP GET. A disseminator is associated with these DataStreams that enforces the policy on the remote content (*e.g.*, sends an alert when a preservation state change occurs).

An important related issue of this research is the tension between varying levels of control over distributed content and services and the types of policies that need to be enforced. For example, it may be necessary to "assert" full control over an object in certain situations in order to achieve certain policies (*e.g.*, copy the object locally to ensure its full preservation).

Metadata Interoperability

The work of the CDLRG in metadata interoperability builds on several years of active participation in the DCMI (Dublin Core Metadata Initiative). Our primary interest in DCMI has been the role of the Dublin Core Element Set in a broader metadata fabric.

This is the issue addressed by the WF (Warwick Framework), which describes a container architecture for associating multiple metadata vocabularies (packages) with digital objects. We note that this container architecture and subsequent work on it provided the foundation for the FEDORA architecture.

The motivation for the WF is the belief that metadata should be modular – individual communities should create and maintain metadata vocabularies appropriate to their areas of expertise. For example, whereas bibliographic metadata should be created and administered by the information management (library) community, metadata governing terms and conditions for access should be the jurisdiction of the rights management (legal) community.

This modularity encourages metadata communities to scope their individual efforts and encourages them to avoid attempts at developing a universal ontology. Instead, individual metadata commu-nities should concentrate on classifying and expressing semantics tailored towards distinct functional and community needs. Warwick Framework-like modularity underlies the design of the W3C's Resource Description Framework (RDF), which is a modeling framework for the integration of diverse application and community-specific metadata vocabularies.

While the Warwick Framework proposes modularity as fundamental to a workable metadata strategy, it recognizes a number of challenges in the implementation of such. An outstanding one is the interoperability of multiple metadata packages that may be associated with and across resources.

These packages are by nature not semantically distinct, but overlap and relate to each other in numerous ways. Achieving interoperability between these packages via one-to-one *crosswalks* is useful, but this approach does not scale to the many metadata vocabularies that will inevitably develop.

A more scalable solution is to exploit the fact that many entities and relationships for example, people, places, creations, organizations, events, certain relationships and the like are so frequently encountered that they do not fall clearly into the domain of any particular metadata vocabulary but apply across all of them.

We are currently investigating a logical model for metadata interoperability with the rather insipid title ABC that is examining the nature of these common entities and relationships.

ABC is an attempt to:

- Formally define these underlying common entities and relationships;
- Describe them (and their inter-relationships) in a simple logical model;
- Provide the framework for extending these common semantics to domain and application-specific metadata vocabularies.

The concepts and inter-relationships modeled in ABC could be used in a number of ways.

In particular:

- Individual metadata communities could use these underlying concepts (the ABC vocabulary) to guide the development of community-specific vocabularies. These individual communities could use formalisms such as RDF to express the possibly complex relationships between the ABC model and their community-specific vocabularies.
- The formal expression of the relationships between community-specific vocabularies and the ABC model could provide the basis for a more scalable approach to interoperability among multiple metadata sets. Rather than one-to-one mappings among metadata vocabulary semantics, a more scalable basis for interoperability could be achieved by mapping through this common logical model.

This research is in its early stages but will be the subject of a workshop held at the end of January 2000. This workshop will bring together a small number of experts from the metadata and data modeling community and will produce a document that refines a conceptual model that could be used and refined by individual metadata initiatives and application developers.

SCHOLARLY PUBLISHING

These are tumultuous times for scholarly publishing On the one hand, there is a sense of serious economic imbalance as subscription prices for scholarly journals rise at a rate far exceeding inflation and put tremendous pressure on flat research library budgets.

On the other hand, the rapid pace of advances in a number of disciplines (e.g, computer science, physics, law) conflicts with the relatively slow turn-around of the traditional scholarly publishing model.

A number of exciting initiatives are responding to these pressures. Several scholarly disciplines, especially the hard sciences, have launched ambitious e-print efforts. The most notable example is the physics archive (arxiv) hosted by Los Alamos National Laboratory. We at Cornell have been active in e-print initiatives within the computer science community both with NCSTRL and CoRR (the Computer Resource Repository).

In addition, a number of scholarly publications have been started that are only available in digital form. For example, Cornell and CNRI jointly publish D-Lib Magazine, a monthly publication documenting digital library research. Finally, many members of the traditional publishing community now make their publications available in electronic form (for example, the ACM digital library).

A prevailing meta-question in these digital publishing efforts is what is the proper model for interoperability amongst them? Researchers, who often cross disciplinary boundaries, will suffer a loss if the traditional single point of access offered by the print library catalog transitions in the digital age to a plethora of individual entry points.

These questions of interoperability are fundamentally those that we are examining in the context of our infrastructure research. As part of this research, we are involved in the OAI (Open Archives Initiative).

OAI developed at a meeting held in October 1999 in Santa Fe that was attended by a number of people already running digital scholarly archives or actively interested in the issue.

The purpose of the meeting was to develop standards for interoperation. The meeting ended with agreement on a *harvesting* model of interoperability, whereby participating sites will follow a standard for making common and specific metadata available.

This metadata can then be used by *mediator services* that build additional layers of functionality using this information. Some examples of these additional layers are federated searching, abstracting and indexing services, and so-called "overlay journals" (which combine documents from multiple resources into a virtual journal). One area of special interest in our research is *reference linking*.

The OAI agreement contains the following components:

- A very simple common metadata standard for coarse granularity resource discovery purposes.
- A simple protocol for harvesting this metadata, site-specific metadata, and other basic information from participating archives. This protocol is a subset of the Dienst protocol.

The OAI is still in very early stages but it has already attracted a significant amount of attention from the scholarly community.

From the standpoint of the research of the CDLRG it provides a number of benefits:

- It raises awareness of the Dienst protocol as a vehicle for richer interoperability.
- The success of the OAI and the adoption of the harvesting standard by a number of content provides will increase the number of collections for our work on policy enforcement.

Nomadic Devices

In general, digital library technology assumes that the user has a networked personal computer that is used to access server computers, which store content and provide information services. In practice, people increasingly use a variety of computing devices in their daily lives not all of which are continuously connected to a network.

This growing proliferation of palm devices, hand-held computers, disconnected laptops, and embedded processors (*e.g.* "smart" mobile telephones) offer exciting opportunities for the creation of *personalized information spaces* – digital libraries with collections and services that correspond to targeted needs and situations. Increasingly, we expect that individuals will want to exploit the mobility of these devices and use them for storage, access, and update of selected information resources when network access is impractical or impossible.

Developing and deploying these nomadic digital libraries will require technology that is sensitive to two critical dimensions of these devices:

- *Device capability*: Each computing device has unique hardware characteristics, including display capability, input mechanisms, presentation software, and hardware capacity.
- *Device Connectivity*: The connections of these devices to the networks vary in both permanence and speed.

These two dimensions can be characterized as *device appropriateness*. The CDLRG is currently undertaking a research and implementation project to investigate a number of the salient problems in realizing nomadic digital libraries that are sensitive to device awareness. This research programme has the following components:

- *Synchronization of Personal Information Spaces*: This research is addressing what constitutes a coherent *collection* in a digital library distributed among multiple device types. We are extending the collection abstraction that we developed for "attached" digital libraries to nomadic devices with varying connectivity and hardware characteristics. This raises fundamental issues related to the synchronization of the collection among devices.
- *Remote Reference Linking*: We are investigating issues of reference linking in the context of disconnected devices. This involves investigating a number of questions in this area. What is the appropriate partitioning of reference linking mechanisms between the mobile device and participating servers? How can this partitioning be done in a device-aware manner? How can this model be extended to a set of occasionally connected mobile devices – for example, how might a group of individuals at a meeting share references through their infrared ports?

- *Disseminations*: The capability of an individual device must be considered when disseminating digital library content to that device. For example, a user of a desktop workstation with a fast network connection may want to see a richly illustrated dissemination of a book, but the user of a palm device may find an abbreviated text-only summary appropriate. We are investigating the mechanisms to allow matching of device characteristics with dissemination capabilities of an individual digital object. This work builds on the FEDORA dissemination characteristics.

MANAGEMENT OF DIGITAL RESOURCES

The global information infrastructure is transforming with the growth in full text digital resources and fast communication facilities. This is so because institutions, agencies and departments in every country are busy capturing, processing, storing and disseminating information in the digital form. One of the primary methods of digital collection building is digitisation.

The digitisation means the conversion of any fixed or analogue media-such as books, journal articles, photos, paintings, microforms- into electronic form through scanning, sampling, or in fact even re-keying. Digital library is a library where the information is made available in electronic form and access to it is provided through computers and other media like Local area network or Internet.

Digitising information has become a boon to many including library and information professionals. It reduces storage space, increases efficiency of retrieval of information. The digital library offers users the prospects of access to electronic resources at there convenience temporarily and spatially. Users don't have to be concern with the physical library hours of operation and users don't have to go physically to the library to access resources. Some of the Digital library initiatives undertaken so far world-over are highlighted: Medoc in Germany, Digital library projects at the National diet library in Japan, Tsinghua University Central Library in China, Biblio theca Universalis – G7 Project, Library of Congress USA, NSW Parliament News paper clippings and press releases imaging project in Austraila, Internet Archives USA, California digital libraries.

In India, the major initiatives undertaken in this direction: Million Book Universal Digital Library project, Vidyanidhi project, National Mission of Manuscripts, Traditional Knowledge Digital Library (TKDL), Gyan Nidhi and Indian National Digital Library in Engineering Science and Technology (INDEST). The initiatives undertaken so far clearly indicate that there is a boom in funding for digital library projects.

IGM LIBRARY, UNIVERSITY OF HYDERA BAD AND DIGITAL INITIATIVES

The University of Hyderabad came into existence in 1974 to promote teaching and research. The University at present has eight schools of study–

Chemistry, Life science, Physics, Mathematics and computer/information science, Humanities, Social science, fine arts and communication and management studies. It offer postgraduate and research programme across a wide spectrum of discipline in area of Science, Art and Technology.

The IGM library was established in 1975 as a central facility supports teaching and research activities of the university. The library has been over years successfully catering to the information needs of the Schools/departments and students of all subjects.

It is the first University library in India to computerise all its operations and services. With modernisation and networking of the library and information system the university campus has been networked with fibre optic cable and 2MB bandwidth Internet connectivity for creating local resources, cataloguing and repackaging web resources.

All school/departments are catered network. Library holdings can now be accessed through this Local Network and Internet.

DIGITAL RESOURCES

IGM library provide access to in – house digital resources as well as external digital resources. In – house resources are stored in web server and made accessible through Network. They are books, serials, theses and dissertations, current and back volumes of periodicals, university publication, faculty publication, theses and dissertations, project reports, Lectures of visiting experts, conferences/workshops, seminars/proceedings.

The external resources are not stored in web server. Here the digital library only act as an intermediary by subscribing these e-books, databases and provide hyperlinks to the respective databases in the web server. IGM library is subscribing to over 8000 ejournals from several publishers like EBSCO, Elsevier, UGC-Infonet, SCOPUS- A&I database, Royal Society of Chemistry, Institute of Physics and Mathscinet have given campus-wide IP based access.

OBJECTIVES OF THE STUDY

The Study was intended to collect information from the Librarian and Library staff who are involved in digitisation activity. Also to know whether they are satisfied with the digital resources currently available in IGM library.

The specific objectives of the study were the following:

- To ascertain information about the digitisation initiatives in IGM Library.
- To gather details about the existing digital library facilities in terms of collection, organisation and dissemination of the information to students, Research Scholars and Staff.
- To collect information about provisions of financial assistance and grants and other facilities.

- To review the present position of digital library facility in terms of access, preservation, retrieval of digital material.
- To find out the activities, services and area of digitalisation.
- To know the problem faced by the library staff in digitisation activity and user accessing digital material.
- To ascertain details about the future plans of the libraries in digitisation material.
- To collect the opinion and suggestions of librarians and users of digital library for improving digital library services.

METHODOLOGY

For collection of data combination of data collection was used. The data analysed on the nature and type of digital collection, the policies and programmes, planning, formats, standardisation for digital preservation. The study employed questionnaire method and discussions were made with the librarian, library staff and users to collect additional information about existing facilities in libraries. Separate questionnaires were administered to the librarian, library staff and users of the IGM library to gather data.

The survey questionnaire for the library staff covers areas like:

- Digital material policy
- Digital holdings
- Storage methods and formats
- Digital knowledge/training and
- Future needs for the services

Areas covered by the questionnaire for the users include their preferences and opinion on:

- Access to digital material
- Mode of access
- Type of material
- Problems and training
- Future needs

The scope of study includes:

- Information created originally in digital form and acquired by a repository through purchase, transfer, or legal deposit;
- Digital material created through programmes or projects that convert print, photographic and manuscript materials to digital form. The digital conversion projects mainly to improve access to material and in terms of preservation;
- The nature of accessing, type of materials accessed and problem in accessing digital material.The present study is a case study taken up to analyse the electronic and digital library management strategies adopted by I.G.M. Library of the University of Hyderabad. Due to

limitations of time the researcher could not gather the results based on the surveys of other library(s) of similar nature to evaluate and compare the services of IGML.

FINDINGS

- *Library Survey*: IGM Library is the first University Library in South India that has developed a full-fledged digital library and provide global access to it. Present study makes an attempt to study various digitisation activities of the library – Planning, Creation, Preservation and Management of digital resources.
- *Planning*: IGM library adheres to the authorised written policy documents approved by the library committee for managing digital material. The policies provide guide lines for acquiring material in digital form, converting the material from print to digital form, storage, Refreshing and migrating of material. It is ongoing and continuous. The policies of the institution meets well with the current needs. The materials selected for digitisation are not under copyright and published in house.
- *Creation of Digital Collections*: IGM Library has started creating and storing of books, serials, theses and dissertations, current and back volumes of periodicals, University publication, faculty publication, Lectures of visiting experts, conferences/workshops, and Seminars/ convention proceedings in digital form. The Library is well equipped with necessary Hardware High end book scanners both flat bedded and hand held scanners, printers, P IV PCs for processing, i2s Digibook scanner, Sony digital camera, SUN server for storage, UPS backups.
- *Different Softwares used by the library includes*: VTLS: Digital library application software, OCR fine reader 7, cleaning and editing software, scanner software, LINUX, ORACLE, Publishing software, Search Engines, etc. The pages are scanned and a computer readable (digital) image of pages are produced and stored in computer. The Optical character Recognition (OCR) software convert the text image in ASCII format for editing and manipulation of information and digital document is stored in server for online access.
- *Preservation of Digital material*: IGM digital library holds the responsibility of long term preservation of digital material. They are stored in hard disk, magnetic tapes, CD ROM, Optical disk(rewritable) and WORM Optical disk (write once and read many). It accepts electronic records in any format and convert into standard format and store them in hard disk, CD ROM, Optical disc Rewritable, WORM. Digital materials are archived in TIFF, JPEG or PDF formats.

- *Access Control*: IGM Library provides access to digital resources to its students, faculty and staff. User can access the digital material through ID and Password. There is no limitation for access to the materials provided if he/she is an authorised user. The institution has chosen to mount the digital reproduction (content) for Internet access in order to support searching across the collection. Digitisation work is an ongoing, there is no specific time schedule. The IGM library receives funds from University of Hyderabad, UGC, Vidyanidhi project, Universal digital library project and SUN Micro system. It also holds preservation responsibility of digital material. Currently, approximately 621 documents with 7200 MB has been stored in PDF format. The digital library supports the metadata standards.
- *Training of Staff*: The staff are trained in digitisation work. They are given training in IIIT, Hyderabad and IIIT, Bangalore from time to time. There are training programmes to increase the level of staff expertise with digitisation of material and preservation. The Library is also a member of digital consortia–Universal digital library (UDL), Vidyanidhi and UGC – infonet.
- *User Survey*: The IGM Digital library is large depository of information collected and stored in digital form. The study has examined the use of the digital collection by potential users (such as students, Research scholars, and faculty). A structured questionnaire was prepared taking into consideration all parameters regarding digital library use.

It may be observed from the findings that majority (53 per cent) of users suggested that the Internet connectivity speed should be increased. Users have also requested to organise training programme on down loading, saving and printing of digital materials. Some of the users requested to increase the number of computers in the campus for accessing of digital materials. Some of the users even suggested to adopt more user friendly software for down loading of digital materials in any format *i.e.,* PDF, HTML or XML.

The 21st century witnessing a knowledge revolution resulting from rapid growth in information and communication technology, acceleration of technical change and intensification of globalisation. Creating digital resources for providing wider and seamless global access to digital information to the users in distributed environment became a challenging task for any contemporary librarian.

The present study is an attempt to analyse the present situation in IGM library, University of Hyderabad. Regarding the frequency of use of library and digital material in the library, it is observed that a large number of faculty and research scholars are accessing and using regularly both in-house and external digital resources.

This indicates the optimum utilisation of library resources. IGM Library has framed regulations to allow access to the digital material to the registered users of the university. The library provides access to the digital material to its users regardless of their geographical location.

It is also observed that the problems faced by users using Digital Libraries are quite similar to the traditional libraries with some changes due to electronic rather than physical resources. The nature of problem can be broadly categorised as slow access, inadequate number of systems, inefficient display of information and lack of awareness in access, use and downloading information from digital resources. There are number of managerial and technical issues that are to be addressed by the digital librarians to provide satisfactory services to the users. The workflows and processes are only one aspect of digital libraries but there are number of issues that need to be considered. When creating a digital library like users, management support, staff authority and responsibility, policy related to IPR, security, finance, leadership and coordination, etc. Before starting to create a digital library it is important to evaluate the hardware and software aspect so that the digitisation process can run smoothly without further investment for it. There is another important aspect of the digital library, *i.e.,* preservation of digital contents. Therefore, the preservation technology must also be addressed while planning the creation of a digital library. There are two main methods for transferring information contained on magnetic or optical media onto new media; harvesting and migration seem to be the only logical answers to preserve the information. Migration is an active system-based approach.

Migration preserves information by continually moving it between one system and its replacement. The difference between the two methods is that migration preserves the structure of the file and its information while harvesting merely copies the information. Building a digital information is a complex process involving requirements analysis, careful planning, and well informed choices. Ultimately, every library's goal is to meet the information needs of its users. The digital library infrastructure will assist staff in creating the tools and supporting applications to manage a growing collection of library work in digital form, will help to ensure long term preservation, and will provide new and innovative library services to the users.

Acquiring and implementing application development tools for programming staff, testing implementation of digital content that use the core software defining the library's corporate requirements for electronic document management and determining the best approach for implementing an electronic document management system. All hardware and software dependencies should be avoided and all digitisation equipment must be capable to support the requirements for long-term preservation. The library professionals should pay keen interest to understand the various provisions about the copyright act, patterns, and designs, etc.

The liabilities and safeguards in regards to the librarians and libraries should be taken care of to avoid the infringement of the copyright act. The Government of India has passed the copyright law before attaining independence and amended in different periods to protect the copyright till date. In digital and new worked environment, it would be ideal if there is a single world law on copyright to safeguard the intellectual property rights, at the national, and international level. The role of Library professional is also changing in the digital library environment. Library professionals with their expertise, knowledge and techniques of where to look up and how to find out information for a given query can help the users in their search for information by extending personal help and assistance. Library professionals should acquire such skills in handling the information sources and users tactfully and render satisfactory information service in the fast changing digital library environment.

It is also necessary for their very survival and survival of the library profession. In a Country like India where resources are limited, funds are inadequate; librarians have to take careful and judicious decisions in selecting library materials for digitisation. However, taking into consideration the user's information needs other requirements, university libraries may plan for digitisation projects. Only through digitised information, university libraries can share their resources with other libraries and make their resources available to a large number of users through the web.

IMPACT OF DIGITAL LIBRARY ON HIGHER EDUCATION AND RESEARCH

The library has, since long, been considered to be the source and power of knowledge and also the knowledge base. In higher education ands research, the library has specific functions to facilitate the extensive use of learning resources by students, teachers, and researchers.

With the growth of literature in large numbers even in the same field, these groups of library users have faced problems in identifying the appropriate literature for their use and consultation in a desired timeframe.

Information and communications technology (ICT), particularly during the last two decades, has significantly contributed to open the door of accessing, hidden, knowledge in a highly efficient manner. Initially, the ICT was used in the library environment for developing databases of in-formation resources mainly aiming at storing and retrieving information on various types of publication resources and also to organize various types of information services.

The ICT has put us in the electronic environment to help identify, assess, acquire, record, store, organize, and disseminate information and information resources according to the need of specific requirements and/or of an organization or an individual requirement.

The use of IT in libraries has enhanced efficiency in all aspects of information acquisition, storage, and transfer. Its magical opportunities have dramatically changed the operations of the library and its information services.

With the new facilities, the traditional libraries have been modernized to make these as well-equipped and inter-connected electronic resource centres.

In the library and publication fields, computer-based communications have extensively facilitated the transmission of messages, transfer, and exchange of files and text, such as online submission of papers for publication in books and journals, uploading/downloading, access to databases, conduct of interactions, provision of bulletin boards and newsletters, journals, and publications, online orders, inter-library loans, creation of user profiles, consolidation and repackaging of information for specific needs, dissemination of information, and so on.

Uncountable numbers of monographic materials, journals, learning resources, documents, reports, data, databases, and audiovisual materials generated and published by government and non-governmental organizations and commercial agencies/publishers are now available in electronic formats to access even from the remote corner of a country, thereby increasing the use of these materials and enhancing the efficiency of information dissemination.

PURPOSE, SCOPE, AND LIMITATIONS OF THE PAPER

The concept of developing the digital library system is very new in Bangladesh. In Bangladesh, we have 77 (54 private) universities, about 1,800 university colleges, institutes, and colleges, and about 600 organizations and institutions involved in research and related activities.

These organizations and institutions have libraries, but most are run in a traditional way. About 100 libraries have been using IT to carry out various library-related activities, including creation of databases.

Most publications in various fields coming out from Bangladesh are still in printed formats; as a result, the people remain uninformed of these materials.

There have been no formal survey or studies to know the potentials of digital libraries in Bangladesh where the conditions of libraries and information services are rather deplorable in most cases. In Bangladesh, we are moving at database level but not at digital level, except a few cases. The purpose of the present paper is to highlight the potentials and various aspects of digital library and also to highlight its benefits for and impacts in Bangladesh, particularly in higher education and research.

The paper is not based on any research study, rather it is of educative nature. While writing the paper, we had to depend heavily on various publications, particularly the book titled "Introduction to digital libraries" by G.G. Chowdhury and Sudatta Chowdhury published in 2003.

Change in Library-access and use Patterns

Library is used by various categories of people who need to read literature to keep themselves informed, to enhance their knowledge, to meet specific need(s), to educate themselves, to teach and for learning, practical applications, research, and dissemination.

Their major interest is that their desired information/materials are made available at a minimum effort in an appropriate format and when they need these. Library patrons need information, use literature and knowledge, and again apply that knowledge to generate new knowledge and information. Information and knowledge can be obtained from print materials, audiovisual materials, databases, and the Internet.

With the change in the information-provision system over the last few years, libraries are becoming information resource-access centres, while maintaining also the traditional library and modern library services. With the advent and applications of ICT, libraries are now gradually becoming dependent on web-based resources available through the Internet (network of networks), which was first developed and launched in the USA in 1969.

Full-text journals, publications, data, and audiovisuals are available through the Internet, thereby facilitating access to free and priced online information and learning resources. But monitoring and tracking the availability of, and searching for, needed papers and publications are major problems in the web-based information system because the system is invisible. Library patrons and library professionals can easily register with publishers of journals and other materials through the Internet to be alerted electronically on a regular basis.

These have warranted that both information users and information professionals are well-oriented with the Internet, with web addresses of those organizations/institutions which put materials in their websites, and with searching mechanisms.

Users are now more independent than before, they are self-learners and self-accessors, and they can access web-based information resources even from their home computers and search databases according to their needs.

The technology has been gradually making the traditional libraries to become universal for all those who need, and seek for, information and information resources either from within or out-side the organization or the country where they are located.

Transitions in Library Development

The history of development of libraries started with the preservation of knowledge on bones, wood surfaces, bark, hides, textiles, stones, clay tablets, papyrus, parchment, vellum, etc. and subsequently on paper with the advent of printing machine. The use of paper in recording knowledge helped spread out the use of knowledge all over the world, even spreading up to rural areas. This also helped preserve knowledge for a longer time.

The mechanism for preservation of knowledge on paper has gradually been transferred to the electronic medium since the advent of the computer system which is used all over the world, including Bangladesh. Now, most publishing houses, national, regional and international organizations are putting their publications and public records in the Internet.

In the early stage of human communication and while transferring knowledge, "man may have even developed an 'oral literature' that was handed down from generation to generation." Initially, library was usually conceived of graphics forms of recorded information, and the library was only one of many means of communication. "The library is a means of communication in the sense that it is a storehouse of recorded information..."

So, the library is the fundamental source of organized recorded or stored information. The process of communication, thus, started first with speech, then writing, then printing, and finally with electronic devices.

Each stage of the development of speech/language, writing, books, earlier libraries, and modern libraries passed though a process of considerable time-span to establish each stage of the conceptualization of each process to development, to organization, to implementation, and to management. "The earliest form of library was what we would consider today an archive, since it was really a collection of government or religious documents."

Based on the growth and change in library systems within the traditional and modern concepts, we have, like computers, several generations in the development of the library system since its inception to up till now.

The generations are:

- *First generation*: Generation of the early archival library system with early writing materials
- *Second generation*: Generation of the traditional library system with collection of printed materials and without the use of modern tools of library organization, such as cataloguing rules and classification schemes
- *Third generation*: Generation of the traditional library system organized with modern tools of library organization
- *Fourth generation*: Generation of the computerized library system with the use of IT/ICT
- *Fifth generation*: Generation of the digital library system without any space, time and language barriers and highly depending on the Internet/web-based resources.

Meaning and Scope of Digital Library

The term 'digital library' has synonymously been used for meaning 'automated library', 'electronic library', 'virtual library', and 'digital library'. The concept of digital library began initially with modernization of libraries with electronic devices.

GG and S Chowdhury reports that "Borgman suggests that the first research-oriented definition of digital libraries appeared in 1992 when the phrase 'electronic libraries' was used for what is now called digital libraries." Another name that we come across is 'hybrid library'.

A hybrid library is a library where both "digital and printed information resources co-exist and are brought together in an integrated information service accessible locally as well as remotely." Whatever may be the name, all mean almost the same, which "support full life cycle of creation, storage, preservation, dissemination, and use of data, information and knowledge." The scope of the functionality of these terminologies is almost same.

Unfortunately, as of now, concerned professionals could not conclude an acceptable definition of digital library. Various researchers and information professionals have proposed various definitions. GG and S Chowdhury say, "Two major categories of definitions are available, one focusing on the access and retrieval of digital content and the other focusing on the collection, organization and service aspects of digital libraries." Borgman presents the scope of a digital library (then defined as electronic library) as a combination of: "

- A service;
- An architecture;
- A set of information resources, databases of text, numbers, graphics, sound, video, etc.
- A set of tools and capabilities to locate, retrieve and utilize the information resources available."

He further says, "Digital libraries encompass two comprehensive ideas, one emphasizing that they extend and enhance existing information storage and retrieval systems, incorporating digital data and metadata in any form; the other emphasizing that the design, policy, and practice should reflect the social context in which they exist."

The 1994 IEEE CAIA Workshop on Intelligent Access to On-line Digital Libraries defined "A digital library is an assemblage of digital computing, storage, and communications machinery together with the content and software needed to reproduce, emulate, and extend the services provided by conventional libraries based on paper and other material means of collecting, cataloging, finding, and disseminating information.

A full service digital library must accomplish all essential services of traditional libraries and also exploit the well-known advantages of digital storage, searching, and communication." The Stanford digital library research team defined a digital library as "coordinated collection of services that are based on collections of materials, some of which may not be directly under the control of the organization providing a service in which they play a role".

Oppenheim and Smithson defined a "digital library as an information service in which all the information resources are available in computer processable form and the functions of acquisition, storage, preservation, retrieval, access and display are carried out through the use of digital technol-ogies."

According to Arms, a digital library is a "managed collection of information, with associated services, where the information is stored in digital formats and accessible over a network."

The Digital Library Federation in the USA defines the digital library as "Digital libraries are organizations that provide the resources, including the specialized staff, to select, structure, offer intellectual access to, interpret, distribute, preserve the integrity of, and ensure the persistence over time of collections of digital works so that they are readily and economically available for use by a defined community or set of communities." Access to the entire collection is globally available directly or indirectly across a network.

Review of the above concepts and definitions suggest that the digital library is "the collection of services and the collection of information objects that support users in dealing with information objects and the organization and presentation of those objects available directly or in-directly via electronic/digital means."

A digital library may contain materials that are already available in digitized format, such as electronic online journals, electronic information resources, or may contain materials that were originally produced in another form, but subsequently digitized.

Need of Digital Library

Many academic and research organizations and libraries in developed countries are building institutional repositories of the institution's books, papers, theses, and other works. Institutional repositories are often referred to as digital libraries.

Cornell University and the Wisconsin State Historical Society are considered leaders in the field of digital archive creation and management. The ICDDR,B in Bangladesh is also in the process of developing an institutional repository of its publications.

With the gradual change in the library-accessing system and with the increased use of IT in libraries, the libraries in Bangladesh will, in the near future, be in a position to put linkages to international online resources and develop their own digital libraries with collection that are relevant to their library patrons.

This is imminent because of the absence of the needed infra-structural facilities in libraries, urgency of the need for information and information resources, information resource-accessing problems in the local environment, *e.g.*, home, shortage of man-power and budget, scarcity of foreign currencies, and pressure from library users and also from the higher authority.

If we consider the advantages and disadvantages of the digital library system, it also guides us to think of developing and establishing the digital library system without wasting any more time.

Benefits and Impact of Digital Library vis-à-vis Traditional Library

A digital library being in the web is not limited by any space/location and time, resulting in an easy and open access to web-based information resources compared to the traditional library system. Any user may access to information resources round the clock, provided he/she has the access facility.

The major important benefits are that users from various locations within and outside the country can simultaneously access the required document without any serious hindrances and download the needed documents without loosing the quality. They can also search for documents by word, by subject, by phrase, by author, by title, etc. as the providers of the digital library system facilitate user-friendly search interfaces. The digital library system takes very little space in storing information resources, allowing unlimited networking benefits, link-age of documents in any site at a lower cost, handling of the system with minimum staff and at a lesser cost, and adoption of new developments compared to the traditional library system where budget, space, and skilled manpower are the important constraints. The traditional library system is demarked and/or highly constrained by space and print collection and by provision of time-needed traditional library services. In this system, information-seekers and library users are generally required to personally visit libraries to meet their needs of information and literature and to get services.

Unfortunately, the services do not reach them in our country. On the other hand, the open access or digital libraries are demarked by electronic collection, electronic preservation system, and online access facilities. Time and access problems are important factors in the traditional library system, whereas time and access are not barriers in the digital library system.

Digital libraries can serve the user population very fast and with easy access to online resources. The digital library system can cope with the problem of handling information explosion and can manage large amounts of digital contents.

Implementation of the digital library system has treme-ndous benefits and impacts. It brings in-formation and information resources to users, provides a one-stop service, facilitates improved searching, manipulation of information, improved information-sharing, timely access to information, improved use of information, and improved collaboration, and reduces the digital divide.

The digital library system permits offering of digital library services, including personalized information services, reference services, SDI and current awareness services, literature-searching services, bibliographic services, transmission and exchange of literature search results, files, and publications, library-to-library cooperation, removal of barriers of space, time, and language, avoidance of dependence on others, improved communications between receivers and providers, e-alerts of table of contents of journals and publications, and many more.

The digital library helps build own personal collection according to need, lessens the dependence on information professionals or intermediaries, facilitates access to information resources wherever they are located, facilitates the use of same information resources simultaneously by various users, and provides access to information resources not owned by the service-providing organizations.

It brings paradigm shift in the creation, distribution, management, and use of information and facilitates the consumption, creation, and sharing of knowledge. It also facilitates better delivery of information than was possible in the traditional library system.

Limitations, and Constraints in Development, of Digital Library

Digital libraries cannot possibly replace the environment of a physical library as we still like to see and browse reading materials physically and get attracted more to read these. Lack of skills in handling computer viruses and lack of standardization for digitized materials are important limitations. While there are obvious benefits of digitization, the major problem is, however, ensuring the quality of digitized materials. The other problems are access management, determination of authenticity of materials, and control of unauthorized access and use. Access being open, through the Internet, many people may be indulged in browsing vulgar resources. Sometimes, it may take a long time to access literature that are immediately needed.

It may happen that computers and other related facilities remain paralyzed in absence of regular maintenance and replacements of necessary equipment.

The development of the digital library system at least involves:

- Digitization (data conversion, data organization, etc.)
- Establishment of linkages to digitized publications. Development of databases only does not mean digital library.

Digitization also involves hardware and software costs, staff cost, outsourcing cost, cost of various related activities before and after digitization, such as movement of physical items, copyright clearance, creation of records, indexes, and so on. The development of a digital library system demands incurring of "large costs for the conversion of print materials into digital format, for the technical skills of staff to maintain them, and for the costs of maintaining online access (*i.e.,* servers, bandwidth costs, etc.)."

Data from the old system to the new system would also need additional costs. The initial cost (cost of hardware, software, groundstations or leasing communication circuit, etc.) is rather high. For fast access and transmit files, the system needs high bandwidth. In the Internet environment, it is difficult to monitor and keep track of information resources used for subsequent use. Users face the problem of 'information overload', receive unwanted information, data, or resources, and provision of services may be disrupted unless access or facilities are ensured.

5

Research and Technological in Diligent

DILIGENT (DIgital Library Infrastructure on Grid ENabled Technology) is a three-year Integrated Project funded by the European Commission under the 6th Framework Programme for Research and Technological a Digital Library Infrastructure that will enable members of dynamic virtual research organisations to create on-demand transient digital libraries that exploit shared resources.

Resources in this context are multimedia and multi-type content repositories, applications, and computing and storage elements. Following the understanding of DLs expressed in Borgman *et al.*, this project focuses on the development of DLs that "are not ends in themselves; rather they are enabling technologies for digital asset management, electronic commerce, electronic publishing, teaching and learning, and other activities". From an abstract point of view, the DILIGENT infrastructure can be understood as a broker serving DL resource providers and consumers.

The providers are the individuals and the organisations that decide to publish their resources under the supervision of the broker, according to certain access and use policies. The consumers are the user communities that want to build their own DLs. The resources managed by this broker are content sources (*i.e.* repositories of information searchable and accessible through a single "entrance"), services (*i.e.* software tools that implement a specific functionality and whose descriptions, interfaces and bindings are defined and publicly available) and hosting nodes (*i.e.* networked entities that offer computing and storage capabilities and supply an environment for hosting content sources and services). Providers register their resources and give a description of them by exploiting appropriate mechanisms provided by the infrastructure.

The infrastructure also automatically derives other properties of the resources that are used to enrich the explicit description. The infrastructure manages the registered resources by supporting their discovery, monitoring and usage, and by implementing a number of other functionalities that aim at realising the required controlled sharing and quality of service. A user community can create one or more DLs by specifying a set of requirements.

These requirements specify conditions for the information space (*e.g.* publishing institutions, subject of the content, document types), for the operations that manipulate the information space (*e.g.* type of search, tool for data analysis), for the services for supporting the work of the users (*e.g.* type of personalised dissemination, type of collaboration), for the quality of service (*e.g.* configuration, availability, response time) and for many other aspects, like the maximum cost, or lifetime. The broker satisfies the community's requirements by selecting, and in many cases also deploying, a number of resources among those accessible to the community, gluing them appropriately and, finally, making the new DL application accessible through a portal.

The composition of a DL is dynamic since the DL broker continuously monitors the status of the DL resources and, if necessary, changes them in order to offer the best quality of service. By relying on the shared resources many DLs, serving different communities, can be created and modified on-the-fly, without big investments and changes in the organisations that set them up. In order to support the transactions between the providers and the consumers, the DILIGENT infrastructure exploits the virtual organisations (VOs) mechanism that has been introduced in the Grid research area. This mechanism models sets of users and resources aggregated together by highly controlled sharing rules, usually based on an authentication framework. VOs have a limited lifetime, are dynamically created and satisfy specific needs by allocating and providing resources on demand.

Through the VOs mechanism the DILIGENT infrastructure glues together the users and the resources of a DL. The consumers, *i.e.* the user communities that require DLs to support their needs. The providers, each of which makes a number of resources available, are on the right. The infrastructure acts as a mediator by maintaining a framework where multiple virtual organisations, active on the same shared resources, can co-exist. The DL development model proposed by DILIGENT is radically new. Within the described framework each DL consumes the required resources only for the time it needs them. This opens a lot of new opportunities for the creation of the functionalities required by the new "knowledge commons" environments. In particular, the exploitation of more effective, but also very computationally expensive algorithms becomes viable at an acceptable cost for many communities.

For example, thanks to sharing, the use of the high processconsuming algorithms that automatically extract features from multi-media objects can be exploited in a large number of DLs. Moreover, in the framework established by the new development model, the user communities can easily, and in a timely manner, create and maintain their own DLs with limited resources since the management of the DL is automatically and transparently carried out by the infrastructure. The system that implements the functionality of the DILIGENT infrastructure is being built by integrating DL and Grid technologies. The motivation for this design choice relies on the similarity between many of the problems encountered through our new notion of DLs and the issues addressed by the most recent research in the Grid domain.

From the functional point of view, the DILIGENT system is divided into five functionality clusters:

- *DL Creation and Management:* is responsible for the dynamic construction and maintenance of the transient DLs and for the controlled sharing and management of the resources that are used to implement them. The functionalities offered by this cluster allow users to express the requirements that the DL must fulfil. Moreover, they automatically identify and arrange the pool of resources needed to satisfy these needs.
- *Index and Search Management:* is responsible for enabling cost-efficient search and retrieval of information in DLs, while satisfying the level of quality required for the overall data retrieval and delivery operations.
- *Content and Metadata Management:* implements the handling of DL content and related metadata, the consistent and distributed management of annotations, and the integration of external content and metadata sources.
- *Process Management:* manages the creation of user processes composed of existing services, the validation of their correctness, the automatic optimisation of their definition according to the resources available and the service characteristics, and their reliable execution. Thanks to this feature, the DILIGENT system can easily be enriched with additional operational workflows to meet new user requirements.
- *Application Specific Functionality:* provides the functionality needed to support user-specific scenarios, like portals, document visualisation, or features extraction.

From the architectural point of view, the DILIGENT system is designed as a Web Services Resource Framework (WSRF) application built on top of the gLite Grid middleware released by the Enabling Grids for Escience in Europe (EGEE) project. gLite hides the heterogeneous nature of the computing elements (*i.e.* services representing a computing resource) on the one hand and storage elements (*i.e.* services representing a storage resource) on the other hand by providing an environment that facilitates and controls their sharing. The DILIGENT services are being initially deployed on a project-proprietary gLite infrastructure. Architecturally, this infrastructure is completely interoperable with the EGEE infrastructure. EGEE is currently the largest European Grid infrastructure ever built.

A number of other recently funded projects will extend this infrastructure to other geographic regions, like Mediterranean countries, Latin America, or

China. The interoperability with the EGEE infrastructure will allow any authorised virtual community that wishes to create DLs to also exploit the resources made available by this vast Grid infrastructure. During the project timeframe, the DILIGENT infrastructure will be populated with a number of important archives and software applications provided by the two communities that are participating in the experimentation with the results of the project, one from the environmental e-science domain and one from the cultural heritage domain. The first community is ImpECt (Implementation of Environmental Conventions) and includes leading players in the environmental sector. This community will use DILIGENT to support the organisation of conferences and the preparation of projects and periodical reports.

Through DILIGENT this community expects to improve accessibility, interoperability and usability of environmental data, models, tools, algorithms and instruments, integrating the distributed data sources with specialised data handling services. The second community, ARTE, is a community of scholars located in different parts of the world, working together to establish a new discipline that merges experiences from research in medicine, humanities, social sciences and communication. In order to achieve their objectives, these researchers require instruments to ease the construction of multimedia artefacts and to improve support for education.

At the time of the writing of this paper initial experimentation with the features of a DILIGENT DL has already been conducted by implementing simplified services for preparing environmental reports, as required by the ImpECt environmental agencies. Through the exploiting of rich information sources, ranging from raw data sets to maps and graphs archives, these agencies periodically prepare reports on the status of the environment. Currently, this task is performed by first selecting the relevant information from each of the multiple and heterogeneous sources available, then launching complex processing on large amounts of data to obtain "products", like graphs, tables and other summarised information and, finally, producing the required report by assembling all the different parts together. This process, which is repeated periodically, requires a lot of work due to the complexity of interfacing the different sources and tools.

Despite the effort expended, the resulting reports do not completely fulfil the requirements of their readers, who would like to have a picture of the environmental status which is updated at the time the report is accessed. A DILIGENT DL offers a more effective framework for the creation and maintenance of these reports. In our experimentation, for example, we have built a DL which exploits content maintained in both repositories including textual documents and archives of Earth observation raw data provided by the European Space Agency. In this DL, which is accessible through a single user interface, all the different kinds of information necessary for creating the reports can be found. By combining this information and by defining how to derive the associated "products" (images, tables, or graphs) from raw data, the users can create their reports much more easily.

Moreover, a specialised user interface allows authorised users to access these composite reports by choosing static or dynamic generation. The selection of dynamic generation triggers associated process workflows which, by combining appropriate applications, generate the required products on demand by processing both the raw data and other intermediate products stored in the DL repositories. The dynamically generated products are obtained by running those applications that are computationally intensive on the Grid. In this way the complex processes required to generate the products are executed in few minutes at a limited cost to the community that is exploiting them. In order to obtain the same performance without the Grid, an institution would have to equip its digital library with a great number of computers, while in the case of DILIGENT the institution can also exploit computer capabilities made available by third party organisations. The same is true for storage capacity. Maintaining raw data, intermediate products and high resolution images requires a large amount of storage capacity. By exploiting the Grid technology, part of this information, especially the temporary part, can be maintained in third-party storage systems.

DIGITAL STORAGE IN LIBRARIES

The relatively recent change from the term *Information Technology* (IT) to *Information and Communication Technology* (ICT) due to the convergence of IT and ICT has open up new challenges for libraries. Information Technology is the collective name for a group of technologies that are concerned with the storage, retrieval, manipulation, analysis, and transmission of information. Since the fabrication of the first modern computer in the mid 1940's, computer technology has developed at a tremendous pace to the point where it has penetrated almost all occupations and has spread to the far concerns of the world.

Similarly, communication technology has made rapid progress in the post World War II period. But it is the development of this technology in the last 15 years that has made IT so important. The development in this area have been brining about a revolutionary change in the way humans work, and in the way they interact with each others. The spread of telecommunications has brought into limelight the Internet, the global intercommunication of computer networks. This has made available a large store information to all concerns of the world. Information Technology provides the following services for information:

- Storage of large amounts of information in a cost effective manner.
- Structuring of information to enable quick retrieval of what is required.

- Analysis of stored information to help in decision making.
- Sharing of information among people geographically dispersed.
- Quick transmission of information over large distances.

IT consists of five components, *i.e.*, electronic science, computer science, tele-communication science, artificial language and human interface.

INFORMATION TECHNOLOGY USE IN LIBRARY MANAGEMENT SYSTEM

The IT revolution has also embraud the library system. A massive and rapid computerization process throughout the levels of the library system has made IT an integral part of the library management scene in many countries all over the world. The incorporation of IT into the day-to-day activity of libraries has a strong impact on virtually every aspect of their management processes. Although there is no agreed definition of IT, the term "IT" includes three main components – *management information system* (MIS) or *decision support system* (DSS), hardware, and human factors. A management information system is the set of structure and procedures that govern the collection, processing, analysis, presentation and use of information within an organization.

IMPACT OF ICTS IN LIBRARIES

Technology is changing the nature of libraries and librarians, and it continues to exert a major influence on the strategic direction of libraries in society. Today the library services are transitioning from local traditional collections to global resources provided on demand via the most advanced networking technologies.

DIGITAL DATA STORAGE IN LIBRARIES

Digital data storage media for storing digital data are constantly being developed, improved or superseded, and any discussion of them here can only be taken as description of the current situation i. e., optical discs, magnetic media, other media for digital data storage. The concept of the "digital library" evolved out of potential for digitization of all forms of media: print, image, sound, complex data sets, and computer simulations of non-time-bound sequences, otherwise not demonstrable events, etc., and retrieving them in context of multiple networked information systems.

The digital library often serves as a multidimensional catalogue or index to bring together the resource discovery information of every resource that was topically, creatively, or by reason of other connections generatively related. A digital library does not only consist of digitized and digitally born information resources, but also of electronic metadata on non-digital objects. Digital Data: Considerable attention is now being paid to the possibility of converting the intellectual content of items in library collection into digital data by electronic means and storing it on magnetic tapes or discs. Both textual and pictorial information can be converted. For example by using optical character recognition devices which convert texts into their digital code equivalent, or by using scanners to convert text or, more usually, pictures into an analogue form.

Text can also be input by keyboarding. In addition to information already in another format being converted to digital format, much information is now originated in digital form and may appear only in that form in the library. Digital data have considerable advantages. They can be rapidly duplicated and speedily transmitted without deterioration through electronic communications networks to whatever the user is working. Storage: It is a mainly technical requirement, although new media may complicate storage decisions and costing. Today's large digital repositories use multiple level of mass storage media and mechanical robots to locate and mount the media.

Phases of Digitization: Undoubtedly, digital media will have to co-exit with print media. Different kinds of collection could be digitized at different times depending on the priorities of the library. To start with, any one type of collection, for example, important out of print publications could be made available in digital form. Feedback of its usage can be sengut and analyzed. In the next phase, another type of data could be converted into digital form. Digitization Process: Digitization is a process of converting paper documents to electronic format. Scanning process does the conversion.

Digital information can be transmitted and received anywhere in the world where the infrastructure to send and received is in place. Due to the implementation of the IT, the librarian need to be well aware of the technical issues, potential problems involved, trained manpower available, the hardware required, document management systems, *optical character recognization* (OCR) technology for implementing digitization of the collection and services. As been know the concept of digital library is growing very fast globally. It is a welcome trained that various institutions and professional societies are involved to provide opportunities for the library and librarians to upgrade and enhance the professional knowledge about digital library. Various important aspects like digital libraries issues, architecture, electronic publishing, collection building, storage, organization, transmission of digital information, creation and use of hypertext and hypermedia system, networks and their implications, manpower development etc. We are in the early stage of a transmition from a print-based to a digital society.

The latest technologies offer cheap computer processing power, cheap mass storage, inexpensive and ubiquitous access to high speed networks and retrieval devices give us the ability to create, to manipulate, to storage and especially to transfer large quantities of information in digital form at low costs. Digital information can be stored on any medium that is able to represent binary digits 0 and 1. Conversion from the conventional storage to digitized format required discrete analysis as the primary function, based on user electronic storage and retrieval system. Some of the common digitized storage media that are presently used world over are the Hyper books, CD-ROM, Multimedia. New media are constantly being developed. Some that are still in experimental stages or have been only very recently introduced are digital videotape, digital audiotape and digital paper.

CREATING NETWORKS WITH GROWING REACH

It involves rapid advances in two technologies – digital storage and processing of information and satellite and optical fibre transmission of information– are creating new and faster ways of storing, handling, distributing and accessing information. These innovations enable the processing and storage of enormous amount of information, along with rapid distribution information through communication networks. For example in 2001 more information can be sent over a single cable in a second than in 1997 was sent over the entire internet in a month.

Linking computing devices and allowing them to communicate with each other creates networked information systems based on a common protocol. Individuals, households and institutions are linked in processing and executing a huge number of instructions in imperceptible time spans. This radically alters access to information and the structure of communication extending the networked reach to all corners of the world.

TECHNOLOGICAL TRANSFORMATIONS

Today's technological transformations are intertwined with another transformation, globalization and together they are creating a new paradigm – the network age. These transformations expand opportunities and increase the social and economic rewards of creating and using technology. They are also altering how and by whom technology is created and owned, and how it is made accessible and used. Technology is not inherently good or bad the outcome depends on how it is used.

SOME INITIATIVES IN IT SECTOR

The Department of Information Technology has setup Community Centre (CICs) at 487 blocks in the seven North Eastern States 9 Arunachal Pradesh, Assam, manipur, Meghalaya, Mizoram, Nagaland, Tripura) and Sikkim to provide connectivity at the block level and thus promote application of Information Technology for accelerating socio economic development of the region.

INFORMATION TECHNOLOGY ACT

The Government of India has created the necessary legal and administrative framework through the enactment of the Information Technology

Act, 2000. While on the one hand it seeks to create the public key infrastructure for electronic authentication through digital signatures.

DIGITAL LIBRARY

Digital Libraries are a form of information Technology in which social impact matters as much as technological advancements. Future knowledge networks will rely on scalable semantics, to automatically indexing the community collections so that users can effectively search of billion repositories.

NATIONAL INFORMATION CENTRE (NIC)

It provides informatics services for decision support to government offices/ bodies at national, state, district and block levels. It offers network services. NIC also provides video conferencing facilities.

INFRASTRUCTURE FOR DIGITAL MANAGEMENT

We are living to-day in a world of change and the changes we see all around us due to availability of information quicker than before, faster communication through E-mail, voice mail and video conferencing and the great influence of the Internet and web pages. The use of computer-based system in the libraries and information units is now commonplace all over the world. Computers are used to assist in a variety of functions such as maintaining and providing access to the catalogue of items in the collection, managing the issuing and returning of items from the collection, the acquisition of new items for the collection, controlling the serial publications and allowing the retrieval of information from the databases relating to bibliographic data financial or numeric data or the full text of documents.

DIGITAL ASSETS

- Floppies: Certain Books are accompanying floppies; such floppies are assigned the concerned Book Accession Numbers. These floppies are arranged serially and kept in the floppy boxes. J.N.N. College of Engineering Library has 200 floppies. Users lend and read these floppies in OPAC systems.
- CDs: Some new books contain CDs also. Such CDs are assigned the Concerned accession Number and kept in CD container. There are about 1,400 CDs available in Library. Users refer these CDs through OPAC system.
- Software used in J.N.N. College of Engineering: There was one software, which was developed by one programmer of computer science Dept. It had some limitations. Now, 'LIBRIS SOFTWARE' has been purchased and installed. This software put into use.
- LAN: Local Area Network was established by connecting all 6 systems

in Library with a Main Server. Each system was connected Ethernet and Win proxy Card through Co-Axial cables.

- UPS: An UPS was purchased and connected with all 6 terminals in the Library.
- Computers: There are 7 computers available in the Library. PC's Configuration: -
  - Pentium III/650 MHZ and above, 512 KB internal and external
  - Cache memory 815 E-Intel
  - Chipset motherboard 128 MB SD RAM.
  - Minimum 17.1 GB/HDD IDE Drive.
  - 1.44 MB FDD, 32 Bit Graphic Card 52*CD Drive, 17 inch Colour
  - Monitor with electronic turner and energy saving windows
  - Keyboard, Logitech Mouse, ATX Cabinet with preloaded and O.S.Windows 95/98.
- Printers: There are one Dot Matrix and one Laser Printer available in the Library.
- Bar-Code Printer: One Bar-Code Printer is also printing in barcode labels in Laser Printer was purchased along with 2,500 Book Barcode sheets and 5000 ID Barcode Label Sticker Sheets.
- Book Database: A book database was created with 53,500 records. Bibliographic information about each Access No. Title, Author, Call Number, Keywords, Publisher, Price, etc.
- Periodical Database: A periodical database was created entering all current journal's bibliographic information. The data entry for receipt of periodicals is being entered into computer. Reminders for non-receipt of periodicals is taken as print out and sent to the periodical suppliers.

ADVANTAGES

Computerization of Library operations saves much time of the Library Staff and users. Students and Staff members feel happy to handle Bar-coded Membership Card. Bar-coding facilities stock verification of books and journals.

DRAWBACKS

Since we implement computerization, our library staff does dual job entering all operations manually and through computer. Staff finds this as a job. In the beginning it may be do their, jobs through computer only. During power failure time, staff face problems to operate computer. These problems can be solved using UPS. An UPS* was purchased and connected to all systems in the library. This UPS solves power problem up to some extent.

HOW TO IMPLEMENT IN FUTURE

Our library staff will prepare bar-coded identity cards for fresh students in future using the barcode equipments. Similarly barcode labels will be generated and pasted in three places of each new book purchased in future. Stock verification will be done online using the barcode scanner in future.

PURCHASING CD CABINET

To preserve CDs it is proposed to purchase a CD Cabinet. All CDs will be serially arranged and kept in proper order. Whenever a user requires particular CD, Library Staff can provide the same for reference purpose.

DIGITAL INITIATIVES AT J.N.N. COLLEGE OF ENGINEERING LIBRARY

It is experienced that Bar-coding has revolutioned the library activities globally. A Laser Barcode printer was purchased and Bar-coding software was also installed. The Bar-coding labels for each book were generated.

BAR-CODING OF BOOKS

Printing barcode labels and pasting in three places of each book, *viz.,* Title page, Secrete page and due date slip were entrusted with a contractor. This generating of Bar-coding labels and pasting the labels for all 53,500 volumes were completed within five months. Retrieving of information through barcode labels using barcode scanner was tested.

The computer displayed the Accession Number and the relevant bibliographic information was retrieved from the book database. The bibliographic information includes Accession Number, Author, Title, Call Number, Publisher and Keywords.

BAR-CODED IDENTITY CARDS

The work of bar-coding of identity cards for all users J.N.N. College of Engineering. College was entrusted to the Frontier Information Technology, Secundarbad. The identity card contains the attributes: Class, Dept, Eligibility, Valid up to, Blood group, Residential address, residence phone number. A stamp size photo of each member was scanned and printed on each card. Both Librarian and Principal are signed on this ID card. The identity cards looked good rather than the old traditional plastic card. Each user used to carry this card and produce the same in the issue counter along with the books and get it issued. Now user feels happy in handling this bar-coded identity card. They also feel proud in producing the same card wherever he visits either inside the college or outside the campus.

NETWORKING AND MANPOWER TRAINING

J. N. N. College of Engineering, Library is a member of the DELNET. The users of the library access the resources listed in this network through the net connectivity. The library staff had their sufficient training at Frontier Information Technology, Secundarbad on various divisions of the library such as Acquisition,

Cataloguing, Circulation and Periodicals control. They received special training with regard to preparation of Bar-coded identity card. Various processes include:

- Scanning of the User's Photo.
- Printing the photo in the special art paper using the colour printer.
- Composing various fields, *viz.*, name class, branch, valid up to, eligibility, blood group, residential address, residence phone.
- Laminating the above paper using laminating machine.
- Books issue through scanner.
- Books return through scanner.

Our Library staffs were sent to nearest libraries to have practical exposure towards developing of barcoded identity cards. J.N.N. College of Engineering Library staff underwent hands on training nearest libraries studied the system form all perspectives. The hands on training assisted the Library staff to develop the barcode identity cards. For this purpose the following equipments have been identified.

- Digital camera.
- Colour printer.
- Scanner.
- Laminating Machine.

J. N. N. College of Engineering Library staff has also studied various operations in DRTC Library, Bangalore.

DISTRIBUTED SERVICES ARCHITECTURE IN DLIBRA DIGITAL LIBRARY FRAMEWORK

The dLibra Digital Library Framework has been developed in Poznan Supercomputing and Networking Center since 1999. The first dLibra-based digital library (DL) was the Digital Library of the Wielkopolska Region (WBC). It was started in October 2002 and now it consists of over 3000 various publications grouped into four thematic collections: cultural heritage, regional materials, educational materials and music notes. Such number of publications makes from WBC one of the largest Polish digital libraries. In the end of November 2004 the second dLibra-based digital library was deployed – the Wroclaw University of Technology Digital Library. There are also four other test dLibra installations academic libraries, and in the nearest future three new regional digital libraries will be started. Due to the diversity of mentioned digital libraries, many different aspects must be taken into account during the dLibra development. Each DL has its own specific publications – for example the majority of WBC publications are relicts of writing and old documents associated with social life of the Wielkopolska Region. Such resources are mostly stored in a graphical form, in formats like DjVu, PDF or JPG scans. All that publications consist of quite large files and their content is often not searchable. On the other hand, there are academic DL systems, like one of test dLibra installations in AGH University of Science and Technology, where a typical publication is an academic script stored as a set of

HTML pages or small PDF file with searchable text content. Such differences requires support in many areas – from format dependent publication structure analysis during the publication upload process, to sophisticated mechanisms for content indexing and searching, to different publication view and download possibilities. Another important element is the amount of stored publications.

When there are many gathered resources, and a large number of readers accessing it, the overall system performance becomes a crucial parameter. We want to show the way in which we designed the internal dLibra architecture and its basic mechanisms to create an efficient, flexible, distributed and error-resistant digital library system. The structure of distributed services architecture developed in the dLibra Digital Library Framework. We also show an overview of these services functionality. We try to demonstrate our approach to improving the dLibra stability in some extreme situations, like very heavy user requests load or network communication errors. Those mechanisms are an integral part of dLibra services and service management system.

IMPROVING SERVICES AVAILABILITY IN dLIBRA FRAMEWORK

The distributed architecture of the described dLibra services requires additional mechanisms for improving system reliability and availability. When one of the services stops responding, the library may become less functional or may not be functional at all - when the User Server or Metadata Server fails. To prevent such situations, a number of mechanisms were introduced. The first of them is the way of service resolving done by the System Services. There is a possibility to create such services configuration, in which multiple instances of the most crucial services are started.

Before the System Services gives one service access to another service, it tests the requested service functionality. When the tested instance of a given service fails, the System Services can return reference to other instance. Such instance switch is transparent to other services. With addition of services load monitoring functionality, this mechanism can also be used for load balancing between service instances. The second mechanism is internal services monitoring. Each service is periodically checked if it is responding or has enough processor time for its tasks. This check is performed by a special service wrapper based on an open-source Java Service Wrapper project. The Wrapper can restart or shutdown the service when, for some reason, it stops responding or when host processors are overloaded for a longer period of time. This service monitoring is done locally so it is independent of the state of network connections. Another reliability improving mechanism is implemented in events sending and receiving parts of the dLibra framework. When service generates an event, it is not directly sent to the Event Server, but it is stored in a persistent storage. This storage is implemented with Hibernate, so it can be based on many types of relational databases.

All stored events are read by a specialised Event Sender thread. This thread tries to send events to the Event Server. If connection to the Event Server is lost, all events stay in the storage until there is a possibility to send them again. On the other hand, when the Event Server retrieves an event, it also stores the event before trying to send it to registered services. Each service, while registering for events, gives the Event Server special timeout parameter. This parameter describes how long the events should be stored in the Event Server, if the registered service becomes unavailable. If the registered service becomes available again, all events stored for this service will be passed to it.

FUTURE WORKS

We think that next dLibra development stages will bring this distributed digital library framework closer to grid technologies. In order to do so, it will be necessary to extend our services model. Each service should gain the ability of describing itself with metadata. On top of the System Services there must be some kind of a new, much more advanced service – a dynamic distributed digital library services broker. This should allow automated service discovery and creation of virtual DL organisations. Such active organisations of services could be used to create distributed digital collections from resources gathered in heterogeneous DL systems. We can also imagine Information Retrieval Grid services based on different distributed digital libraries. By creating an environment for advanced cooperation of computational grid services, grid data management systems and digital libraries we want to give an opportunity for advanced usage of digital libraries in sophisticated grid scenarios.

dLIBRA ARCHITECTURE

The initial dLibra architecture and design was based on experiences from previous PSNC projects. We assumed that the dLibra environment should consist of a number of portable, distributed services. Portability was achieved by choosing Java™ as the programming language. Further works and practice from dLibra deployments formed the current dLibra structure.

This structure is based on a set of cooperating remote services. All these services together create the complete dLibra-based digital library. Each service can be started on a separate computer, but they can also be connected into service groups running on the same machine.

When services are started on different hosts, they use Java RMI technology to communicate with each other. Six of dLibra services give together the entire dLibra server functionality.

These services are:

- *The Metadata Server*—gives a possibility to define, modify and remove metadata attributes that are used to describe digital library publications. It also gives access to dictionaries and thesauri with values of all attributes. It is responsible for managing digital library directories and collections. In addition, it allows adding, modifying and deleting publications, and it has possibilities to manage lists of languages defined in the DL system. Moreover, it has a module for performing periodic metadata consistency test.

- *The Content Server*—gives access to all gathered digital content. Before sending content to the client, this service is able to compress it or encrypt and send securely. The Content Server is also used to store the publications content. Resuming is supported during both publication upload and download.
- *The Search server*—allows users to search through all gathered content and metadata. It also contains indexing functionality, which prepares indexes used during search.
- *The Distributed Search Server*—is used to harvest remote dLibra instances by means of the OAI-PMH protocol. It also gives the user a possibility to search through gathered remote metadata. In fact, any OAI-PMH-enabled repository can be harvested and searched using that service.
- *The User Server*—contains all user-related data and allows users authentication and authorisation. It is also used to create groups of users and to grant users different digital library rights, from library administration to simple publication view.

All the services give together the entire dLibra digital library functionality. However, at least two more elements are required to create a fully functional system. There must be a possibility to connect all these services and create an entry point to the system for both external applications and users.

The first of them is a service called the System Services. It can be treated as a broker of services for single instance of the distributed digital library. It allows inter service communication and handles services addresses resolving, connecting and authorisation. For example, when the Search Server wants to refresh its indexes, it asks the System Services for the Content Server and the Metadata Server. The System Service checks if such services are registered, if they are available and if the Search Server is authorised to access them. If all those conditions are met, as a response the Search Server receives references to the requested services. In order to become available to other services, each service must register itself in the chosen System Services. Services registered in one System Services create a digital library. The second additional system level service is the Event Server. It allows services to communicate with the event messaging system. It is very useful when one service wants to notify some other services about a particular event. A good example of this mechanism can again be a process of refreshing search indexes.

Just after start, the Search Server registers in the Event Server for events related with the modification of gathered content and metadata. When a new publication is added, modified or removed, the Metadata Server sends an event notification to the Event Server. Next, the Event Server forwards this event to all services registered for this event type. After receiving such event, the Search Server can decide if index refreshing is required or maybe just some data should be removed from the index.

This corresponds to two additional parts of the dLibra Framework. One of them is WWW Service and the second is the Editor/Administrator application. The WWW Service is designed as a read only entry point to the system. It can be used by readers to access gathered resources. Content browse and searching are the main functionality of this service, but it is also an OAI-PMH data provider, and it has many user-friendly features like RSS feeds with information newly added publications, publications ranking etc. This functionality is realised with the use of all other dLibra services reached through the System Services. The Editor/Administrator Application is an application for librarians and library administrators. It allows adding and modifying library resources and managing all library items.

DIGITAL REFERENCE SERVICES AND LIBRARIES

A number of libraries have now begun to offer Web-based reference services and a number of recent studies report the current practice of reference services provided by libraries. Although this is not an exhaustive review of all the Web-based reference services provided by libraries, the following section provides a quick overview of some that are currently available.

ROLE OF OPEN SOURCE IN HIGHER EDUCATION

Traditionally, a programme is defined as a set of instructions which tells a computer what to do. For example, the Windows operating system by Microsoft is a programme, or a set of instructions, which tells the user's computer how to send information to the disk drive, how to take information from the user, and how to communicate with pieces of hardware such as the modem or the network card. However, these programmes are compiled, which means that they are translated into the binary code which the computer understands. The lines of instructions, which are translated into the binary code, are called the source code of the programme. If a user or a programmer has access to the source code behind the programme, then the user is able to alter the programme, changing the way that it works.

For most proprietary, or closed source, programmes, the source code is not available for users or programmers to alter. This means that if a user encounters a bug in the closed source programme, they will not be able to fix it themselves, but must rely on the software vendor to fix the error. As many frustrated users know, this can often take a very long time. Open source software, by contrast, is software for which the source code is freely available. The web server Apache, for example, is a programme which runs as many as two-thirds of the web servers on the Internet. Apache is open source, which means that anyone can access the source code for Apache and make changes in how the programme works.

ATTRIBUTE OPEN SOURCE PROPRIETARY

License Licensed to provide freedom to use for any purpose, modify, and redistribute.Licensed to restrict use to "acceptable uses", protect against modification and redistribution.Control Balanced. Consumers and providers of commercial offerings have equal access. Vendor is in control. Often large up-front investments in the software, training, and other implementation costs create a lock-in situation that strips the consumer of control. Innovation Rapid and diverse. Leverages a very large community of users and developers working in parallel. Limited to vendor investments. Typically caters to the features sought by the largest audience. Low levels of innovation. Longevity/ Risk of abandonmentSoftware will always be available as long as it serves a useful purpose. The larger the adoption the safer the investment. No single point of failure. Dependent on the success of the vendor. Single point of failure.Security and reliability As the great tradition of peer review produces high quality academic and scientific works, open source projects produce software that is generally more secure and reliable. Like peer reviewed papers, open source software is subject to greater scrutiny and leverages a larger collective intelligence than proprietary software. *Total cost of ownership* (TCO) Acquisition cost Low or no initial license cost. License costs on the rise in education. Implementation and support costs OS community support and competition for commercial support keeps costs low.

Choice allows consumer to bear costs internally which may further decrease cost. Costs determined by and coupled to vendor. Lack of choice. Alternative service organizations often lead to higher costs. Costs of scale No additional license cost with additional users, servers, etc. License costs generally rise with increased use. Platform support Broader platform and server support increases leveraged investments in existing institutional infrastructure. Platform support limited to what the vendor offers. May not fit well with institutional infrastructure. As we can see from the comparison, open source promises some impressive advantages over proprietary software. While open source has a rich history in education, a recent convergence of powerful drivers and enablers are precipitating a strong movement towards open source in higher education.

ROLE OF OPEN SOURCE IN HIGHER EDUCATION

Open source is changing the nature of the software business in many settings, but the movement is particularly impressive in education. While open source has nearly a 20 year history of success producing leading software, it has mostly been in the infrastructure domain-the protocol implementations, servers, development frameworks, and utilities that enable the e-mail programmes, browsers, and other applications we all depend on. Open source has not been a significant model for producing application software-until recently. In the past few years colleges and universities have begun to produce enterprise open source applications like course management systems and electronic portfolios that compete directly with their proprietary counterparts. These e-learning applications are leading a movement in higher education from proprietary software towards open source. A snapshot of the current proprietary software environment in education reveals some compelling drivers.

- Tight budgets have focused attention on software acquisition costs, and total cost of ownership
- Growing resentment of vendor power, particularly in the wake of price increases and licensing changes that many institutions felt powerless to reject.
- Lack of innovation. Learning technology has not lived up to its potential to improve learning. and some enablers of a more effective model:
- Collaboration technology has made large-scale collaborative work across institutional, geographic, and cultural boundaries more effective.
- Software design patterns, development technologies, and standards have evolved in a way that facilitates modular, interoperable software components.
- Proven business models and education focused companies that embrace open source.
- Strong cultural appeal of open source in academia

We observe many of these drivers and enablers beyond the context of higher education. Perhaps the cultural appeal in academia represents the 'tipping point' for a powerful movement unique to colleges and universities. At the heart of the cultural fit between academia and open source are common philosophy and values. Creating and sharing knowledge for public good is a key part of the mission of colleges and universities, and a core part of the philosophy driving open source software. Colleges and universities are also home to some of the best software engineers in the world. Yet most institutions don't have a plentiful supply of available talent to meet evolving needs-individually. The open source model provides colleges and universities a way to leverage cultural values of collaboration and sharing to gather resources and work together for the common good. Unlike contexts outside of education, working together doesn't blur institutional brand or threaten a school's income. As a result, higher education not only boasts some of the best software engineers, but also has a plentiful supply of willing talent- a critical success factor for open source. A common challenge to developing software is understanding the needs of the users and turning that understanding into a suitable software design. While there are many different approaches and software methodologies, the open source model clearly has an advantage since the individuals most involved in teaching and learning are deeply involved in the development of the software for teaching and learning.

Another critical success factor for open source is the emergence of education-focused companies that embrace open source as the preferred model for business. Although colleges and universities are well suited to develop world class enterprise software, supporting that software for other institutions isn't an activity that helps fulfill their mission. A new ecology has emerged where commercial organizations, colleges, and universities play complimentary and collaborative roles. The Andrew W. Mellon foundation, the William and Flora Hewlett Foundation, and others have recognized the need and the potential and have made considerable financial resources available to seed open source projects and help create the new ecology. While there are literally thousands of active open source projects all over the world addressing most application domains, there are a number of notable projects particularly interesting for institutions of higher education.

OPEN SOURCE PLAIN AND SIMPLE

Open source software (OSS) refers to software programmes that are distributed with the source codehence open source. The open source license allows users the freedom to run the programme for any purpose, to study and modify the programme, and to freely redistribute copies of the original or modified programme.

Open source is a way of building software

Open source software is often constructed using the same time-tested methodologies and practices used to construct proprietary software. However there are a number of interesting differences that result from the difference in rights conferred by the license:

- The software evolves more rapidly and organically. Many individuals and teams working in parallel produce advances beyond the capacity of a single team. The improvements are managed into releases by a core team much like the proprietary alternative.
- Users' needs are rapidly met as the OSS model harnesses their collective expertise and contribution. Improvements to the software are often contributed by users who have fixed a problem or added new features.
- New versions are released very often and rely on the community of users and developers to test it, resulting in superior quality software tested on more platforms, and in more environments than most commercial software.

- The development "team" is often largely volunteers, distributed, many in numbers, and diverse. Often, paid members of the development team will manage the project and organize the work of the volunteers.
- Security is enhanced because the code is exposed to the world. In proprietary packages, shortcuts and poor programming are more easily overlooked because only a select few see the code. Like peer reviewed papers, open source code is subject to much greater scrutiny and thus produces a higher calibre result.

Open Source is a Way of doing Business

Open source is often thought of as free software. In fact, one of the benefits is that anyone can use, modify, and redistribute the software without a license fee. While the code is free, the benefits have much more to do with the freedoms than the cost. On the surface it may appear that free software is in opposition to the 'business' of software and, while the open source model challenges the traditional models, open source represents great opportunity for customers and businesses alike. Without the restrictions of a proprietary software license, any institution or company with the skills can use the software to solve their own needs or offer products and services of value to others. Businesses based on open source software typically add value by:

- Offering services such as implementation, training, and support;
- Packaging and integrating open source software to make its installation and use easier for a wider market;
- Creating complementary, add-on, or enhanced software for sale. Open source affords institutions, as consumers of software, unparalleled control over the use of software to meet business demands and control over where they deploy their budget dollars. Taking into consideration its core competencies and available resources, an institution may use its own people and resources, hire external resources, or partner to share costs. The principles of open source software-freedom to run the programme for any purpose, to study and modify the programme, and to freely redistribute copies and modifications-are simple, yet have powerful and far reaching implications.

COMPARISON TO PROPRIETARY SOFTWARE

One of the great misconceptions about open source is that it is an alternative to commercial software. Rather, open source software is an alternative to proprietary software, but often acquired through or supported by a company-in other words commercial. Fundamentally, the difference between open source and proprietary software has to do with control. Where the open source license imparts freedoms to use, modify, and redistribute the software, the proprietary license restricts use, modification, distribution, and more.

Vendors of proprietary software restrict access to and use of the source code because the source is knowledge-and knowledge is power.The open source license corrects the balance of power between producers and consumers of software. Access to the source code is about freedom and choice. After all, most of us aren't software engineers-we can't start adding features and fixing bugs just because we have access. Yet access to the source code is important to all of us because access is control. Open source clearly offers advantages for the consumer, but it also represents a significant competitive advantage to companies that adopt compatible strategies. IBM, HP, Sun Microsystems, Apple Computer, Red Hat, Novell, and many other companies attribute significant revenue from strategies built on commercialization of open source software. Mainstream press coverage of open source has been accelerating all over the world, but the press coverage in higher education has been nothing short of explosive in recent months. Vendors of proprietary software have been carefully crafting their powerful and influential messages about open source. Some attempt to categorize open source as something applicable to research and experimentation. Others cast open source as comparable to open standards. Still others warn about considering open source software for mission critical applications. Each of these messages uses generalizations that distort the truth.

THE ROLE OF LIBRARIES IN FUTURE DLs

In the framework envisaged by DILIGENT, libraries play an important role at the organisational level. In particular:

- As providers of resources, they can help to enhance the amount of available resources by making stakeholders aware of the importance of sharing. In particular, as far as the sharing of content is concerned, they can operate by promoting digitisation campaigns and the Open Access approach. These actions may result in a vast amount of new digital information accessible online which can be exploited by advanced services.
- Also within a digital framework, libraries are certainly the best candidates for carrying out content description, maintenance and preservation of resources. By exploiting their large experience acquired in the past, they can contribute to the long-term availability and to the quality of the resources disseminated by the DLs.
- Long-term availability also requires the implementation of models able to support the sustainability of the resources provided. Libraries, either alone or as members of library consortia, can also act as the organisations deputed to define and put in place these models.
- As main resource providers, libraries can work jointly on the definition of common policies and standards. An agreement on these aspects would strongly contribute towards facilitating the design and

development of the new complex services required to fulfil the emerging user needs.

- In the future envisaged by DILIGENT, libraries can also play an important role as mediators between the infrastructure and the user communities. In particular, they can proactively promote and facilitate the creation of DLs that respond to the needs of the user communities. They can also assist users by providing, if necessary, the skills required to select, update and exploit the DL content and services.

ADDING NEW MODES OF UNDERSTANDING TO THE DIGITAL LIBRARY

People perceive the world through many modes, including textual and graphical. Some people comprehend information more easily in one mode than another. Most people benefit from a variety of modes that reinforce one another or that can be used when appropriate to the context. Many digital library projects remain text-based; however, this text-only dimension is changing as digital libraries become oriented more to multimedia and as other modes of information presentation become viable on the Internet. KOSs can be used to bring new dimensions to an information resource or a collection in a digital library.

In the digital library environment, these dimensions can be viewed as layers that can be added on top of one or more objects. Various tools and services can be developed that are geared to a particular mode. For example, the results of a text search can be presented in graphical or visual form, based on the number of occurrences of a term or concept or on the occurrences of documents from a particular country, journal title, or author. A more complex dimension that can be added is the geospatial dimension, which emphasizes access by place.

A "geolibrary" is defined as a digital library consisting of "geoinformation", or material that can be accessed by place. This so-called geo-referencing can be either direct or indirect. Georeferencing of textual objects is facilitated by a gazetteer, which brings together the place name and the spatial footprint for its location. Many gazetteers also include feature types for each footprint. The vocabulary used for the feature types varies among gazetteers, but may include terms such as "airport", "harbour", and "railroad station".

Although many organizations, including federal and state agencies, are currently required to provide geospatial referencing as part of the National Spatial Data Infrastructure Programme, the geospatial referencing is not readily available for older works. How can the data sets of today be integrated with the textual information of yesterday? The answer is by adding geospatial referencing to the text resource. Geospatial referencing requires that the text name for a place have an associated spatial footprint. This can be achieved by using a georeferenced, digital gazetteer that provides geospatial footprints for place names.

Through this type of knowledge organization system, place names in a library catalog or bibliographic database can have footprints assigned. If one or more of the library's resources have latitude or longitude coordinates in the catalog record or in the full text but no place name, the coordinates can be extracted and submitted to the gazetteer service. The service will return the place name for the footprint.

Alternatively, the resource may have a textual place name. This place name can be extracted and searched against the gazetteer, and the footprint can be provided to a mapping application. The latter search may result in more than one footprint, since place names may be ambiguous. Therefore, it is important that the user interface be designed to allow the user to distinguish the locations. Once the footprint has been determined, a user can access the text resource through a geographic mapping tool. Alternatively, a user of the text resource can find a set of results and have the place names displayed as footprints on a map.

In disciplines such as ecology, environmental science, and even public health and epidemiology, it would be beneficial to build a digital library with access to such a digital gazetteer service. Users could then access the system through the text mode or the geographic mode, depending on their comfort level and the type of information needed. Presenting the results on a map allows users to make new associations and analyse the results more easily. Through a geospatial KOS, they can see connections between disparate data, because the data are presented in an alternate mode.

PROVIDING MULTILINGUAL ACCESS

A third way that KOSs can support the use of digital libraries by disparate communities is to provide multilingual access. A variety of sources, including multilingual dictionaries and multilingual thesauri, can support this type of access. One of the most extensive multilingual thesaurus efforts is the *Generalized Multilingual Environmental Thesaurus* (GEMET) from the *European Environment Agency* (EEA), produced by Italy's research council, the *Consiglio Nazionale delle Ricerche* (CNR).

The GEMET is available in 12 languages, and plans for a global environmental thesaurus in many more languages were recently announced. GEMET is available by agreement with the EEA. The European Topic Centre on Catalogue of Data Sources in Germany is developing a system that will link data sources and metadata information in a virtual library. GEMET will be used to convert a search in one language into searches for the same concepts in other languages.

Users will retrieve documents not only in their native language but also in other languages. This will allow data systems from throughout the EEA and beyond to be accessed as a virtual library collection with both controlled vocabulary and free-text term searching in multiple languages.

EXPANDING FREE-TEXT SEARCH TERMS

Free-text searching is the main method of searching on the Web. Only a small percentage of Web resources have metadata, and an even smaller percentage have controlled vocabulary assigned. However, variations in natural language make free-text searching problematic. Even a knowledgeable user may not know all the terminology that can be used in the literature to express a concept. The problem is exacerbated when the user is unfamiliar with the topic or is interested in an interdisciplinary area. How can the user expand his or her search to overcome these terminology differences? One possibility is to use KOSs as aids to the selection of free-text keywords. The Getty Vocabulary Project emphasizes support for searching as a significant application of its vocabularies. Harpring reports that the vocabularies are increasingly being used in search engines to look for different terms that refer to the same concept.

The Getty vocabularies are particularly rich in equivalence relationships. "When these equivalence relationships are exploited in search engines, there are typically two possible scenarios: the user may be allowed to first query the vocabulary database, locating appropriate terms, and then applying those chosen terms in a query across target databases; or there may be little or no user interaction with the vocabulary, when the vocabularies are used behind the scenes..."

Getty developed a prototype called *a.k.a.* to experiment with the use of equivalence terms to broaden or narrow searches across databases on the Web. In addition to expanding routine search queries, KOSs can be used in Web mining tools. Northern Light has developed a Web mining tool that reportedly returns a high degree of relevant hits. The KOS that supports the Northern Light site was built by ingesting large existing vocabularies and thesauri.

The result was then organized under an extensive classification scheme developed by Northern Light. The terms can be used to extend a user's search or to distinguish between multiple meanings of the terms supplied by the user. The results of a search are organized into "folders" based on the classification scheme. These high-level categories, represented by the folders, help distinguish multiple meanings of the same term. For example, an ambiguous word such as "pitcher" might result in two folders being presented to the user. One folder would be titled "Sports", the second "Decorative Arts". The user who chooses only the Sports folder will be presented with only those Web resources that use "pitcher" in the baseball sense.

The user who selects the folder called "Decorative Arts" will be presented only with those resources that are related to water pitchers. KOSs can be very powerful in supporting free-text searching within digital libraries and in integrating Web resources into existing digital libraries. However, these systems must be used with caution. KOSs have generally been developed for a specific discipline, task, or function, or for the indexing of a specific collection or database. Therefore, depending on the domain in which the KOS is being used and the complexity of the system, it may or may not suggest relevant free-text terms. Expanding a search with related terms, rather than pure synonyms, may return hits that are only peripherally relevant to the user.

SORTING SEARCH RESULTS OF ONLINE LITERATURE DIGITAL LIBRARY

An OLDL (Online Literature Digital Library) is a library in which collections, *i.e.*, publications from one or more domains of study, are stored in digital formats and accessible by users through the Internet.

Examples of well-known OLDLs are:

- IEEE Xplore
- CiteSeer
- Google Scholar
- PubMed

Digital libraries are rapidly growing in popularity. For instance, ScienceDirect, the world's leading scientific, technical and medical information resource celebrated its billionth article download in November'06 since, launched in 1999. Besides usage, digital libraries are also rapidly growing in terms of size and diversity of topics.

For instance:

- In Computer Science, ACM Digital Library has close to one million full-text publications collected over 50 years, to search and download.
- In Electrical Engineering and Computer Science, IEEE Xplore, another OLDL, provides users with on-line access to more than 1,700 selected conferences proceedings.

These high growth rates introduced several challenges facing the information access capability of OLDLs. Next we list few challenges that probably guides future research related to LDLs.

LARGE SIZES AND TOPIC DIVERSITY OF SEARCH OUTPUT RESULTS

Search outputs of OLDLs tend to suffer from the 'topic diffusion' problem, where commonly, keyword-based searches produce a large number of publications over a large number of topics, where not all topics are of interest to the user. One way to solve this problem is to assign scores to search results. Assigning scores to publications helps OLDLs to present the most important relevant publications to the user first, Citation-based publication score measures are commonly used for ranking publications. At the present time, OLDLs lack effective and accurate publication ranking.

LACK OF EFFECTIVE SCORING FUNCTIONS FOR PUBLICATIONS

At the present time, OLDLs lack effective and accurate publication rankings. Providing accurate publication scores can help users in reducing the time spent in searching OLDLs, and thus enhances the scalability of OLDL usage as users can quickly identify important relevant publications to their topic of interest.

LACK OF EFFECTIVE SCORING FUNCTIONS FOR SEARCH OUTPUTS

In the field of literature digital libraries, citation analysis is employed to order digital library search outputs. Examples of citation-based measures are citation-count and PageRank. However, as noticed by, citation-based measures compute popularity of publications based on the 'current' state of a citation graph that continuously changes and evolves.

Thus PageRank is effective in capturing the popularity of publications based on the current citation-graph inhand. We show that PageRank may assign inaccurate popularity scores for both old and recent publications. And thus PageRank cannot be used to rank OLDL search outputs. We therefore need effective techniques to order search results based on their importance and relevance to users' interests.

EVALUATING PUBLICATION SCORING F UNCTIONS IN DIGITAL LIBRARIES

This section deals with the issues of defining score functions for publications in digital libraries, and evaluating how good they are.

Presently, digital libraries do not assign scores to publications, even though they are potentially useful for:

- Providing comparative assessment, or 'importance', of papers; and
- Anking papers returned in search outputs.

Using social networks or bibliometrics, one can define a number of publication score functions. Existing citation-based publication score functions are all based on the notion of prestige in social networks and bibliometry. The well-known PageRank algorithm determines the importance of a publication by the number and importances of publications with links to it. The Hyperlink Induced Topic Search (HITS) algorithm is similar to the PageRank algorithm in that HITS involves computing two scores for each publication; hub and authority scores. Authorities represent high-prestige publications, whereas hubs are publications that have links to authorities.

Other citation-based score functions can be derived as follows:

- Use normalised citation count as the basis for a score function.
- Revise the score of a paper using the score of its publication venue.
- Add weights to citations, *e.g.*, citations by an 'important' author's work are more significant.
- Revise the score of a paper using temporal distributions of citations;

e.g., citations in the last 10 years are more significant than earlier citations.

- Revise a paper score using the score of its citation venue; that is, capture the notion of a hub or an authority, *e.g.*, survey journal represents a hub, whereas a research paper represents an authority.
- Revise a paper score by the score of its author.

Citation-based Publication Score Functions

PageRank

Importance of papers that cite a particular paper determines its importance. PageRank and HITS were designed based on this assumption. PageRank scores is computed recursively using the formula

Where *Pi* and *Pi+1* are the current and next iteration PageRank vectors respectively. *M* is a matrix derived from the citation matrix *C* by normalising all row-sums in *C* to *1. C,* in turn, is the adjacency matrix of the graph *G* formed as follows; the papers represent the graph nodes, and the citation relationships between these papers represent the edges. *C* is of size *NxN,* where *N* is the total number of papers in the system. Finally, *d* and (*1-d*) are the future citation probability. Given that an author *A* who is writing a new paper and already cited paper *u* which in turn cites paper *v,* and let *w* be a paper in AnthP selected randomly. The parameter *d* represents the probability that A will cite *w,* and (*1-d*) is the probability that *A* will cite *v*. To guarantee the algorithm convergence, it is assumed to have a hidden link between each pair of the graph nodes. This link is represented by the user-defined parameter *E*. A variation of *E* is simply *E1=d*. Another variation of E that is used in is,

Hubs and Authorities

Authority score of paper *P* is computed by summing up the hub scores of the papers citing *P*. Hub score of *P* is computed by summing up the authority scores of the papers that *P* cites. Computation is recursive until results converge after a number of iterations. One difference between HITS and PageRank is that the first one works on papers in the result set of a query, while the latter considers all the papers independent of the query.

Citation Count

A paper, normally, does not cite another paper unless the cited paper is relevant. And, large number of citations to a paper gives an indication that the paper is important. Based on this fact, one can use citation count as a measure for paper importance. For a given paper *P*, let CitationCount (*P*) be the number of times paper *P* is cited by other papers. Using the number of citations, paper *P* is as important as those papers that have the same number of citations and more important than those papers that have fewer citations. As suggested, refer to this paper ranking measure as PCitation_Count.

Evaluating Publication Score Functions

Figure shows the three score functions, namely, PageRank (PPgRank), Authorities scores of HITS (PAuth) and, the Citation-count (PCitCnt). As it is clear from the figure the three functions are highly skewed, and do not separate scores well over the interval. This figure is based on the AnthP digital collection from the field of data management. In the author observed the skewness and inseparability of these functions independently in computer science and life sciences publications as well. And, it is shown that distributions of citation-based score functions are also highly skewed and decay very fast. Studies show that the cause is topic diffusion since, scores are computed with respect to the full publication set.

In the authors compared and evaluated several publication score functions, including PageRank and Authorities scores, both adopted from the www search domain, and citation-count scores from the bibliometrics domain. The authors observed the separability problem with all of these functions which is that none of these scoring functions assigns scores that distribute well over a given scale, *e.g.* Instead, distributions of existing publication score functions are highly skewed, and decay very fast resulting in a much less useful comparative publication assessment capability for users.

This lack of separability is caused by the 'rich gets richer' phenomena, *i.e.*, a very small number of publications with relatively high numbers of in-citations have even higher chances of receiving new citations. Yet, these scoring functions are still not very accurate, probably caused by topic diffusion in search outputs. In the following section, and by using the research-pyramid model proposed in, the authors in normalise scores of publications within their own research pyramids, which allows for a fair comparative assessment of publications as publications are compared to their peers in their own research pyramids.

6

Library Information and Information Science

LIBRARY INFORMATION

Information, in its most restricted technical sense, is a sequence of symbols that can be interpreted as a message. Information can be recorded as signs, or transmitted as signals. Information is any kind of event that affects the state of a dynamic system.

Conceptually, information is the message being conveyed. This concept has numerous other meanings in different contexts. Moreover, the concept of information is closely related to notions of constraint, communication, control, data, form, instruction, knowledge, meaning, mental stimulus, pattern, perception, representation, and especially entropy.

ETYMOLOGY

The English word was apparently derived from the Latin stem (*information-*) of the nominative (*informatio*): this noun is in its turn derived from the verb "informare" (to inform) in the sense of "to give form to the mind", "to discipline", "instruct", "teach": "Men so wise should go and inform their kings." *Inform* itself comes from the Latin verb *informare*, to give form, to form an idea of.

Furthermore, Latin itself already contained the word *information* meaning concept or idea, but the extent to which this may have influenced the development of the word *information* in English is not clear. The ancient Greek word for *form* was (morph) and also (*eidos*) "kind, idea, shape, set", the latter word was famously used in a technical philosophical sense by Plato (and later Aristotle) to denote the ideal identity or essence of something. "Eidos" can also be associated with thought, proposition or even concept.

INFORMATION THEORY APPROACH

From the stance of information theory, *information* is taken as a sequence of symbols from an alphabet, say an input alphabet χ, and an output alphabet Υ. Information processing consists of an input-output function that maps any input sequence from χ into an output sequence from Υ. The mapping may be probabilistic or determinate. It may have memory or be memoryless.

AS SENSORY INPUT

Often information is viewed as a type of input to an organism or system. Inputs are of two kinds. Some inputs are important to the function of the organism or system by themselves. In his book *Sensory Ecology,* Dusenbery called these causal inputs. Other inputs are important only because they are associated with causal inputs and can be used to predict the occurrence of a causal input at a later time. Some information is important because of association with other information but eventually there must be a connection to a causal input.

In practice, information is usually carried by weak stimuli that must be detected by specialized sensory systems and amplified by energy inputs before they can be functional to the organism or system. For example, light is often a causal input to plants but provides information to animals.

The coloured light reflected from a flower is too weak to do much photosynthetic work but the visual system of the bee detects it and the bee's nervous system uses the information to guide the bee to the flower, where the bee often finds nectar or pollen, which are causal inputs, serving a nutritional function.

AS REPRESENTATION AND COMPLEXITY

The cognitive scientist and applied mathematician Ronaldo Vigo argues that information is a relative concept that involves at least two related entities in order to make quantitative sense.

These are: any dimensionally-defined category of objects S, and any of its subsets R. R, in essence, is a representation of S, or, in other words, carries or conveys representational information about S. Vigo then defines the amount of information that R conveys about S as the rate of change in the complexity of S whenever the objects in R are removed from S. Under "Vigo information", pattern, invariance, complexity, representation, and information—five fundamental constructs of universal science—are unified under a novel mathematical framework. Among other things, the framework aims to overcome the limitations of Shannon-Weaver information when attempting to characterize and measure subjective information.

AS AN INFLUENCE WHICH LEADS TO A TRANSFORMATION

Information is any type of pattern that influences the formation or transformation of other patterns. In this sense, there is no need for a conscious mind to perceive, much less appreciate, the pattern. Consider, for example, DNA. The sequence of nucleotides is a pattern that influences the formation and development of an organism without any need for a conscious mind.

Systems theory at times seems to refer to information in this sense, assuming information does not necessarily involve any conscious mind, and patterns circulating in the system can be called information. In other words, it can be said that information in this sense is something potentially perceived as representation, though not created or presented for that purpose. For example, Gregory Bateson defines "information" as a "difference that makes a difference".

If, however, the premise of "influence" implies that information has been perceived by a conscious mind and also interpreted by it, the specific context associated with this interpretation may cause the transformation of the information into knowledge. Complex definitions of both "information" and "knowledge" make such semantic and logical analysis difficult, but the condition of "transformation" is an important point in the study of information as it relates to knowledge, especially in the business discipline of knowledge management.

In this practice, tools and processes are used to assist a knowledge worker in performing research and making decisions, including steps such as:

- Reviewing information in order to effectively derive value and meaning
- Referencing metadata if any is available
- Establishing a relevant context, often selecting from many possible contexts
- Deriving new knowledge from the information
- Making decisions or recommendations from the resulting knowledge.

Stewart argues that the transformation of information into knowledge is a critical one, lying at the core of value creation and competitive advantage for the modern enterprise. The Danish Dictionary of Information Terms argues that information only provides an answer to a posed question. Whether the answer provides knowledge depends on the informed person.

So a generalized definition of the concept should be:

"Information" = An answer to a specific question"

When Marshall McLuhan speaks of media and their effects on human cultures, he refers to the structure of artifacts that in turn shape our behaviours and mindsets. Also, pheromones are often said to be "information" in this sense.

AS A PROPERTY IN PHYSICS

In 2003 J. D. Bekenstein claimed there is a growing trend in physics to define the physical world as being made of information itself. Information has a well-defined meaning in physics. Examples of this include the phenomenon of quantum entanglement where particles can interact without reference to their separation or the speed of light.

Information itself cannot travel faster than light even if the information is transmitted indirectly. This could lead to the fact that all attempts at physically observing a particle with an "entangled" relationship to another are slowed down, even though the particles are not connected in any other way other than by the information they carry. Another link is demonstrated by the Maxwell's demon thought experiment. In this experiment, a direct relationship between information and another physical property, entropy, is demonstrated. A consequence is that it is impossible to destroy information without increasing the entropy of a system; in practical terms this often means generating heat.

Another, more philosophical outcome is that information could be thought of as interchangeable with energy. Thus, in the study of logic gates, the theoretical lower bound of thermal energy released by an *AND gate* is higher than for the *NOT gate*. Physical information is of particular importance in the theory of quantum computers.

NATURE OF INFORMATION

Information as a resource has been a topic of discussion of academics and practitioners in various subject fields-especially in the field of economics. Economists such as Machlup, Porat and Bell pioneered the ideas of information economy with information as the transforming resource for postindustrial society. Authors such as Horton pioneered the view of information as a corporate resource, which like other resources such as people, money, raw materials, equipment and energy, should be managed to give a competitive edge. These authors helped develop both the idea of information as a resource and the idea of information-resources management.

In the wake of information and communication technologies, Hawkins confirmed that information has become a commodity. Yet requirements for economic enhancement are not necessarily requirements for development in rural communities when it comes to the basic survival of people.

This immediately raises the question of what prerequisites a resource should comply with in order to be useful for development purposes. Of course, many other resources are needed for developing people in rural communities with which information as a resource should favourably compare-for example, farming practices in rural communities will require input resources, farming implements (tractors, ploughs), credit, markets, infrastructure, and natural resources (soil, water, climatic conditions).

At first glance, when comparing information with these resources, it seems that most of them are tangible in nature, while information is not. And yet, many view information as one of the most important resources needed for rural development. Although information is recognised as an important, yet still under-utilised, development resource, one needs to look critically at the attributes of information to determine whether they could aggravate the problem of under-utilisation.

Attributes of Information

While investigating the validity of information as a resource, the natural approach would be to compare attributes of information with those of other resources, in order to find some commonality. A comparison of this nature necessitates a closer look at the attributes of the different resources.

To this end, Burk and Horton give eight basic similarities between information and other traditional resources to fit into a resource-management framework, namely:

- Information is acquired at a definite, measurable cost.
- Information has a definite value, which may be quantified and treated as an accountable asset.
- Information consumption can be quantified.
- Cost-accounting techniques can be applied to help control the costs of information.
- *Information has a Clear Life Cycle:* Definition of requirements, collection, transmission, processing, storage, dissemination, use, and disposal.
- Information may be processed and refined, so that raw materials (*e.g.*, databases) are converted into finished products (*e.g.*, published directories).
- Substitutes for any specific item or collection of information are available, and may be quantified as more expensive, or less expensive.
- Choices are available to management in making trade-offs between different grades, types and costs of information.

From this it is clear that Burk and Horton felt that information should be seen as something tangible, physical and concrete, while viewpoints from within the information profession emphasise the intangibility of information. Counter-arguments from authors such as Vickers, White, Cleveland, Boulding, Repo, Cronin and Gudrim show that information differs from tangible things generally thought of as valuable resources.

In classifying resources needed for development, Boon distinguishes between material resources and know-how resources. Information, together with data and knowledge, is listed as a know-how resource. There is also the viewpoint of Boulding that information should be seen as a dynamic force, which constantly alters and extends a store of knowledge. Shannon was probably the first to state that information can alleviate uncertainty-another intangible attribute.

In trying to identify those attributes of information that focus on its intangibility, Eaton and Bawden combine the viewpoints of various authors to come to the following key distinctions:

- *Value of Information*: Unlike other tangible resources, information is not readily quantifiable-that is, it is impossible to predict the ultimate value of information to its users. Also, over time, there is no predictable change in the value of information.
- *Multiplicative Quality of Information*: The results produced by the use of information differ greatly from those produced by the use of other

resources-for instance, information is not lost when given to others, and does not decrease when 'consumed': sharing information will almost always cause it to increase-that is, information has a self-multiplicative quality.

- *Dynamics of Information*: Information cannot be regarded as a static resource to be accumulated and stored within the confines of a static system. It is a dynamic force for change to the system within which it operates. It adds value to an organisation through encouraging innovation and change without being tangible.
- *Life Cycle of Information*: Information seems to have an unpredictable life cycle. Ideas come into, go out of, and finally come back into, fashion.
- *Individuality of Information*: Information comes in many different forms, and is expressed in many different ways. Information can take on any value in the context of an individual situation. This proves that, as a resource, information is different from most other resources. The very fact that information is characterised as a dynamic force, 'constantly altering and extending a store of knowledge', corresponds with situations in development in which outside information is offered to focus groups to alter their understanding of certain practices, which in turn can help them solve problems.

Apart from the attributes identified by Eaton and Bawden, the following, also containing elements of intangibility, may be added to the list:

- *Alleviation of Uncertainty:* Mark and Pierce, Shannon, as long ago as 1948, defined information as the resolution of uncertainty. This is perhaps one of the intangible attributes best known among a variety of researchers.
- *Interdependency*: Information almost always forms part of technology-it is the "soft" part. Without its information component, technology has little value as a resource for potential users who are not familiar with its workings or its background. With regard to developing rural communities, one should bear in mind that it is not necessarily new technology that brings about these achievements. All outside technology applied for the first time could be viewed as *new* to the user group or that particular situation, and could have similar effects.
- *Enhancement of Economic Growth*: A frequent complaint is that information is often denied its role as a resource. Yet, when looking at the effect of information in development situations, there seems to be an underlying awareness of its importance. Kaimowitz refer to the impact of new technology in agriculture on the basis of such aspects as increased farm income, reduced risk, resource conservation, improved health, better (food) security, and overall economic growth.

- *Extension of the Knowledge Base*: From a development point of view, there is more emphasis, first, on improving peoples' lives socially, and only secondly on economic improvement. In development, outside technology is often introduced with the help of education, training and visual demonstrations. Rogers states that training helps people in rural communities to expand horizons, increase perceptions, enhance competencies, enlarge sense of perspective, and enhance self-esteem.

The above seem to emphasise the impact of the dynamic force of information, where the 'extension or altering of people's stores of knowledge' positively affected their social well-being.

Thus, although information is an intangible entity, it has the ability to bring about change for the better; which is the ultimate goal of development:

- *Context Dependency*: The value of information as a resource in rural development depends largely on situation-specific issues: for example, one could argue that agriculture-related information is mostly technical in nature. However, people with little exposure to modern society have many related issues they need to know about. Ozowa, for example, identified certain types of basic information needed for the development of crop production by traditional farmers; *inter alia*, information about agricultural input (seeds, fertilizer, etc.), extension, technology (farming equipment, etc.), implementation techniques (ploughing, sowing, pest and weed control), soil, water and climatic conditions, conservation, credit, marketing and infrastructure.
- *Culture Dependency*: Another attribute of information that can influence its usefulness as a development resource is that it is culture dependent-involving conceptual and cognitive differentiation. Pickering is of the opinion that because information is culture specific, it is incommunicable unless acculturated-that is, adapted for the cultural environment or the cultural mind-set of the recipient group. Here, Shields and Servaes also point out that information is not totally value-free, but is socially conditioned and shaped by the social structures that apply it. This aspect has serious implications for developers' efforts to transfer information to the rural communities of developing countries.
- *Medium Dependency*: Information is not only culture dependent, but also medium dependent. Once information is concretised outside the human memory it should be packaged in some or other format to be communicated to someone else. Unless receivers know how to use that particular format, the information will remain inaccessible and rendered useless; for example, an electronic medium directed at users who are unfamiliar with such facilities can impede access to available information.

Thus, medium dependency of information can have serious implications for quite a number of rural people who are dependent on oral communication, owing to their oral tradition and the fact that many of them are not literate.

This attribute could cause information to be a less useful resource when compared with other resources needed for development purposes:

Conversion Dependency: It is a well-known fact that information is not used in the original form offered by its creator alone-.often, it needs to be adapted to suit a particular situation or specific circumstances. It can also happen that only a small chunk of the original information is used together with other chunks of information to form a new information package needed for a particular situation. In this way, more value can be added to the appropriateness of information. Particularly in a situation where outside information from the industrialised world is used to improve a practice in rural development, the information content needs to be adapted to bring it to the level of understanding of potential recipients.

Suitability of Attributes

It is evident that information differs phenomenally from other resources needed for development-especially because it is intangible in nature. Although some of its attributes make it a suitable development resource (such as its ability to act as a dynamic force), others render it less suitable (such as its inaccessibility owing to its dependency on culture and media). As far as the requirements for rural development are concerned, it seems that the attributes can be divided into two categories, those suitable for development, and those less suitable for development:

A comparison of the attributes of information:

- Attributes suitable for development:
- Dynamic force
- Extends the knowledge base
- Increases perceptions
- Enhances competencies
- Enhances self-esteem
- Enhances growth
- Multiplicative
- Versatile
- Attributes less suitable for development:
- Intangible
- Interdependent
- Culture dependent
- Medium dependent
- Content dependent
- Conversion dependent

ORIGIN AND SOCIAL CONTEXT OF INFORMATION SCIENCE

Information science is a field that emerged in the after-math of the Second World War (WW II), along with a number of new fields, with computer science being but one example. The rapid pace of scientific and technical advances that were accumu-lating since the start of the 20th century, produced by mid-century a scientific and technical revolution. A most visible manifestation of this revolution was the phenomenon of "information explosion," referring to the exponential and unabated growth of scientific and technical publications and information records of all kinds, so masterfully synthesized and illuminated by de Solla Price.

In a remarkable turn of events, the impetus for the development of information science, and even for its very origin and agenda, a respected MIT scientist and, even more importantly, the head of the U.S. scientific effort during WW II.

Bush did two things:

- He succinctly defined a critical and strategic problem that was on the minds of many, and
- Proposed a solution that was a "technological fix", and thus in tune with the spirit of the times.

Both had wide appeal and Bush was listened to because of his stature. He defined the problem in almost poetic terms as "the massive task of making more accessible a bewildering store of knowledge". In other words, Bush addressed the problem of information explosion. The problem is still with us. His solution was to use the emerging computing and other information technology to combat the problem. But he went even further. He proposed a machine named Memex, incorporating a capability for "association of ideas," and duplication of "mental processes artificially." A prescient anticipation of information science and artificial intelligence is evident.

Memex, needless to say, was never built, but to this day is an ideal, a wish list, an agenda, and, some think, a utopia. We are still challenged by the ever-worsening problem of the information explosion, now universal and in a variety of digital formats.

We are still trying to fix things techno-logically. We are still aspiring to incorporate Memex's basic ideas in our solutions. A number of scientists and professi-onals in many fields around the globe listened and took up Bush's challenge.

Governments listened as well and provided funding. The reasoning went something like this: Because science and technology are strategically important for society, efforts that help them, information activities in particular, are also important and need support. In the U.S., the *National Science Foundation* (NSF) Act of 1950 established NSF and provided a number of mandates, among them "to foster the interchange of scientific information among scientists in the U.S.

and foreign countries" and "to further the full dissemination of information of scientific value consistent with the national interest".

The 1958 National Defence Education Act enlarged the mandate:

"The National Science Foundation shall..undertake programme to develop new or improved methods, including mechanized systems, for making scientific information available".

By those mandates, an NSF division, which after a number of name and direction changes is now called the Division of *Information and Intelligent Systems* (IIS), has supported research in these areas since the 1950s. Importantly, the field-defining studies that NSF supported included, among others, Cranfield IR evaluation studies in the 1950s and 1960s, large chunks of SMART studies from the 1960s to 1990s, and now the Digital Libraries Initiatives.

In the U.S., information science developed and began flourishing on its own in a large part due to government support by a host of agencies, as did many other fields. Historically, the support was a success—it was instrumental in creation of the whole enterprise of information science and even of the information online industry based on IR. But to the credit of information science it kept growing on its own even after government support slackened substantially. This cannot be said of a number of other fields or areas that floundered after government stopped being their main source and resource.

Social Context

It is a truism to state that information was always important for any society in any historical period. But the role of information and its degree of importance differed. With the evolution of the social order to a "post-industrial" society, or "post-capitalist" society or what we now commonly also call "information society," knowledge and information is assuming an increasing central role in every aspect of life. The classic study by Machlup, followed by a number of similar studies, documented the startling structural changes in the economy and society as driven by the growth of information and knowledge production and processing.

Popularly, they were summarized by Drucker:

The change in the meaning of knowledge that began two hundred fifty years ago has transformed society and economy. Formal knowledge is seen as both the key personal and the key economic resource. . . [K]nowledge proves itself in action. What we now mean by knowledge is information effective in action, information focused on results.... The actual products of the pharmaceutical industry is knowledge; pill and prescription ointment are no more than packaging for knowledge.

Addressing the problem of information explosion, information science found a niche within the broader context in the evolution of the information society. In its various manifestations and attempted solutions, the niche is getting broader and bigger. But by no means does information science hold a monopoly in that niche. As the importance of infor-mation is increasing in society, more and more resources and expenditures are channeled into various information-related activities. More and more research funds, projects, and initia-tives are devoted to information in various disguises. It is not surprising then that more and more fields, researchers, professionals, and businesses are turning to information, and even "discovering" information. There is gold in information. Information science has many competitors—it may be even swamped by them.

TECHNOLOGICALLY MEDIATED INFORMATION

It is estimated that the world's technological capacity to store information grew from 2.6 exabytes in 1986, which is the informational equivalent to less than one 730-MB CD-ROM per person in 1986 to 295 exabytes in 2007. This is the informational equivalent of almost 61 CD-ROM per person in 2007.

The world's combined technological capacity to receive information through one-way broadcast networks was the informational equivalent of 174 newspapers per person per day in 2007. The world's combined effective capacity to exchange information through two-way telecommunication networks was the informational equivalent of 6 newspapers per person per day in 2007.

AS RECORDS

Records are a specialized form of information. Essentially, records are information produced consciously or as by-products of business activities or transactions and retained because of their value. Primarily their value is as evidence of the activities of the organization but they may also be retained for their informational value. Sound records management ensures that the integrity of records is preserved for as long as they are required.

The international standard on records management, ISO 15489, defines records as "information created, received, and maintained as evidence and information by an organization or person, in pursuance of legal obligations or in the transaction of business".

The *International Committee on Archives* (ICA) Committee on electronic records defined a record as, "a specific piece of recorded information generated, collected or received in the initiation, conduct or completion of an activity and that comprises sufficient content, context and structure to provide proof or evidence of that activity".

Records may be maintained to retain corporate memory of the organization or to meet legal, fiscal or accountability requirements imposed on the organization. Willis expressed the view that sound management of business records and information delivered "...six key requirements for good corporate governance...transparency; accountability; due process; compliance; meeting statutory and common law requirements; and security of personal and corporate information."

INFORMATION AND SEMIOTICS

Beynon-Davies explains the multi-faceted concept of information in terms of signs and signal-sign systems. Signs themselves can be considered in terms of four inter-dependent levels, layers or branches of semiotics: pragmatics, semantics, syntax, and empirics. These four layers serve to connect the social world on the one hand with the physical or technical world on the other...

Pragmatics is concerned with the purpose of communication. Pragmatics links the issue of signs with the context within which signs are used. The focus of pragmatics is on the intentions of living agents underlying communicative behaviour. In other words, pragmatics link language to action.

Semantics is concerned with the meaning of a message conveyed in a communicative act. Semantics considers the content of communication. Semantics is the study of the meaning of signs-the association between signs and behaviour. Semantics can be considered as the study of the link between symbols and their referents or concepts; particularly the way in which signs relate to human behaviour.

Syntax is concerned with the formalism used to represent a message. Syntax as an area studies the form of communication in terms of the logic and grammar of sign systems. Syntax is devoted to the study of the form rather than the content of signs and sign-systems. Empirics is the study of the signals used to carry a message; the physical characteristics of the medium of communication. Empirics is devoted to the study of communication channels and their characteristics, *e.g.*, sound, light, electronic transmission etc..

Nielsen discusses the relationship between semiotics and information in relation to dictionaries. The concept of lexicographic information costs is introduced and refers to the efforts users of dictionaries need to make in order to, first, find the data sought and, secondly, understand the data so that they can generate information. Communication normally exists within the context of some social situation.

The social situation sets the context for the intentions conveyed and the form in which communication takes place. In a communicative situation intentions are expressed through messages which comprise collections of inter-related signs taken from a language which is mutually understood by the agents involved in the communication.

Mutual understanding implies that agents involved understand the chosen language in terms of its agreed syntax and semantics. The sender codes the message in the language and sends the message as signals along some communication channel. The chosen communication channel will have inherent properties which determine outcomes such as the speed with which communication can take place and over what distance. More recently Shu-Kun Lin proposed a simple definition of information: Information is the amount of the data after data compression.

CHARACTERISTICS OF INFORMATION

A central theme in books and articles within different areas of the field of business administration is that the world is changing at a faster and faster pace. The reasons given for this is globalization, investments in ITtechnology and the rapid pace of technological change in combination with escalating costs of research and development. Therefore, companies are believed to need information about environmental events. Information is important since it is believed to be a cornerstone for long-term company survival.

Information can reduce uncertainty, risks in decision-making are an important input in the process of strategy formulation, serve as a base for competence development and so on. But the process of gathering information is not trouble free. A theme stressed in the literature is the paradoxical situation that, although there is an abundance of information available, it is often difficult to obtain useful, relevant information when it is needed. Useful, relevant and needed are the keywords here.

By consulting the literature, a tentative conclusion may be that companies do not necessarily need more information; what they need is useful and relevant information in time. This fact has been noticed by researchers within different academic disciplines, not to mention the variety of consulting firms within this area. But the area is blurred, we feel. The reason for this is that there are a lot of different terms used to describe how useful and relevant information might be collected, interpreted, analysed, distributed and so forth. Some of the more popular terms used are Business intelligence, Information management, Marketing research, and Environ-mental scanning. These terms or approaches have a lot in common, but also there are significant differences.

Purpose

Thus, the purpose of this paper is to identify similarities and differences in these terms, relate them to and compare them with each other, but also to identify their underlying concepts and the course of events they represent. The intent with this paper is not to present a complete list of references on the subject, but rather to study some of the literature at hand as a first step towards a mapping of the characteristics stressed in the different terms/approaches.

Terms, Concepts and Course of Events

It is important to look behind terms to discover their meaning. Carl Hempel made this point clear; it is very important to make a distinction between terms and concepts. By looking behind the terms we mean trying to locate the domain(s) they are supposed to reflect, but also to try to identify the concept(s) underlying the terms.

A term is believed to represent a certain object or a course of events. The object or course of events is contained in a certain concept; the term means this concept. In this paper, Marketing research is an example of a term. The term is represented by the Marketing research process, which is a course of events or a domain. Marketing research may be defined as "the function that links the consumer, customer, and public to the marketer through information", which is the concept that the term Marketing research means. The purpose with this distinction is basically to facilitate communication and exchange of meaning. This idea is shown visually in figure.

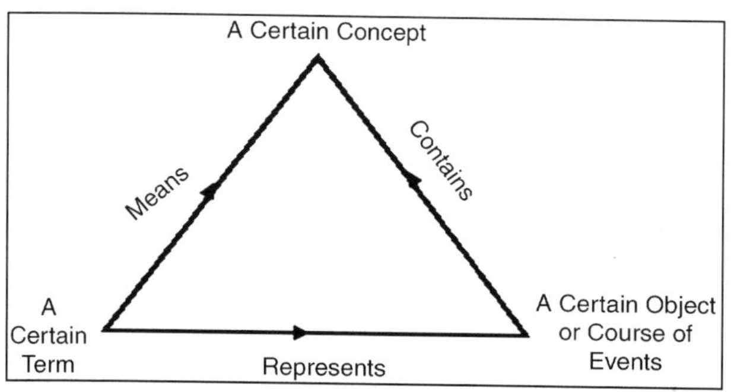

Fig The Difference between Terms, Concepts and Course of Events.

Information Processing Approaches

The terms or approaches Environmental scanning, Business, Competitive, Competitor, Market, and Political intelligence, Marketing research, and Information management will be described. The information system approach is described together with the term Information management. Our intent was originally also to include *Management information systems* (MIS) as an approach here.

This proved very difficult since there seems to be no consensus with regard to how the term is used. Lee and Gosain claim that the MIS discipline is "a fragmented adhocracy characterized by research that is rather personal, weakly coordinated in the field as a whole, with weak entry barriers from one fragment to the other and common sense language dominating". Based on our limited knowledge of the field, we agree with these authors and therefore choose to exclude the term/approach MIS in this paper.

Environmental Scanning

Augilar, Environmental scanning is defined as "the activity of acquiring information". Hamrefors has a somewhat complementary view and claims, "by scanning I mean the behaviour of attending to the events and phenomena in the environment". Under the term scanning Augilar includes not only purposeful search but also undirected viewing.

Aguilar maintains that the importance of scanning derives from the importance of the decisions involved. He further argues that information is useful for making decisions about strategy and long-range plans. The dependence of decision-making on scanning becomes apparent as soon as one examines the various steps of the decision-making process.

The most important type of information received through Environmental scanning is external strategic information, and information is classified as such when it refers to information about events or relationships in the firms outside environment that unveil opportunities to exploit the firms strengths, accentuate the firms weaknesses, or highlight potential threats facing the firm. Before proceeding, what is actually being scanned? How can "environment" be defined? Stewart, and Sweo most research definitions of organizational or business environment has been based on the work of Duncan. Duncan defines the environment as all of the relevant factors outside an organization's boundary that are incorporated into its decision-making.

Further, the environment could be anything material or social in the surroundings, close or distant to an individual. Considering these relevant factors, the environment can be divided into two distinct strata named task and general environment.

The task environment involves sectors in which there is direct interaction with other organizations, suppliers, customers, and competitors being good examples. The general environment includes sectors with indirect interaction with the organization such as government, economic conditions, and socio-cultural factors. Environmental scanning is a quite new phenomenon on the organizational scene. Only in the latest 15 years has this topic started to be of importance on the agenda of many organizations, even if it is by no means a new phenomenon. When consulting the literature, we can see that from the 1960s onwards a lot has been written using the term Environmental scanning in such prominent magazines as ASQ, Management Science, Academy of Management Journal, and the Strategic Management Journal. Issues that were addressed among others were environmental uncertainty environmental characteristics, scanning behaviour of executives and scanning behaviour in relation to competence development.

Business, Competitive, Competitor, Market and Political Intelligence

The question of Environmental scanning has been raised in several contexts. One is the need to identify changes in the organizational environment that the management thinks is important for the organization. This kind of Environmental scanning is often labeled *Business intelligence* (BI), a wording that reflects that it is often inspired by Military intelligence. Business intelligence could be broadly defined as systematized Information management aimed at generating insight into the future developments that are assumed to have an impact on the organization as decision support in organizations.

Usually, the term intelligence is used for indicating that it is an organized activity and an interpretation of the environmental events, rather than sheer information about them. To put it another way, intelligence is actionable, processed, and organized information. Another characteristic of intelligence is that it is future oriented.

By using organized intelligence activities one tries to forecast how relevant parts of the environment will develop in the future. In the literature the term intelligence is often used to capture the process and organization of transforming information into something that makes sense and that could be used in decision-making. Almost all major corporations have Business intelligence units today. The purpose of BI is proactively to support information to decision-makers for their actions.

Often a distinction is made between tactical and strategic intelligence, which originates from the military intelligence tradition that the authors of BI often come from. Furthermore, the proactivity of BI often distinguishes between the ability of finding critical information, without the decision-makers having to ask for it, and the proactivity to anticipate future questions from the management.

Methodologically, the BI operations are based on the intelligence cycle. This cycle has been described by many authors all having their own version of the same basic cycle. The cycle used here is adopted from Ashton and Stacey.

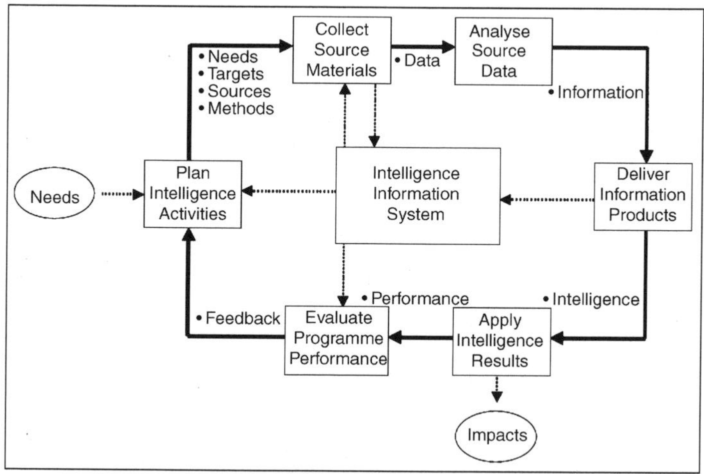

Fig The S&T Intellegence Process.

The first step includes planning the intelligence activities. Effective intelligence is based on clear identification of user or customer needs to be served by the intelligence activity and careful forethought about information gathering and analysis. The second step is to collect source materials.

Sources of information can be internal or external, formal or informal, personal or electronic. The secret lies primarily in narrowing down what information are relevant, identifying where to find it, and knowing how to analyse it in order to support decision-making. The third step involves analysis of the materials and sources to interpret their meaning in the light of intelligence objectives or user needs.

This includes, for example, interpreting the meaning of information, to develop results, and to assess implications. The fourth step is to deliver the information products. This can be done through formal presentation, through e-mail, or by other means. Once developed and disseminated, intelligence results are applied or used in some way to affect organizational decisions or actions. Typically, the findings are either used as the basis for specific action or simply stored for possible later use in actions.

Finally, in step 6, the intelligence process and results should be evaluated with regard to whether they serve user needs and ultimately have beneficial impacts on the organization. The purpose of the evaluation is to improve future operations by making them more responsive to company needs, to further clarify those needs and to adjust practices accordingly. By looking at the model, it is easy to get the impression that the activities are sequential, starting with the planning of intelligence activities. It should be emphasized though that the intelligence cycle describes a continuous activity; a never-ending process oscillating between search and decision.

Marketing Research

Effective decision-making depends on the quality of the information input, and Marketing research plays an essential role in providing accurate and useful information. Marketing research is the firm's formal communication link with the environment. It is the means by which the firm generates, transmits, and interprets information from the environment about or relating to the success of the firms marketing plans. Marketing research is broadly concerned with the application of theories, problem-solving methods and techniques to the identification and solution of problems in marketing. Marketing research may be defined as "the function which links the consumer, customer, and public to the marketer through information Finformation used to identify and define marketing opportunities and problems; generate, refine, and evaluate marketing actions; monitor marketing performance; and improve our understanding of marketing as a process".

Marketing research links the organization with its market environment. It involves the specification, gathering, analysis, and interpretation of information to help management understand that particular market environment, to identify its problems and opportunities, and to develop and evaluate courses of marketing action.

As with the Business intelligence cycle, the Marketing research process has been described by several authors, for example, Churchill, Kumar. Except some minor differences, the process seems to be quite similar, independent of the author. Step 1 in the research process, agree on research process, comprises a shared understanding between the manager and the researcher of problems or opportunities to be studied, decision alternatives to be evaluated and users of the research results.

Then, the research objectives are established. The research objective is a statement, in as precise terminology as possible, of what information is needed. A research objective has three components. The first is the research question. It specifies the information the decision-maker needs.

The second and third elements help the researcher make the research question as specific and precise as possible. After establishing objectives, it is necessary to have an estimate of the value of the informationFthat is, the value of obtaining answers to the research questions.

Such an estimate will help determine how much if anything should be spent on research. The research is then designed, the data collected, the data analysed, and the results are reported together with recommendations.

Over the last ten years, research within the area of Marketing research has been concerned with advertising and media research, brand evaluation and choice, brand management, buyer and consumer behaviour, channels of distribution, new product research, pricing research, and other marketing-related activities.

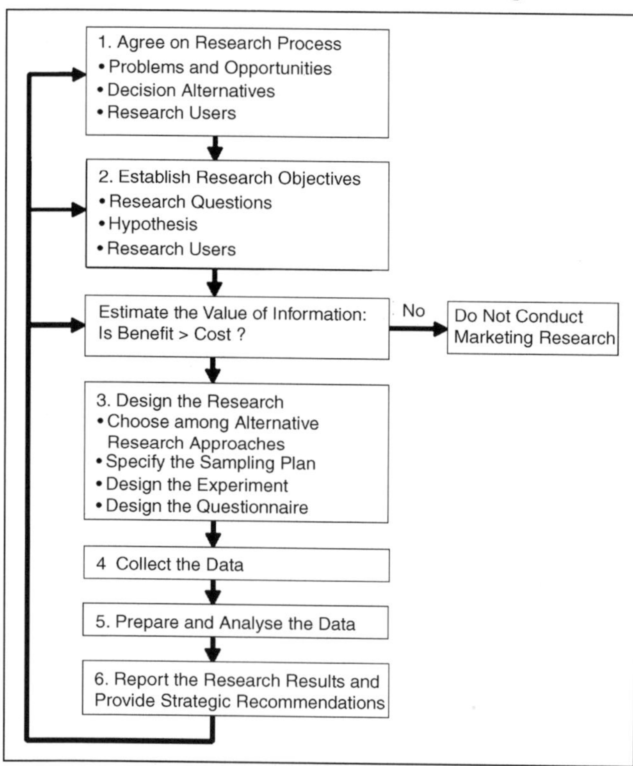

Fig The Marketing Research Process.

INFORMATION MANAGEMENT AND INFORMATION SYSTEMS

Information management has emerged as the most common brief name for the management of the use of information technology in an organization. In this context, information technology refers to the hardware and software of computing and telecom, and associated resources. A central theme in Information management, independent of perspective, is information processing. Information processing might be viewed as doing something to information to make it into something else, *e.g.* subjective knowledge, differently arranged information or summary information.

In general terms, Information management can be viewed as a response to, and a search for new and improved means of controlling the information explosion and the resultant increasing complexity of decision-making by improving the flow, the control, the analysis and the synthesis of information for decision-makers.

The following definition of Information management may be used:

- "The aim of Information management is to promote organizational effectiveness by enhancing the capabilities of the organization to cope with the demands of its internal and external environment in dynamic as well as stable conditions. Information management includes organizational wide information policy planning, the development and maintenance of integrated systems and services, the optimization of information flows and the harnessing of leading edge technologies to the functional requirements of end-users, whatever their status in the parent organization. Information management has two dimensions, the management of the information process and the management of data resources".

Rowley has also suggested a framework for Information management, with the intention of presenting a structure of the knowledge, research and practice within the area of IM. This framework can be found below.

The framework shows the different levels at which Information management can be studied. Outside the circles we find the information environmentF the environment that surrounds information contexts; it consists of political, legal, regulatory, societal, economic and technological forces. In the same way business or marketing systems exist in a wider environment, so the contexts in which Information management occurs can be placed in a wider context.

The outer circle Finformation contextFis the context in which information systems are encountered. The context influences system design, and encompasses the user. Organizations and businesses are an important category of context, but other contexts are also possible, including education, home and community.

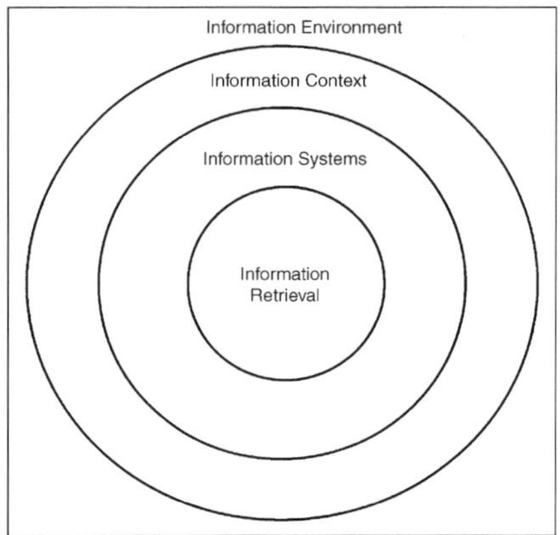

Fig. A Framework for Information Management Environments.

Information contexts are the contexts in which information processing and management take place. As can be read in the definition of IM, part of Information management is information systems, a point also made by Cronin and Davenport. These systems are used in many organizations for daily operations.

An information system may be defined as an organized combination of people, hardware, software, communication networks, and data resources that collects, transforms, and disseminates information in an organization. Information systems are the systems designed to enter information, store it and facilitate effective retrieval. Facilities to support efficient and accurate data entry must be coupled with adequate physical storage capacity and appropriate logical database structures.

Systems include hardware and software, and data, and in some models, users. Information systems should be the invisible tools that support the information processing of individuals or organizations.

The impact of such systems on information processing and developments in information processing in recent years have been so significant that it is appropriate to consider this level in the framework explicitly. An alternative perspective might actually be that the entire framework is concerned with information systems, since either an organization or an individual can be regarded as an information system.

The key issues in IS from IS-managers perspectives are:

- Improving the links between information systems strategy and business strategy,
- Developing and implementing information infrastructure,
- Implementation of knowledge management systems, and
- Reducing IT projects completion time and budget deviations.

Recent academic research has centered on IS development, studies of decision support systems, IS evaluation, IS implemen-tation, and studies of expert systems/ artificial intelligence. Finally, the inner circleFthe information retrieval circleFis concerned with the individual interfacing with a system or range of systems or sources with a view to meet specific conscious or unconscious information requirements. It concerns the actions, methods, and procedures for recovering information from stored data. Information retrieval commences with an individual's explicit or implicit need for information. Typically, the individual will then select one or more sources which on the basis of previous experience might expect to offer access to the required information. Once an appropriate source has been selected the user interacts with that source.

Comparison of the Different Approaches

After describing the different terms/approaches used to describe how information might be collected, interpreted, analysed, distributed and so forth, it is now time to compare these approaches with the characteristics mentioned in each approach. As will be soon evident, there are a lot of similarities between these approaches even if the terms used seem to differ a lot at first glance. The comparison of the different approaches and their characteristics are summarized in figure.

First, as suggested, claim that all the approaches are future oriented in the sense that they aim at generating insight into future developments. Augilar claimed that the most important type of information received through Environmental scanning is information that let the firm exploit its strengths, accentuate weaknesses, or highlight potential threats.

This information can be used for making decisions about strategy and long-range plans, something that appears in a close or remote future. Svensson-Kling claims that one characteristic of Business intelligence is that it is future oriented. By using organized intelligence activities a company tries to forecast how relevant parts of the environment will develop in the future.

This should not be surprising, since BI is viewed as a part of the broader area named Environmental scanning. Further, the purpose of the evaluation step in the intelligence cycle is to improve future operations by making them more responsive.

Since Market, Competitor, Technological, and Political intelligence are viewed as subgroups to the approach Business intelligence, they too are future oriented, trying to generate insights from various areas. And so is the approach Marketing research. Marketing research may help a decision-maker to understand a particular marketing environment in order to evaluate courses of action for the future that might concern new product research or consumer behaviour, for example.

The approach Information management is also future oriented, at least to some extent, although this is not explicitly stated in the preceding description.

Although a lot of emphasis is put on IT-technology and infrastructure, the aim is to support decisionmaking, aiming at better future decisions. Information management has its prime focus on the management of the use of information technology in organizations.

Here, information technology refers to hardware and software of computing and telecom, and associated resources. Information management also focuses on information policy planning, information systems and optimization of information flows. Here, the issue is not what kind of information that is at stake; the issue is, for example, how information is distributed to end-usersFby which means.

Some of the approaches but not all are based around a certain methodology, *i.e.* how the activities are carried out. Environmental scanning is, according to Augilar based around the scanning process. This process is comprehensive and extensive, looks like an enormous blueprint, and is not contained in this report. Business intelligence, and its subgroups Compe-titive, Competitor, Market, and Political intelligence all seem to be based around the intelligence cycle, described by Ashton and Stacey, Collins and Lagerstam among others.

The cycle may vary from author to author, but the basic idea remains the same. Marketing research is based on the Marketing research process. It is worth to note that the Marketing research process can be cyclical; provided results and recommendations may trigger new problems or opportunities, thus starting the process all over again. But the process may also be carried out just on a one-time basis.

In contrast, the intelligence cycle describes a continuous activity; a never-ending process oscillating between search and decision. Information management is not, based on our limited research, based on a certain common methodology. This might be due to the fact that the IM approach is focused more on infrastructure, and that the IM approach is more diverse than for example Marketing research.

Moreover, most of the approaches appear not to be able to avoid the consideration of the processing of information in one way or the other, *i.e.* making information ennobled. In the Environmental scanning approach, the issue of information processing is not addressed explicitly.

However, Augilar talks about purposeful search for information, which can be interpreted as separating important information from less important. In the different intelligence approaches, ennobling of information is central. Intelligence usually indicates an interpretation of environmental events, rather than sheer information. Intelligence is actionable, processed and organized information.

When information is transferred into something that makes sense it is often called intelligence. Marketing research, too, is concerned with ennobling of information. It involves, among other things, interpretation of information and so is Information management, to some extent.

Information processing is considered a central theme, and is viewed as doing something to information to make it into something else. Further, all approaches have strong ties to decision-making. The dependence of decisionmaking becomes apparent as soon as one examines the various steps of the decision-making process, according to Augilar.

The tie to decision-making is also apparent in Duncan's definition of environment. Business intelligence, as well as the other intelligence approaches, is tied to decision-making too. The aim of BI is to generate insight into future developments as decision support in organizations or as Hamrefors puts it, the purpose of BI is to proactively support information to decision-makers for their actions.

Ashton and Stacey has similar thoughts and thinks that once developed and disseminated, intelligence results are applied or used in some way to affect organizational decisions or actions. This is not surprising since adequate information is a prerequisite for rational decision-making.

The Marketing research approach is also strongly tied to decision-making. Churchill claims, for example, that effective decision-making depends on the quality of the information input, and that Marketing research plays an essential role in providing accurate and useful information. Finally, Information management is concerned with decision-making too. Rowley claims, for example, that IM is a means for controlling the information explosion and the resultant increasing complexity of decision-making by improving the flow, the control, the analysis and the synthesis of information for decision-makers.

Finally, each approach has a distinct scope, marking the boundaries or frame of the approach. Environmental scanning has a broad scope, and contains the approach of Business intelligence within its scope. The approach of Business intelligence, in turn, contains all the other intelligence terms or approaches within its scope. The scope of Information management can also be said to be broad, and contains within its boundaries the term information systems.

With regard to some issues, for example the purpose of making information ennobled and future orientation, these two approaches touches on each other in terms of scope. Marketing research might also be related to these two in terms of scope, since there might be similarities with, for example, Marketing intelligence and Information management in terms on ties to decisionmaking.

DICIPLINE OF INFORMATION SCIENCE

Information science (or information studies) is an interdisciplinary field primarily concerned with the analysis, collection, classification, manipulation, storage, retrieval and dissemination of information. Practitioners within the field study the application and usage of knowledge in organizations, along with the interaction between people, organizations and any existing information systems, with the aim of creating, replacing, improving or understanding information systems.

Information science is often (mistakenly) considered a branch of computer science. However, it is actually a broad, interdisciplinary field, incorporating not only aspects of computer science, but often diverse fields such as archival science, cognitive science, commerce, communications, law, library science, museology, management, mathematics, philosophy, public policy, and the social sciences.

Information science should not be confused with information theory, the study of a particular mathematical concept of information, or with library science, a field related to libraries which uses some of the principles of information science.

SCOPE AND APPROACH

Information science focuses on understanding problems from the perspective of the stakeholders involved and then applying information and other technologies as needed. In other words, it tackles systemic problems first rather than individual pieces of technology within that system.

In this respect, information science can be seen as a response to technological determinism, the belief that technology "develops by its own laws, that it realises its own potential, limited only by the material resources available and the creativity of its developers. It must therefore be regarded as an autonomous system controlling and ultimately permeating all other subsystems of society."

Many universities have entire colleges, departments or schools devoted to the study of information science, while numerous information science scholars can be found in disciplines such as communication, computer science, law, library science, and sociology. Several institutions have formed an I-School Caucus but there are numerous others besides these with comprehensive information foci.

Within information science, attention has been given in recent years to human–computer interaction, groupware, the semantic web, value sensitive design, iterative design processes and to the ways people generate, use and find information.

DEFINITIONS OF INFORMATION SCIENCE

An early definition of Information science is:

- "Information science is that discipline that investigates the properties and behaviour of information, the forces governing the flow of information, and the means of processing information for optimum accessibility and usability.
- It is concerned with that body of knowledge relating to the origination, collection, organization, storage, retrieval, interpretation, transmission, transformation, and utilization of information. This includes the investigation of information representations in both

natural and artificial systems, the use of codes for efficient message transmission, and the study of information processing devices and techniques such as computers and their programming systems. It is an interdisciplinary science derived from and related to such fields as mathematics, logic, linguistics, psychology, computer technology, operations research, the graphic arts, communications, library science, management, and other similar fields. It has both a pure science component, which enquires into the subject without regard to its application, and an applied science component, which develops

Some authors treat informatics as a synonym for *information science*, especially related to the concept developed by A.I. Mikhailov and other Soviet authors in the mid sixties, which suggested that informatics is a discipline related to the study of Scientific Information. Because of the rapidly evolving, interdisciplinary nature of informatics, a precise meaning of the term "informatics" is presently difficult to pin down.

Regional differences and international terminology complicate the problem. Some people note that much of what is called "Informatics" today was once called "Information Science" at least in fields such as Medical Informatics.

For example, when library scientists began also to use the phrase "Information Science" to refer to their work, the term informatics emerged:

- In the United States as a response by computer scientists to distinguish their work from that of library science, and
- In Britain as a term for a science of information that studies natural, as well as artificial or engineered, information-processing systems.

There is considerably differences between what is considered a subfield of information science and what is not (or what belongs to one information science and what belongs to another. If we take *information systems* as an example, Vickery is a book written by a leading information scientist and that book places information systems within IS. Ellis, Allen, and Wilson is, on the other hand a bibliometric investigation describing the relation between two different fields: "Information science" and "information systems".

A Multitude of Information Sciences

Michael Buckland wrote an article *What Kind of Science Can Information Science Be?* from the perspective of Library and information science: "other important fields have also used the name "information science." One is computer science, concerned with the theory and application of algorithms. Another, concerned with entropy, probability, Shannon-Weaver information theory, physical patterns, and related topics, is sometimes referred to as the "physics of information."

Also, the word information is, of course, used in information technology, but largely restricted in practice to the use of electronics for communication and computation. These other areas are not considered here. Instead, we are concerned with those areas generally understood as being within the scope of *library and information science* (LIS) and the interests of the American Society for Information Science and Technology."

PHILOSOPHY OF INFORMATION

Philosophy of information (PI) studies conceptual issues arising at the intersection of computer science, information technology, and philosophy. It includes the investigation of the conceptual nature and basic principles of information, including its dynamics, utilisation and sciences, as well as the elaboration and application of information-theoretic and computational methodologies to its philosophical problems.

ONTOLOGY

In computer science and information science, an ontology formally represents knowledge as a set of concepts within a domain, and the relationships between those concepts. It can be used to reason about the entities within that domain and may be used to describe the domain.

More specifically, an ontology is a model for describing the world that consists of a set of types, properties, and relationship types. Exactly what is provided around these varies, but they are the essentials of an ontology. There is also generally an expectation that there be a close resemblance between the real world and the features of the model in an ontology.

In theory, an ontology is a "formal, explicit specification of a shared conceptualisation". An ontology renders shared vocabulary and taxonomy which models a domain with the definition of objects and/or concepts and their properties and relations.

Ontologies are the structural frameworks for organizing information and are used in artificial intelligence, the Semantic Web, systems engineering, software engineering, biomedical informatics, library science, enterprise bookmarking, and information architecture as a form of knowledge representation about the world or some part of it. The creation of domain ontologies is also fundamental to the definition and use of an enterprise architecture framework.

HISTORY OF INFORMATION SCIENCE

EARLY BEGINNINGS

Information science, in studying the collection, classification, manipulation, storage, retrieval and dissemination of infor-mation has origins in the common stock of human knowledge. Information analysis has been carried out by scholars at least as early as the time of the Abyssinian Empire with the emergence of cultural depositories, what is today known as libraries and archives. Institutionally, information science emerged in the 19th century along with many other social science disciplines. As a science, however, it finds its institutional roots in the history of science, beginning with publication of the first issues of *Philosophical Transactions,* generally considered the first scientific journal, in 1665 by the Royal Society.

The institutionalization of science occurred throughout the 18th Century. In 1731, Benjamin Franklin established the Library Company of Philadelphia, the first library owned by a group of public citizens, which quickly expanded beyond the realm of books and became a center of scientific experiment, and which hosted public exhibitions of scientific experiments.

Benjamin Franklin did invest a town in Massachusetts with a collection of books that the town voted to make available to all free of charge, which formed the first Public Library. Academie de Chirurgia (Paris) published *Memoires pour les Chirurgiens*, generally considered to be the first medical journal, in 1736.

The American Philosophical Society, patterned on the Royal Society (London), was founded in Philadelphia in 1743. As numerous other scientific journals and societies are founded, Alois Senefelder develops the concept of lithography for use in mass printing work in Germany in 1796.

19th Century

By the 19th Century the first signs of information science emerged as separate and distinct from other sciences and social sciences but in conjunction with communication and computation. In 1801, Joseph Marie Jacquard invented a punched card system to control operations of the cloth weaving loom in France. It was the first use of "memory storage of patterns" system.

As chemistry journals emerged throughout the 1820s and 1830s, Charles Babbage developed his "difference engine," the first step towards the modern computer, in 1822 and his "analytical engine" by 1834. By 1843 Richard Hoe developed the rotary press, and in 1844 Samuel Morse sent the first public telegraph message. By 1848 William F. Poole begins the *Index to Periodical Literature,* the first general periodical literature index in the US.

In 1854 George Boole published *An Investigation into Laws of Thought...,* which lays the foundations for Boolean algebra, which is later used in information retrieval. In 1860 a congress was held at Karlsruhe Technische Hochschule to discuss the feasibility of establishing a systematic and rational nomenclature for chemistry. The congress did not reach any conclusive results, but several key participants returned home with Stanislao Cannizzaro's outline (1858), which ultimately convinces them of the validity of his scheme for calculating atomic weights.

By 1865, the Smithsonian Institution began a catalog of current scientific papers, which became the *International Catalogue of Scientific Papers* in 1902. The following year the Royal Society began publication of its *Catalogue of Papers* in London. In 1868, Christopher Sholes, Carlos Glidden, and S. W. Soule produced the first practical typewriter.

By 1872 Lord Kelvin devised an analogue computer to predict the tides, and by 1875 Frank Stephen Baldwin was granted the first US patent for a practical calculating machine that performs four arithmetic functions.

Alexander Graham Bell and Thomas Edison invented the telephone and phonograph in 1876 and 1877 respectively, and the American Library Association was founded in Philadelphia. In 1879 *Index Medicus* was first issued by the Library of the Surgeon General, U.S. Army, with John Shaw Billings as librarian, and later the library issues *Index Catalogue,* which achieved an international reputation as the most complete catalog of medical literature.

European Documentation

The discipline of *documentation science*, which marks the earliest theoretical foundations of modern information science, emerged in the late part of the 19th Century in Europe together with several more scientific indexes whose purpose was to organize scholarly literature. Many information science historians cite Paul Otlet and Henri La Fontaine as the fathers of information science with the founding of the *International Institute of Bibliography* (IIB) in 1895.

A second generation of European Documentalists emerged after the Second World War, most notably Suzanne Briet. However, "information science" as a term is not popularly used in academia until sometime in the latter part of the 20th Century.

Documentalists emphasized the utilitarian integration of technology and technique towards specific social goals. Ronald Day, "As an organized system of techniques and technologies, documentation was understood as a player in the historical development of global organization in modernity–indeed, a major player inasmuch as that organization was dependent on the organization and transmission of information."

Otlet and Lafontaine (who won the Nobel Prize in 1913) not only envisioned later technical innovations but also projected a global vision for information and information technologies that speaks directly to postwar visions of a global "information society."

Otlet and Lafontaine established numerous organizations dedicated to standardization, bibliography, international associations, and consequently, international cooperation. These organizations were fundamental for ensuring international production in commerce, information, communication and modern economic development, and they later found their global form in such institutions as the League of Nations and the United Nations.

Otlet designed the Universal Decimal Classification, based on Melville Dewey's decimal classification system. Although he lived decades before computers and networks emerged, what he discussed prefigured what ultimately became the World Wide Web. His vision of a great network of knowledge focused on documents and included the notions of hyperlinks, search engines, remote access, and social networks.

Otlet not only imagined that all the world's knowledge should be interlinked and made available remotely to anyone, but he also proceeded to build a structured document collection. This collection involved standardized paper sheets and cards filed in custom-designed cabinets according to a hierarchical index (which culled information worldwide from diverse sources) and a commercial information retrieval service (which answered written requests by copying relevant information from index cards).

Users of this service were even warned if their query was likely to produce more than 50 results per search. By 1937 documentation had formally been institutionalized, as evidenced by the founding of the American Documentation Institute (ADI), later called the American Society for Information Science and Technology.

Transition to Modern Information Science

With the 1950s came increasing awareness of the potential of automatic devices for literature searching and information storage and retrieval. As these concepts grew in magnitude and potential, so did the variety of information science interests. By the 1960s and 70s, there was a move from batch processing to online modes, from mainframe to mini and microcomputers.

Additionally, traditional boundaries among disciplines began to fade and many information science scholars joined with library programmes. They further made themselves multi-disciplinary by incorporating disciplines in the sciences, huma-nities and social sciences, as well as other professional programmes, such as law and medicine in their curriculum. By the 1980s, large databases, such as Grateful Med at the National Library of Medicine, and user-oriented services such as Dialog and Compuserve, were for the first time accessible by individuals from their personal computers.

The 1980s also saw the emergence of numerous special interest groups to respond to the changes. By the end of the decade, special interest groups were available involving non-print media, social sciences, energy and the environment, and community information systems. Today, information science largely examines technical bases, social consequences, and theoretical understanding of online databases, widespread use of databases in government, industry, and education, and the development of the Internet and World Wide Web.

7

Digital Libraries and Personalised Services

INTRODUCTION

While reviewing the definitions of digital libraries, Borgman noted that "in general, researchers (who primarily come from computer science and/or engineering backgrounds) focus on digital libraries as content collected on behalf of user communities, while librarians focus on digital libraries as institutions or services"'. She further stressed that the current state of digital library research and development, especially in the USA, is influenced by the research definition of digital libraries.

The emphasis on the "enabling technologies" for access to digital resources rather than on the services traditionally provided by libraries becomes quite evident when one looks at the two special issues of the *Journal of the American Society for Information Science*, The two issues contain excellent articles reflecting the state of digital library research but none focus on digital library services *per se*. Even the editor of the two special issues did not discuss reference and information services. He mentioned that "digital libraries have the ability to provide a previously unattainable level of service". He emphasised access to information and suggested the various methods, tools and techniques that facilitate improved access to information in digital libraries. However, this is in sharp contrast to the views of the two editors of the special issue of *Information Processing and Management* on digital libraries. Marchionini and Fox in their editorial stated that "digital library work occurs in the context of a complex design space shaped by four dimensions: community, technology, services and content".

The fact that digital libraries should not be regarded only as point of access to digital information was emphasised by a definition of digital libraries given by Borgman as early as in 1992 whereby she contended that a digital library are:

- A service;
- an architecture;
- A set of information resources, databases of text, numbers, graphics, sound, video, etc. and

- A set of tools and capabilities to locate, retrieve and utilise the information resources available.

The definition of a digital library that came up in the March 1994 Digital Library Workshop emphasised that a full service digital library must accomplish all the essential services of traditional libraries and also exploit the well-known advantages of digital storage, searching and communication.

There are many other definitions of digital libraries that mention the services aspect, either explicitly or implicitly. Pointing out the lack of emphasis on reference and information services, Sloan lamented that "human interaction in the digital library is discussed far less frequently. One would almost get the impression that the service tradition of the physical library will be unnecessary and redundant in the digital library environment". He emphasised the point that "technology and information resources, on their own, cannot make up an effective digital library". Emphasising the need for personalised services in digital libraries, Lombardi mentioned that, "helping clients find resources in a digitally chaotic world is the first priority". In a Delphi study of digital libraries it was revealed that "the primary roles librarians play in digital libraries include organisation, selection and acquisition and acting as gateways to the provision of services involving information". This study also revealed that "the best reasons for developing a digital library include: increasing access to information, serving end users' needs and bringing organisation to the unstructured universe of electronically available information".

Thus, this study shows the importance of "serving end users' needs", and the need for the librarians to act as "gateways to the provision of services involving information" in a digital library. Another study conducted by Downs and Friedman indicated that "in the absence of human intermediaries, there is a need for end-user instruction on the use of digital libraries". Covi pointed out that "digital libraries will be used only when workers can readily integrate into social legimitated and legitimatable ways of working". She further suggested that subject specialists, as digital library service providers, help users formulate disciplinary search strategies and provide assistance in developing new resources.

Arms, while trying to answer the question "whether or not we need reference librarians in a digital library", pointed out that automatic tools are steadily reducing the need for reference librarians in fields like medicine that required a significant amount of intermediation in information searching. The essence of Arms' paper is that while computers can do a lot in performing most of the traditional jobs of reference librarians, their skills may be required in case of complex information searches.

Arms, however, believes that there have been significant improvements in the end-user search facilities, provided by electronic database search services and Web search engines, and hence, the need for human intermediaries in information searching has reduced significantly. Perhaps the most comprehensive view of the need for and the nature of personalised services in a digital library has been delineated by researchers.

They maintained that:

- Services reflect the functionality afforded by systems serving the community of users. Access services that facilitate search and browsing have been central to digital library research thus far, but there is great need for attention to reference and question-answering, on-demand help, and fostering of citisenship and literacy and mechanisms to simplify participatory involvement of user communities.

DIGITAL LIBRARY SERVICES

Always library services are followed by library works. But now the advancement in information technology has brought changes in the concept of traditional library work as well as service. The recent trend and change in the information related field especially in collection, storing, processing and dissemination of information have resulted in to the evolution of digital libraries. Now most of the reference books like encyclopaedias, dictionaries, directories, hand books, etc. are published in electronic form.

Similarly about 50 per cent of the existing secondary resources like abstracting and indexing services are available in electronic form for example, Chemical Abstracts Service, Index Medicus, Engineering Index. At present most of the digital libraries have been highlighted mainly on providing access to diverse digital information resources. The provision of personalized reference and information services is considered as one of the important characteristics of the library and information profession.

However reference services include:

- Either finding the required information on behalf of users, or assisting users in finding information themselves;
- Instruction in the use of library resources and services, and
- User guidance in which users are guided in selecting the most appropriate information sources and services.

In this changing scenario, reference works of modern libraries are influenced by a set of related technical and economic factors, especially the increasing use of technology and techniques. To cite some examples, the recent developments in the INTERNET and in Web Technologies have brought significant changes in the concept of traditional reference services and a number of web-based "expert services", that are now offered by many non-library organisation.

Information services are provided to the users on demand as well as anticipating the user needs including various forms of current awareness and selective dissemination of informa-tion services. Such services are provided to the users to keep them abreast of the latest developments in their field of interest through on-line search services in digital information environment, even by the non-library organisations like Dialog.

DIGITAL REFERENCE SERVICES OF ACADEMIC LIBRARIES

Web based reference services are also now being provided by academic libraries, Recently a study report on web-based reference services reflects the current practices of digital library services in seventy academic libraries of USA. The study shows that university libraries allow their patrons to put reference questions in a variety ways: 99 per cent offer e-mail reference, 96 per cent offer reference services by appointment while 29 per cent of the libraries offer real-time virtual reference. These libraries use *customer relationship management* (CRM) software packages for providing web-based reference services in the virtual reference environment.

CO-OPERATIVE DIGITAL LIBRARY SERVICES

The rising cost of digital reference sources and its proper processing by the trained manpower and also the initial infrastructural investment for introducing new services in libraries have influenced different organisations to choose a co-operative model of digital reference services. As a result some co-operative projects have been launched for providing web-based reference services to the users who can ask for such services from a remote location at any time. The Library of Congress, USA has launched the collaborative digital reference service with a mission to provide the users, anywhere anytime through an international digital network of libraries.

This network has three main components consisting of:

- Member Profiles
- Request Manager-Software for entering, routing and answering reference queries; and
- Knowledge Base-a searchable database of questions and answer sets.

In this network a participating library sends a question to the system on behalf of a user and the system looks in to the knowledge base for a match. Then a reply is sent to the relevant library through e-mail. Incase the question and its corresponding answer is not found in the knowledge base, then it is passed on to the Request Manager where using the profiles of participating libraries and their information resources collection, expertise etc, relevant query is passed on to an appropriate library.

This library receives the query, finds an answer and sends back reply to the results store and answer to the knowledge base. Thus the Knowledge Base and Request Manager become able to provide reference service in digital environment. However, the Library of Congress and OCLC have developed a co-operative "Question Point" the advanced generation of *collaborative Digital Reference Service* (CDTS) in June 2002 which integrates local as well as global electronic reference networks.

PERSONALIZED SERVICES

Most of the researches on digital library development have focused on access to and retrieval of digital information but they have overlooked the personalized service aspects, as primary goal of library information services. However the technology and information resources, on their own, can not make up an effective digital library. On priority basis the personalized services in a digital library environment would help the users to find information resources available in a digitally chaotic world.

In a Delphy study it was revealed that:

- The primary roles library professionals play in digital libraries include organization of macro and micro-documents, selection and acquisition and acting as gateways to the provision of information services, and
- The best reasons of developing a digital library include: increasing access to information serving and users needs and bringing organization to the unstructured universe of electronically available information.

However there is a demand for end-user instruction on the use of digital libraries and the digital library professionals who are subject specialists should help users to formulate disciplinary search strategies and provide assistance in developing new digital information resources.

Web-based reference and information services

Several reference and information services are now available on the web and many of these services are provided by non-library organization. Also a web site that provides a categorized listing of libraries that offer real-time reference services using specific software, live interactive communication tools, call centre management software, bulletin board services and other INTERNET technologies.

Of course, most of these services are designed for registered users of some specific libraries in-digital information environment. HodgKin has made an aggregation approach to reference and information services. According to which more than one reference sources is made accessible digitally and also it is more practicable in terms of visibility and profitability than a single reference source.

Further:

- It's reference service becomes much better known to professional users and thus easier to find, by providing access to several reference works,
- By tackling a number of reference works at a time, the publishers can achieve economics of scale in production and development

- The user's search session is likely to be much more powerful and fruitful.

Online reference and information services can be broadly categorized into three groups:

- Those from publishers, database search services and specialized institutions
- Those provided by libraries and/or experts through the INTERNET and
- Where the users need to conduct a search and find information through the web.

Also they have listed several online information services that belong to the first category comprising various current awareness, and SDI services, for example:

- Contents pages services from commercial publishers, such as Elsevier's Contents Direct Service and IDEAL Alert from Academic Press.
- Information on new books available for free from publishers and vendors, such as Wiley Book, Notification Service from Wiley, and Amazon.com.
- SDI services from online search services providers, such as Dialog (Dialog Alerts)
- Current contents and ISI Alerting Services from ISI and so on.

However some of these services, particularly the contents page services from publishers of journals, are free, while for others, such as Dialog Alerts, or Current Contents from ISI, users need to register and pay for the services. There are also some web-based reference services where users need to conduct a search in order to answer their reference query.

For example:

- The Internet Public Library,
- Britannica,
- The Electric Library and
- The Internet Library for librarians.

Most of these web-based reference services are available free of charge but some charge a small amount as fee. For example, the Electric Library charges an annual subscription fee.

SEARCH ENGINE SERVICES

Sherman made a comparision among three web-based reference services like:

- Ask Jeeves basically a search engine, is useful for complex questions and is a good choice for searchers who lack Boolean or other searching skills, because of its strong natural language parser and question-and-answer template structure. The users can ask a question on a

given topic and it comes up with a list of questions on the same or similar topics; the users can select any of those predefined questions and then it provides further answers. It processes each query syntactically and semantically and then its answer processing engine provides the question template response. When the users click on a response, the answer-processing engine retrieves the answer template that contains links to the answer locations. Thus Ask Jeeves can help users to select a query from a pre-defined set of queries on a given topic. So it is considered as a useful model for reference and infor-mation services in digital libraries.
- The Electric Library is an excellent choice for a serious researcher in need of timely content from a wide array of otherwise unavailable sources. It provides access to various on line reference sources and allows users to either select a specific source or conduct a search on a range, or all, of the sources.
- Information please is a suitable tool for students and other researchers, as an authoritative source of facts and pointers for further investigation.

Moreover Chowdhury and Chowdhury have suggested some other useful search engine services like:
- Web help.com that claims to offer real time search assistance with a real live expertany time, day or night,
- About.com is a service that shows a number of pre-defined categories related to a search topic given by the user.

For example, a simple search on 'e-commerce' not only produces a list of sites, but also provides a set of topics related to e-commerce, such as e-commercedefinition, e-commerce security, the advantages and disadvantages of e-commerce, e-commerce statistics and so on.

DIGITAL LIBRARY INFRASTRUCTURE

A digital library has certain technological requirements such as:
- Locally developed database
- Local library system with adequate personal computers having LAN and CD-ROM Drives.
- Electronic mail service
- Network connection to have access to other data bases
- Various functions to coordinate, manage the entry and retrieve data.
- Multimedia Kit
- Well trained manpower
- Computer Hardware with Audio-Visuals, Video Conferencing Kit, Pentium Web Server, Laser Printer, Scanner, Barcode Scanner, Barcode Printer, Digital graphic printer and UPS.
- Software and its accessories.

The super structure of digital library rests on some important factors like:

- The human need for information especially that is timely and relevant and
- Accumulation of information, and all the supporting infrastructure that includes research community, professional associations, libraries and publishers, advances in methods and technology leading to developments in net working, information science, information storage and retireval, hyper-media, human-computer interaction, artificial intelligence and other areas of computer science that make digital libraries a possible proposition.

DIGITAL REFERENCE SERVICES FOR GENERAL PUBLIC

Today web-based digital reference services are being provided by a network of public libraries. The users make their query on an enquiry page and it is automatically routed to one of the participating libraries which records it as an e-mail message to the user containing necessary and available information.

For example, the British Library, London provides special reference services for business, scientific, technical, medical, patent and environmental information which range from answering simple queries up to complex questions involving on line data base searches. Of course some of these services are free if users put simple queries, but for complex queries users need to pay at the prescribed rate which covers the costs of staff time, on-line searching and value added tax (VAT). The British Library provides STM (Science, Technology and Medicine) Search Service for which users need to pay. Similarly New York Public Library (Digital Library), American Library of Congress, Alexandria Digital Library, Berkeley Digital Library, Bibliotheque Nationale de France, Victoria State Library, Vatican Library, etc. are some other libraries which provide digital reference services for users.

PRESENT SCENARIO IN INDIA

All the six IITs (Indian Institute of Technology) created as centres of excellence for higher training, research and development in science, engineering and technology, have automated their libraries and now they have access to more than one thousand electronic journals. The Central Library IIT, Delhi has switched over to the Silver Platter's Electronics Reference Library (ERL) technology for providing access to bibliographic databases subscribed on CD-ROM.

The technology facilitates simultaneous and integrated access to ERL complaint reference databases to multiple users across the LAN/WAN Via TCP/IP. This library offers network-based CD-ROM search services from the CD-ROM databases subscribed in the central library. Most of its databases have now been transferred to ERL technology and its CD-NET system has been installed for searching of CD-ROM databases on the campus intranet. This

Library has started subscribing to the web-based full-text electronic journals with availability of high speed INTERNET connection and about 1330 electronic journals are accessible full text.

In most of the higher learning and research institutes in India such as:

- The Regional Engineering Colleges (RECs),
- Tata Institute of Fundamental Research (TFIR),
- Indian Institute of Science (IIS),
- Indian Statistical Institute (ISI),
- Indian Agricultural Research Institute (IARI),
- Institute of Veterinary Research of India (IVRI),
- All India Institute of Medical Science (AIMS),
- Indian Institute of Management (IIMs),
- Institute of Physics, Institute of Life Science,
- Shaha Institute Nuclear Physics,
- The Medical College Libraries etc., have automated their library systems.

Some of them are in the process of digitization of rare and valuable documents. Digital library services in India are in developing stage. At present most of the university libraries have taken steps to provide web-based reference and information services in digital environment in addition to their traditional library services.

These services include:

- Access to library catalogues and union catalogues.
- Access to bibliographic databases
- Access to subject gate ways in specific disciplines
- Providing links to web sites
- Accessing and procuring e-reference sources
- Subscribing to e-journals
- Reference services provided by librarians and experts on the web
- Document delivery services
- On-line current awareness services
- Digitization of library resources, considering their intellectual value.

The University Grants Commission (UGC) of India has launched the major initiative for setting up nation wide communication network for Indian universities called UGC-Infonet. Each university was to establish a LAN in its campus linking all the teaching departments including library. ERNET of India and INFLIBNET Centre, Ahmedabad are conducting a series of training programmes for technical staff of each participating university library for managing and maintaining the network at their premises. The INFLIBNET Centre will administer and monitor the E-Journal programme and will have independent electronic access to all the publications to help with the process.

The INFLIBNET Centre has carried out training programmes in various places to spread awareness and to develop expertise in the University community in the use of E-Resoures under the networked environment. The INFLIBNET Centre has developed and also recently released library automation software package new version for university libraries (SOUL) for building up digital library services. Soul is Windows based user friendly software, based on client server architecture with multi-user and multi language facilities which supports internationally known standards such as CCF, AACR-II andMARC-21, etc.

Thus INFLIBNET centre is patronizing for digitization of college and university libraries and encouraging e-subscription and e-learning in Indian Universities and colleges. The DELNET (Delhi Library Network) created as a metropolitan network in 1988, has changed its name to Developing Library New Work (DELNET) in 2000. The main objectives of DELNET are to promote resource sharing among its member libraries, develop a network of member libraries, collect store and disseminate information, offer computerized information services in digital environment

The DELNET presently avails the high speed satellite communication facilities of NIC spread across the country and its 620 member libraries can access about 35 lakh bibliographic records in machine readable form. Also it maintains an online union catalogue of books available in its member libraries in CCF format. Its union catalogue is continuously updated. DELNET has been networking the libraries of about 400 affiliated institutes of AICTE, New Delhi. DELNET presents two management software packages *i.e.* DELMARC and DELPLUS.

CURRENT DIGITAL LIBRARY PROJECTS ON DIGITAL REFERENCE SERVICES

Some research projects aimed at providing reference and information services as part of the digital library services have recently begun. The most prominent is the Collaborative Digital Reference Service (CDRS) project launched by the Library of Congress.

CDRS

Researcher commented that "by applying the best of what libraries and librarians have to offer to the labyrinthine universe of unstructured and unverified information on the Internet, we can begin to bridge the gulf that exists between providers and users of information". With this end in view, the Library of Congress has launched the Collaborative Digital Reference Service, the mission of which is to provide "professional reference service to users, anywhere any time, through an international, digital network of libraries".

The CDRS is a library to library network for asking and answering reference questions. It has three main components:

- *Member profiles*: That contain information on member strengths and features.
- *Request Manager*: A software for entering, routing and answering reference questions.

- *Knowledge base*: A searchable database of question and answer sets.

The system is designed to work in a very simple manner. A participating library sends a question to the system on behalf of a user. The system looks into the knowledgebase for a match. If the answer is found, a response is sent to the querying library by e-mail. If the question is not found in the knowledgebase, then it is passed on to the Request Manager, which forwards the query to an appropriate library selected from the profiles of the participating libraries and their collections, expertise, etc. This library receives the query, finds an answer and sends it back to the results store, which then sends the response back to the asking library, and stores the query and the answer in the knowledgebase. Hence, the strength of the system lies in the knowledgebase and the Request Manager. Since, June 2000 CDRS has been a "working" pilot with a current total of 220 active members who are routing real questions and answers. The next generation on CDRS is being co-developed by Library of Congress and OCLC. It will integrate local and global e-reference networks, and will be released as a full production service in June of 2002.

AUTOMATIC REFERENCE LIBRARIANS FOR THE WORLD WIDE WEB

The Automatic Reference Librarians for the World Wide Web, a DLI-2 funded project at the University of Washington. The central objective of this project, according to them, "is to create software agents that posses reference intelligence I a limited understanding of complex technical topics, but a very sophisticated understanding of how and where to find high-quality information on theWorld Wide Web". Etioni and Weld reported the basic working principles of the proposed system, which works on a wrapper technology.

The basic steps involved are:

- The user asks a question;
- The Query Router assigns a topic to the query;
- The topic maps to a number of relevant wrappers;
- The parallel Web search module sends requests via wrappers to the sites;
- Responses from the sites are obtained and sent to the fusion engine for collation;
- User gets the response.

SIFTER is an interdisciplinary research collaboration among faculty and students in the Computer and Information Science Department and the School of Library and Information Science at Indiana University. The broad aim of the project is to develop information agents that would perform a number of functions such as culling information from complex resources residing in diverse locations, and conducting analysis, synthesis and customisation according to the requirements of the user.

The specific objectives are:

- Dealing with heterogeneous information sources that may change over time;
- Handling shifting requirements and interest of users with minimal human involvement;
- Creating a robust agent architecture for reactive, proactive and collaborative filtering;
- Supporting agent collaboration based on natural or artificial economic frameworks for multi-agent tasks.

VIRTUAL REFERENCE DESK

The Virtual Reference Desk (VRD) is a project sponsored by the US Department of Education, and its objective is "the advancement of digital reference and the successful creation and operation of human-mediated, Internet-based information services". VRD defines a digital reference service as Internet-based question-and-answer services that connect users with experts. The basic idea of VRD is that when a given user asks a question that cannot be answered by a participating centre, it is forwarded to the VRD network for assistance.

VRD services include the following:

- *Collaborative AskA Service*: A network of AskA services and volunteer information professionals.
- *The Learning Center*: A Web site for the K-12 community with curriculum-related Web sites, frequently asked questions, and other previously asked questions.
- *AskA+ Locator*: A searchable database of high-quality K-12 AskA services.

VRD also supports research on interoperability standards, metadata and other aspects of digital reference services.

LEVERAGING THE DOCUMENT SELECTIONS OF EXPERT PROBLEM SOLVERS

This is a DLI-2 project at the Oregon Health Sciences University and Oregon Graduate Institute. The goals of this project are "to understand how experts select information in a large and complex information space and to develop tools that assist them in this process", The project aims to capture the trace of information used by experts in the health field, for example medical doctors. The basic idea is that as medical experts traverse the large and diverse collection of documents, they make explicit choices about which information resources to examine more carefully and which ones to ignore.

These choices create a subset of documents relevant to a given problem and this subset of documents may be of interest to other users concerned with the same or similar problem. Thus, by capturing this information that is inherent in the selection of appropriate information resources for problem solving, this project aims to come up with models that may be useful for other users.

The project proposed to develop:

- A trace that describes the path taken by an expert in solving his/her problem by using the available information resources;
- A precis of information about each document, its content, and the history of its use by experts; and
- Navigation tools that would assist subsequent problem solvers using the collection by exploiting the knowledge inherent in the existing traces.

Though the project specifically deals with medical experts and looks into their problem-solving processes, the project team expects that the resulting technology will be scalable, because the value of a set of precis and bundles within a collection should increase as the document collection grows and as more experts use the collection.

BRINGING THE DIGITAL LIBRARY DESIGN INTO THE REALM OF ENTERPRISE ARCHITECTURE

Previous digital library research and initiatives have conceptualised and proposed several frameworks for the design, development, evaluation and interaction of digital library systems. Levy and Marshall discussed a work-oriented perspective of digital library research that is based on the work people do, and how digital libraries assist in the completion of work related tasks. Their framework highlights three crucial characteristics of digital libraries: document, technology and work. Moen and McClure identified a framework of five interacting dimensions in digital library of Government Information Locator Service (GILS): policy, users, technology, contents, and standards. The evaluation framework also includes three perspectives, representing the "views" of the stakeholders in the GILS: users, agencies, and the government. Marchionini and Fox identified four dimensions of digital library development: community, technology, service and content. Researchers presented a framework, consisting seven levels, for examining digital libraries: social, institutional, individual, interface, engineering, processing and content. Another holistic framework is presented by Fuhr consisting four major dimensions, namely data/collection, system/technology, users and usage. Sandusky developed a list of six attributes in framing digital library usability research: audience, institution, access, content, services, and design and development. Soergel offered a digital library research framework consisting of three guiding principles and eleven specific themes for research and development.

Researcher introduced 5S and formalisms for Streams, Structures, Spaces, Scenarios, and Societies - as a framework for providing theoretical and practical unification of digital libraries. All these frameworks emphasise the importance of a holistic approach rather than examine digital libraries as a single view, which would be limited in their utility. However, the absence of common frameworks in the digital library development practices undermines the ability to develop and design digital library systems efficiently, to create large-scale collaborative activities, and to communicate the value of the systems to other communities.

Researcher wrote that the broad and deep requirements of digital libraries demand new frameworks and theories in order to understand better the complex interactions among their components. Supporting this claim, the summary report of the Joint NSF-European Union (EU) Working Groups on Future Directions of Digital 1 Libraries Research recommended that "new frameworks and theories be developed in order to understand the complex interactions between the various components in a globally distributed digital library". Formal frameworks are crucial to specify and understand clearly and unambiguously the characteristics, structure, and behaviour of complex information systems such as digital libraries.

The Digital Library Federation (DLF) in 2005 sponsored the formation of the Service Framework Group (SFG) to consider a more systematic, community-based approach to align the functions of digital libraries in fulfilling the needs of information environments. DLF envisaged that digital library functionalities be generated from the library business processes, considering the architectures as information systems with specific business requirements.

It is in this context, and in recognition of visions already underway to align digital library development with the emerging perspective of the Enterprise Architecture, the authors conducted a study that seeks to understand and model the digital library services adopting a framework that give preference to scopes, goal requirements and processes - those concepts already common in Enterprise Architecture processes Abdullah and Zainab regard a digital library as an enterprise that requires architecting.

An Enterprise Architecture for the digital library is a framework or blueprint which shows how the digital library organisation carries out an intended task and how the digital library will or can improve the processes.

It shows how a digital library represents a special workspace for the user community, not only for search and access but also for the process or workflow management, information creation, sharing and exchange, and distributed workgroup communication. In order to identify what is required of a digital library in a specific context, a sound methodology is needed to establish an understanding of the digital library entire structure.

A multi-faceted information services such as digital libraries may be examined along different dimensions and from different perspectives or views of the stakeholders. There is a need to identify potential users, their involvement and roles in the digital library, their attitude towards the technology, their perception of its potential use and how it fits within the digital library goals in general.

ENTERPRISE ARCHITECTURE

In general, Enterprise Architecture is a framework that describes how an organisation develops, manages and uses information technology to optimally support its business functions. Sometimes, the term refers to the group of people responsible for modeling and then documenting the information architecture; other times the term denotes the process of doing this work.

More commonly, Enterprise Architecture refers to the models, documents and reusable items that reflect the actual architecture. In the EA Community Enterprise Architecture is a framework or blueprint for how the organisation achieves the current and future business objectives.It examines business processes, information technology, software and hardware, local and wide area networks, people, operations and projects with an organisation's overall strategy. Each of these strategies has a separate architectural discipline and Enterprise Architecture is the "glue" that integrates each of these disciplines into a cohesive framework.

From these definitions, it is understood that Enterprise Architecture consists of the various structures and processes of an organisation. Following this understanding, it is known that an Enterprise Architecture model is a representation of those structures and processes. A good Enterprise Architecture model will depict the organisation both as it is today and as it is envisioned in the future, and will map the various views representing the architecture to oneanother.

These views include both business-oriented perspectives as well as technical perspectives. The blueprint or framework of the enterprise would reveal detailed statements and processes that characterised architectural drawings. The detail drawings would be in any form, such as rich pictures, structuredcharts, data flow diagrams, Unified Modelling Language (UML) activity diagrams, database tables and entity-relationship model.

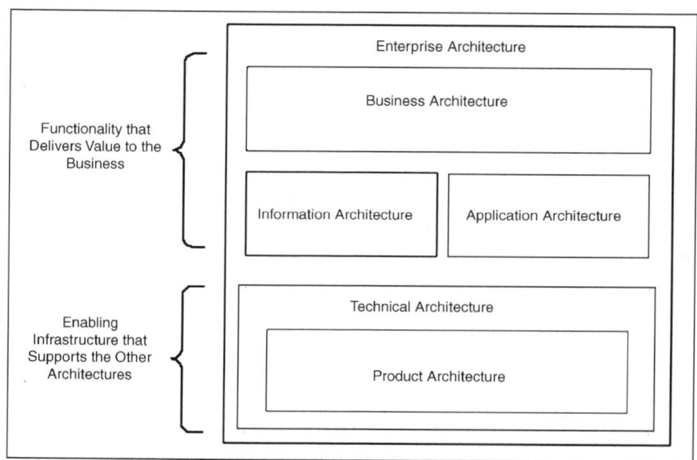

Fig. Enterprise Architecture Relationship.

ZACHMAN FRAMEWORK FOR ENTERPRISE ARCHITECTURE

The Zachman Framework is a logical structure for classifying and organising the descriptive representations of the enterprise that are significant to the management of the enterprise, as well as to the development of the enterprise' systems.

The framework uses a grid model to provide a logical structure for classifying and organising the descriptive representation of an enterprise, in six different dimensions, and each dimension can be perceived in five different perspectives. In this framework, the architecture is described across two independent aspects, the rows represent the views of five different types of stakeholders and the columns represent six different aspects of the architecture.

The points of intersection between the rows and the columns form cells. Each of these cells holds important information of the enterprise that needs to be understood and explicitly declared. The Zachman Framework's enterprise design model is presented in figure.

The Zachman Framework for Enterprise Architecture is found suitable to investigate the initial requirements and define the digital library organisation, processes, technology and information flows, as well as ground the design of digital libraries for the following reasons:

- The framework helps to explicitly show the many perspectives that need to be addressed by the digital library. It requires the planner, owner and designer of the digital library to involve the stakeholders to ensure that it meets their needs and will be used. It holistically controls the approach to investigate the user requirements and guides the data gathering techniques.
- The framework requires the involvement of stakeholders, not just the enterprise architects and developers. and ideally this practice is what digital library designers and developers should follow. This aligns with the need to involve stakeholders in digital library design and development.
- The framework is robust enough. It explicitly shows and requires the designer to consider all aspects of the digital library design.
- The framework is generic in nature and can be applied perfectly to digital library organisation. As such it is a flexible framework and it does not impose a method or restrict any user to a set of pre-defined artifacts.

This chapter shows, through a case study, how the three tiers of Zachman Framework - the contextual or planner's perspectives, the conceptual or the owner's perspectives and the logical or the designer's perspectives– are used to design a digital library.

The first two rows or layers are referred to as the Business Architecture for they describe the functions a business performs and the information it uses.

The third row refers to the information and the application architecture. The planner is concerned with positioning the digital library in the context of its environment.

This is when the planner enquires about the demographics of the stakeholders, ICT individual differences, their readiness to participate and collaborate, their awareness of the concept of digital libraries and their perception of the digital library initiative.

The owner is interested in the digital library's deliverable and how it will be used. The designer is concerned with how the digital library is to perform its functions. This involves investigating the resources that are used, the user behaviour of seeking for resources, the experience of searching, the relevance perceived and the problems encountered.

The possible sets of constructs or artifacts to represent the cell content for each cell in the top three rows or layers of the Zachman Framework are presented in table.What How Where Who When Why SCOPE (Contextual) Planner List of things important to the business List of processes the business perform List of location in which the business operate List of people involved in the business List of events significant to the business List of business goals and objectives SCOPE (Contextual) Planner BUSINESS (Conceptual)

Owner Semantic Model Business Process Model Business Logistic Model Work flow model Master Schedule Business Plan BUSINESS (Conceptual) Owner SYSTEM (Logical) Designer Logical Data Model Application Architecture Distributed System Architecture Human Interface Architecture Processing Structure Business Data Model SYSTEM (Logical) Designer TECHNOLOGY (Physical) Builder DETAILED PRESENTA-TION (Out-of-context view) FUNCTIONING ENTERPRISE–The prototype Data Function Network People Time Motivation FUNCTIONING ENTERPRISE–The prototype table. Zachman Framework at the Contextual, Conceptual and Logical Systems Architecture

FORMULATION OF AN INTEGRATED FRAMEWORK FOR THE COLLABORATIVE DIGITAL LIBRARY

Collaborative digital libraries are constructed, collected and organised by a community of users and their functionalities support the information needs and uses of that community. Researchers viewed a digital library as a collaborative working and meeting space of people sharing common interests. Through a case study method, Zachman Framework is used as a basis to investigate the existing stakeholder's conditions and environment that would ensure the reception of a collaborative digital library for urban secondary schools use in Malaysia.

In this digital library environment, students collaboratively build the digital library resources, which indirectly allow members of the community to be aware and be actively involved in local content development.

The collaborative digital library would benefit both the students who would be the creator and publisher of digital project works and the teachers who would be given the experience of managing digital resources.

The multi-method approach used in the case study, to ensure the consideration of all the aspects (dimensions) of a digital library system and the relationship of these dimensions in the framework used, has been reported elsewhere.

Findings were used to populate the Zachman Framework with contextual, conceptual, logical and module diagrams at every intersection between the columns (why, what, who, how, where, when) and the rows (scope, business model, system model).

The framework abstracts the characteristics and features of the digital library based on the following six dimensions:

- Motivation factor, requiring the planner and owner to solicit answers to the "why" question, why there is need for the digital library? Why does the current business process need special handling such as those provided by the digital library?
- Data factor abstracts the "what" aspects of the digital library. What data that is currently handled by the stakeholders? What format would the data take in the digital library environment? What are the characteristics of the data used, processed, stored and presented or disseminated in terms of quality, accuracy, usability, description and organisation?
- People factor looks at the "who" questions or the roles of people in the digital project environment. Who will be instructing? Who will be handling the data? Who will be reporting the collated or processed data? Are the players in the digital library environment "ready" to participate and contribute to the digital library initiative? Are they able to do so?
- Function or Process factor defines the "how" of the activities in the digital environment. How will users search for data, how will they store the data? How will students write, present and submit their project report? How will the teachers ensure that the students know what is required? How do they grade the reports? How will they keep the reports submitted for the specified time required by the Malaysian Ministry of Education? How can the school library or resource centre accommodate these reports?
- Place or Networks looks at the "where" factor. Where will the digital library be located? Where will it be accessed by the stakeholders?
- Time looks at the "when" aspects of the digital library. When will submission of reports take place? This is useful for designing schedules, the processing and control architecture and timing systems.

The next section illustrates the use of Zachman Framework in design of the digital library, focusing on all six dimensions of the framework from three perspectives. Each of these dimensions is investigated from the perspective of the planner, owner and designer of the digital library.

These perspectives help ensure that everything relevant to the digital library enterprise is covered. The columns, comprising the six dimensions, are arranged so that the most important column or the focus of attention is presented first. At the end, the outcome would be in the form of listings and diagrams depicting the scope, business and system model of the digital library. Rows 4, 5 and 6 are beyond the scope of this chapter.

CASE ANALYSIS OF ZACHMAN FRAMEWORK FOR THE COLLABORATIVE DIGITAL LIBRARY

Motivation: Why the Digital Library is Needed

Why (Motivation) column of Zachman Framework extracts the motivation of the people that support the realisation of the digital library. This reveals the reasons for creating the digital library, as well as the establishment of goals, objectives and business plan of the digital library. The authors felt motivation aspect (stakeholders' motivation) of the framework should be first populated and given the most importance. The case study revealed that the educational community is ready to collaboratively build the digital library as reflected by the following findings:

- Students are "Internet ready", as indicated by:
  - High home computer ownership as such they are ready to utilise the digital library;
  - High Internet penetration either at home, school, cyber cafes or friend's houses;
  - A high number of students either have 3-4 years or more than 5 years experience in computer usage;
  - Students regularly go online, between either every alternate days or everyday.
- Students are "digital ready" as indicated by their awareness, experience in using and preferring digital sources. The survey indicates that all students know how to word process; they know how to prepare slide presentations or draw using the computer, edit images, create multimedia and scan images, create web pages, database or undertake simple programming. This results show that they are aware and competent in handling digital resources, which is necessary when using digital library.
- Students are also moderately "Web ready" as they know how to use the web. Although most had no formal training, they learn how to use the Web by self-teaching, from books and people. The students also learn how to find sources on their own, from their parents and siblings or from their classmates and friends.

- Students are ready to collaboratively develop digital resources as they indicated sharing the resources they create or found with their friends either by e-mailing the URLs of web sites, informing others through chat room or social networks or creating links to web sites.
- Some students are "ready web publishers", as many of them either maintain a group web page, have their own personal web page or have been creating page pages for others. The results also show that the students have experience in creating digital resource over the Internet using webpage creator tools or HTML to develop their sites.
- Students do use the Internet for school related assignments or as a major source for their school project. Students sampled highly use the Internet resources to get information for the following subjects, History, Science and Geography. The results indicate that students believe that the Internet helps them with their school work.
- All students feel that there is a need for digital library of local information and feel that this would definitely benefit them. The results indicated very significant correlation between positive perception of the digital library with high Internet use, length of Internet experience, accessibility of Internet from home high self ratings of Internet skills.
- Teachers in the case study see the value of digital resources and online publishing for their students. They expressed the willingness to play the role as a facilitator in the digital library environment. They were keen on the digital library because students could contribute original works to be shared with other students, especially where some local contents are not available in textbooks. They believed students would be more careful in preparing their project report if they make it available to wider audience in the digital library environment.
- Teachers felt that a digital library would solve problem of storage and retrieval of reports submitted Since, project reports kept in resource room could only be retrieved by class name and level, and difficult to be retrieved by subject or topics of report or by specific student's name.
- The school's infrastructural facilities are ready to support a digital library as students can gain access to computers at self-accessed learning centres, especially for students and teachers who do not have computers or Internet access at their homes.

The findings indicated that the readiness factors serve as motivating indicators, goals and objectives that support the plan for developing the digital library.

Figure presents the motivating factors that support the plan of the collaborative digital library. The findings of the case study were plugged into the first three rows of the motivational aspect of Zachman Framework.

In Row 1, the Planner's goals and objectives are defined in the form of vision statement that provides the strategic direction for the digital library.The digital library will support secondary students' information needs in conducting research projects through project-based learning (PBL).

In PBL, students interpret, analyse, synthesise, generate, and evaluate information about a topic, collaborate with others, and produce a report.To support students in these types of activities, a full complement of tools is needed to meet the unique needs of learners, and Internet technologies such as digital libraries have the affordances to support students in these activities.

Based on this premise, as well as building from various illustrations of digital library initiatives' vision statement, the planner establishes the vision of the collaborative digital library to populate Row 1 of the Motivation column. The planner's vision of the digital library is as follows:

- "The collaborative digital library should enable secondary students conducting history1 school projects to access the information they need any time and any where, in a friendly, efficient and effective way, by overcoming the barriers o distance and language. The digital library should enable students to collaboratively contribute resources as the digital library is seen as a growing repository on Malaysian local history for education".

With the vision in mind, the planner establishes the following goals for developing and implementing the collaborative digital library:

- The development of local historical resources;
- Provision of resources for lifelong learning;
- Provision of round-the clock access; and
- Development of community of users.

School's Technical Readiness	Students' ICT Readiness	Students' Digital Readiness
* ICT Infrastructure is in Place * New Infrastructure is Planned * Awareness of ICT Support System * Implementation of ICT Mediated Learning	* High Computer Ownership * Ease of Internet Access * Home Access to Internet * Frequent Users * Technologically Skilled	* Could Use Digital Resources * Strong Preference for Digital Resources * Adequate Searching Skills * Familiar with Search Agents
Teacher's Ready to Collaborate	**Motivating Factors**	**Acceptance of Digital Library**
* Value of Integrating with Subject Learning * See the Value of Digital Resources * See the Value of Online Publishing	**Strategic Readiness** * Master Plan for ICT Integration * Budget Borne by Government and Parent-Teacher Association	* Perceive Digital Library as Useful * Willingness to Contribute Contents

Fig. Motivating Factors that Support the Plan for Realization of the Digital Library.

In this capacity, it establishes "a digital library service environment" - that is, a networked, online information space in which students can discover, locate, acquire access to and, increasingly, use information.

The objective of the digital library is therefore to provide a learning environment and resources network for history education which is:

- Designed to meet the information needs of learners, in both individual and collaborative settings (enable the creation, organisation and maintaining of local history resources);
- Constructed to enable use of a broad array of materials for local history learning, primarily in digital format submitted by the educational community themselves (they themselves become resource providers); and
- Managed actively to promote reliable access anytime-anywhere to quality collections and services (provided over the Internet), available both within and outside the network.

Row 2 of the figure of the Motivation column identifies the owners' business plan that is the approach to use the collaborative digital library. The digital library is modelled to focus on serving students information needs in conducting research projects. As such, in the implementation of this digital library project, the use of the online resources would be an integral part of history projects-based learning activities.

The digital library may move the student community towards an emerging digital resources and the submission of reports in the electronic form is therefore feasible. The implementation of the business plan is consistent with the Ministry of Education's implementation and evaluation of History project, which will make the accomplishment of the goals and objectives feasible.

The teachers on the other hand will be given the opportunity to validate the quality of submissions to maintain the quality of the digital library, grade the report online and add links to resources found on the Internet.

Row 3 spells out the the designer's perspectives which expressed the motivation of the digital library in the form of behavioural objectives.

The objectives of the collaborative DL from the designer's perspectives are to:

- Enable students to search and browse the digital library resources through various access points regarding the topics they are exploring
- Allow the students to sequence and organise their project reports in various styles, construct references and append digital objects or pictures to their report.
- Provide the students with the experience of publishing their project report, allow teachers grade and their friends to view the repot. The motivation for this is to satisfy their innate need to share their work,

so that their peers can give comments for improvements before the report is finally submitted.

- Allow teachers to check the suitability of submissions, maintain quality of contents of the digital library and grade the submissions.
- Allow teachers and students to provide metadata for resources submitted to the digital library. A metadata schema will be applied for this purpose.
- Enable students and user groups to register as members to login and submit and describe resources
- Allow users to submit feedback or submit useful links to other resources in the Internet.
- Guide and assist users in using the digital library functions and services.
- Allow authorised users to add, modify or delete submitted resources to the digital library.

These behavioural objectives of the digital library would assist the designer in developing the required digital library. The motivation and objective statements subsequently assist in the development of the user requirement and detailed definitions of the digital library services required in the Function column of the Framework.

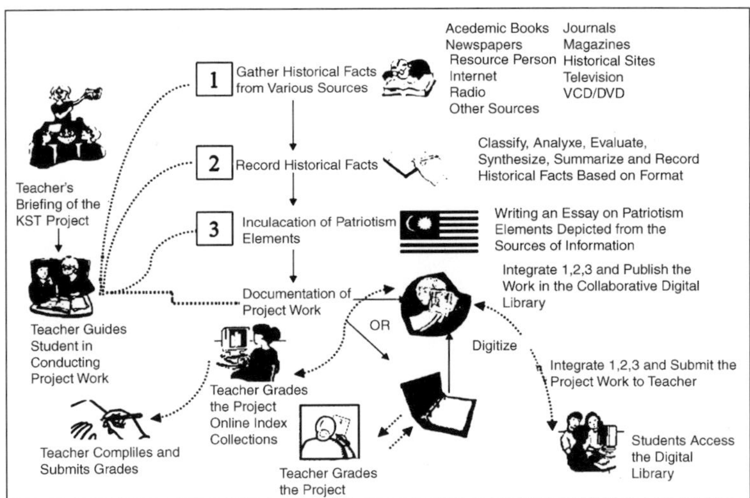

Fig. The Business Plan to Use the Collaborative Digital Library.

Data: What Resources Constitute the Digital Library

What (Data) column of the Zachman Framework describes the digital library resources students used to fulfill their research needs. The data component, at the macro level identifies the information resources included or covered in the collaborative digital library, and at the micro level, concerned the collections, quality, accuracy, usability, description and organisation of the resources in the digital library.

Findings from the case study revealed that the students and teachers emphasised the needs for contents to be "clear, accurate, adequate, organised, valid, reliable, informative and resourceful" To cater for students' information needs, in Row 1, the planner describes the three main categories of resources, without policy-controlled access.

The types of resources are:

- Resources that are born digital;
- Digitised resources or digital proxies for physical items; and
- Links to other resources relevant to the domain focus of the digital libbrary.

The digital library collections incorporates not only digital resources in different media types such as text, images, web documents, audio and video, but also in different formats with different levels of content quality and metadata.

History has been chosen as the domain of the digital library test-bed based on the survey findings that indicated the students surveyed mainly use Internet resources to get information for their History project. Case findings revealed that the project reports are typically made available in the form of collections, which refers to groups of resources organised around three themes or topic namely prominent personalities, historical events and historical buildings.

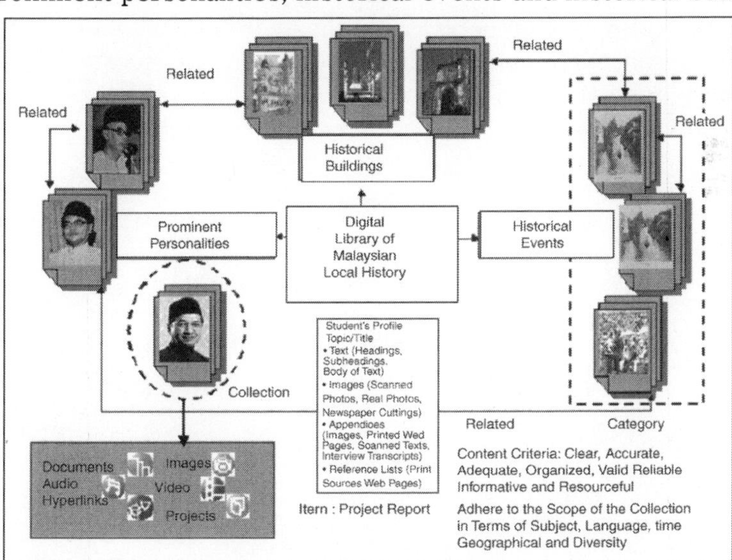

Fig. Domain Focus, Contents, Content Criteria and Scope of the Collaborative Digital Library (Owner's View of Data).

Figure presents the semantic description of the domain focus, contents, content criteria and scope of the collaborative digital library, which populates the Data component of the Zachman Framework. The stakeholders' needs for contents to be "clear, accurate, adequate, organised, valid, reliable, informative and resourceful" are therefore used as a set of general guidelines or selection criteria of resources accepted for submission.

From the designer's perspective, the data of the digital library is expressed as table definition for the digital library data (comprising digital objects data and metadata, user information, annotation and static information pages) and metadata profile for the digital object resource description (comprising administrative, technical and descriptive metadata). Administrative metadata is created by the author, technical metadata is automatically generated and descriptive metadata is assigned by the content access provider (human indexer).

The descriptive metadata schema used for the object data description is the Dublin Core (DC) Metadata.The digital library has altogether 16 metadata elements and incorporates DC's 14 out of 15 elements, namely title, creator, subject, description, publisher, contributor, date, type, format, identifier, language, relation, coverage and rights. The DC source metadata element is not used. Two other elements incorporated are Collection and Ranking metadata.

People: Who Interacts with/within the Digital Library

Who (People) column represents the stakeholders or the people within the digital library enterprise to which the digital library assigns responsibility for work. Thus, this component concerns the identification of the digital library users, their information needs, their usage of the Internet and online digital resources and their roles in the enterprise. The design of the enterprise has to do with the allocation of work and the structure of authority and responsibility.

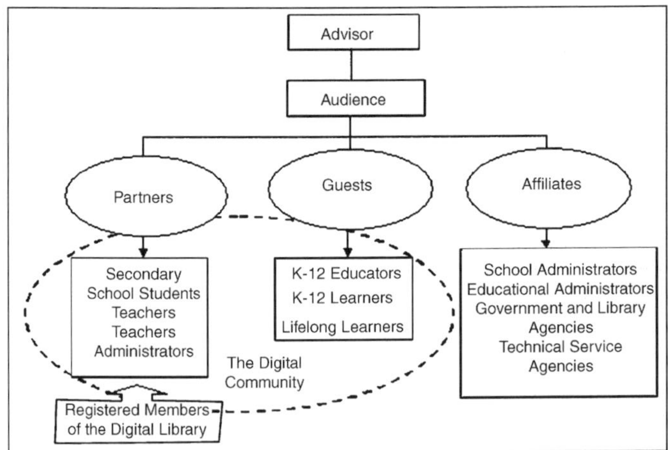

Fig. The Digital Library Organisational Structure (Planner's View of People).

This column also deals with human-machine interfaces and relationships between the people and the work they perform. In Row 1, the planner identifies the audience and the digital library organisation. There are three types of audiences within the collaborative digital library enterprise, categorised as partners, guests and affiliate members. The planner identified these groups of people in the form of digital library organisational structure.

The digital community follows certain rules and their members play different roles, as consumers, content developers or providers, content access providers and content manager.

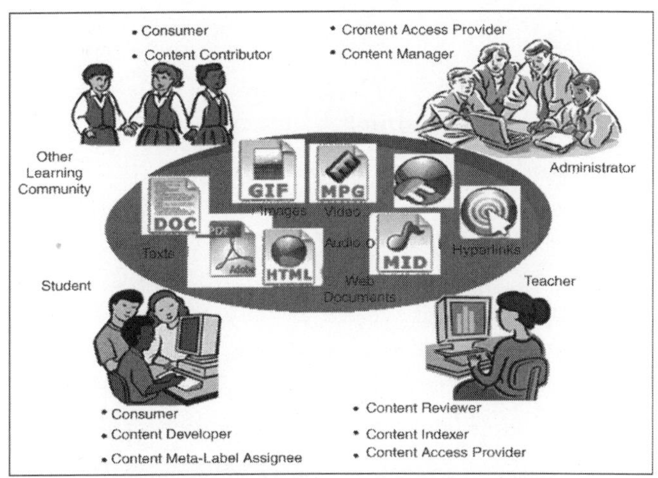

Fig. The Digital Library Actor-Roles Diagram (Owner's View of People).

Here, the digital library community includes people as well as computers, agents, network connections, files and operating systems, user interfaces, communication links, and protocols, which either use or support the digital library services. The communities of autonomous agents and computers instantiate functions upon requests by the actors of the digital library.

To operate, these agents and computers need structures of vocabulary and protocols. They act by sending streams of queries and retrieving streams of results. The digital library system uses the three-tier client-server architecture.

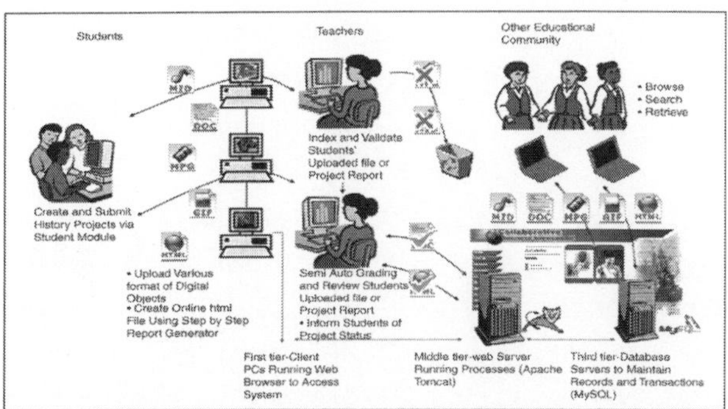

Fig. Actors and Their Roles Depicted in the Digital Library Three-Tier Client-Server Architecture (Designer's View of People).

The client tier comprises computers with web browsers such as Internet Explorer, Netscape Navigator, Mozilla Firefox and Opera. User interfaces are provided for clients to process their application and manipulate their data. All application programmes reside in the middle-tier (web server). The web server processes the request from the client and then returns required result in web page format. It processes data request by linking to a database server (such as authenticating and validating users that login into the system). It is also linked to transaction server, especially when clients are uploading files to the web server. The third tier consists of the database server and transaction for maintaining data records.

Function: What Happens in the Digital Library

How (functions) defines the functions or activities the digital library enterprise is concerned about relative to each perspective. In Row 1, the planner describes the students' research activities that take place, which encompass the entire information seeking process (from recognising the need for information to finding, using and presenting it) and the submission and evaluation of the information in the form of project report. This is presented in the form of rich pictures. Basically, the students do solitary information seeking, have spontaneous interactions with other people such as parents, siblings and friends and ask for help, and work with information in a group. The description of the activities when conducting history projects are then transformed into the online activities the students and teachers would be able to perform in the collaborative digital library. Figure presents the workflows and processes the collaborative digital library enterprise should conduct. These processes are also in line with the owner's plan to use the digital library for school project. The function component refers to the activities students perform in their research, such as choosing topic, searching for information, organising resources, writing, presenting, submitting and teachers grading of project work.

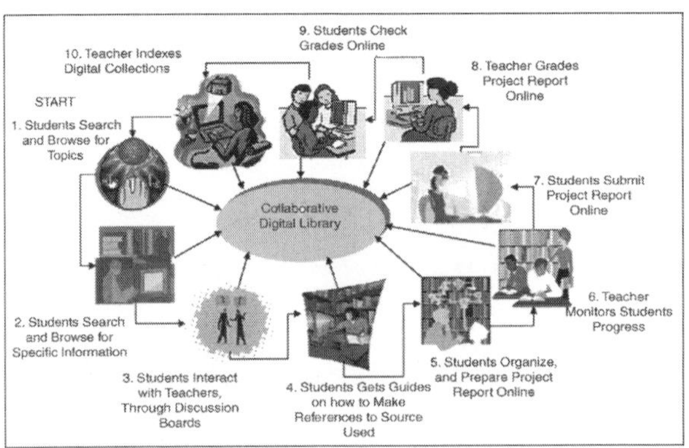

Fig. Activities Performed in the Collaborative Digital Library.

Using data from analysis of the activities culled from the research, formulation of behavioural objectives of the digital library as well as from the analysis of digital library functional requirements, the planner develops the user requirement expressed in terms of functions and present it as services in a contiguous structured chart, The structured chart is comprehensible to the owner as the conceptual model of the digital library services. This structured chart populates Row 2 of the Function Column and describes the process of translating the objectives of the digital library enterprise into successively more detailed definitions of its services. Feedback from the stakeholders on the potential features of a service and digital library design implication derived from the analysis of the case study have helped to ascertain the main features required by the collaborative digital library.

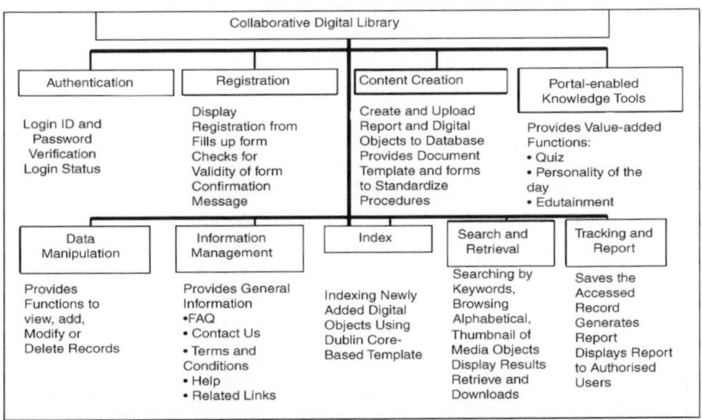

Fig. Conceptual Model of Services in the Digital Library.

In Row 3, the designer portrays the digital services in terms of data transforming processes, described exclusively in terms of definition of programme modules and how they interact with each other. The three system modules, namely administrators (including teachers), students and guests, provide different access types for different level of users. Along with this are specific definitions of security requirements, in terms of who (which role) is permitted access to what function, in the form of structured charts and detailed description of the modules menu.

Network: Where can one Access the Digital Library

Network (Where) shows the sites or geographical locations and the interconnections between activities within the digital library enterprise. It illustrates the network-related aspect of the digital libraries in terms of the physical locations of members in the digital library which spread over a geographical area. The planner provides the big picture of the digital library as a centralised system with the control for the whole structure at the Faculty of Computer Science and Information Technology University of Malaya (FCSIT UM) as the developer of the digital library system. FCSIT UM group manages the centralised database server. School A is the content collaborator and joint owner of the system and other potential future collaborators such as School

B, Education Departments, Ministry of Education, as well as other repositories, would be able to utilise the application server running locally to fetch the required data from the database server.

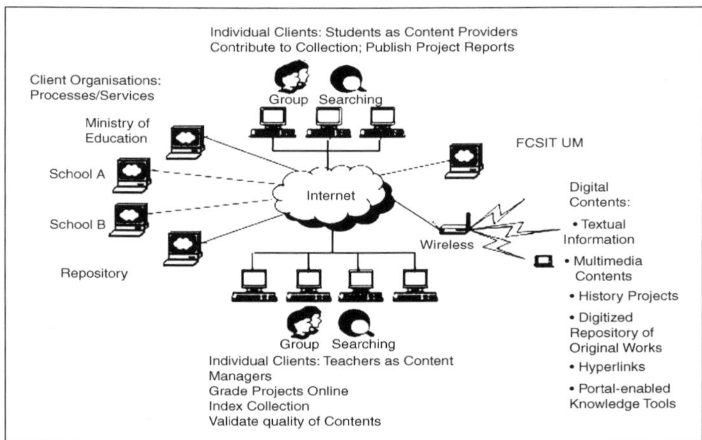

Fig. The Physical Network of the Collaborative Digital Library

The owner is interested in the conceptual model of "Where" which includes the location of access and place where the primary stakeholders, namely the students and teachers use the digital library. It illustrates the collaborative digital library deployment expressed in term of location of access and computing facilities and network. The school community may access the collaborative digital library system from any 10 locations in the school, as all computers there are connected to the network.

From the designer's perspective, the Network Column presents the logical model of the network component of the collaborative digital library which depicts the types of systems facilities and controlling software at the nodes and lines such as processors/operating systems, database and lines/line operation systems.

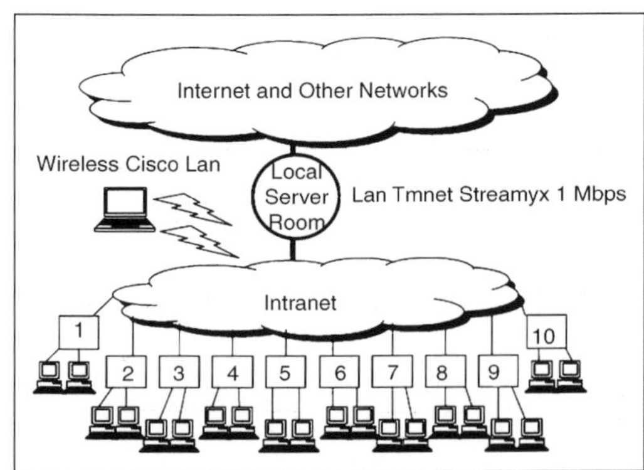

Fig. The School's Network Diagram Positioning the Location of Access for the Digital Library

The notional distributed systems architecture shows servers supporting the digital library services served from the regional (FCSIT) and local data center environment to the school's three primary locations of access. It is referred to as a notional architecture Since, the extent of the ability to remotely serve specific applications in both the baseline state and the target state remains to be established.

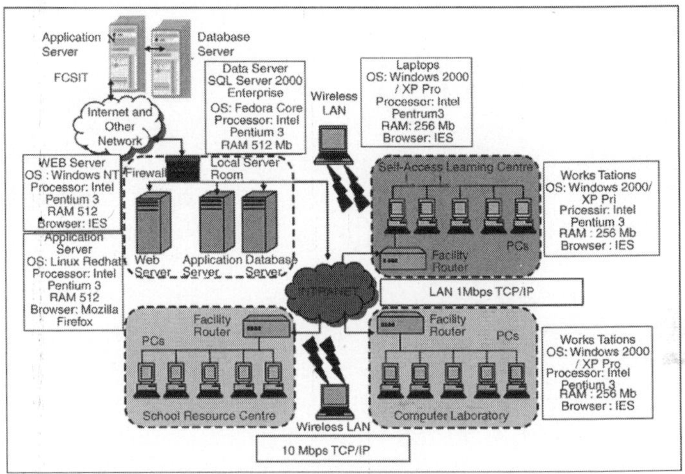

Fig. The Digital Library Notional Distributed Systems Architecture.

DIGITAL REFERENCE SERVICES AND LIBRARIES

A number of libraries have now begun to offer Web-based reference services and a number of recent studies report the current practice of reference services provided by libraries. Although this is not an exhaustive review of all the Web-based reference services provided by libraries, the following section provides a quick overview of some that are currently available.

DIGITAL REFERENCE SERVICES FOR THE GENERAL PUBLIC

Ask A Librarian is a Web-based reference service, primarily designed for UK residents, provided by a network of public libraries in the UK. The site says: "Mail us your factual question and we'll send you an answer within two working days, if not before". A user has to put the query through an enquiry page, which is automatically routed to one of the participating libraries, which receives it as an e-mail message. Within two days the library sends an e-mail message to the user with its response to the enquiry. The British Library provides special reference services for business, patent, scientific, technical, medical and environmental information. These services range from answering simple questions to finding answers to complex questions involving online database searching, etc. While some of these services are free, for others users need to pay. For example, users can ask simple business questions using a form, and can expect an answer within ten working days. Similarly, users can send e-mails with simple environmental queries.

A typical answer in such a case may include:

- A list of bibliographies from a British Library catalogue literature search; and/or;
- A list of organisations to contact for more detailed information, and/ or
- Information retrieved from Internet sources.

Users are not charged for this kind of service. However, for complex queries users need to pay.

For example, the British Library provides a Science Technology Medicine (STM) search service for which users need to pay at the following rate:

- J 82.00 per hour of staff time divided into 15-minute periods;
- Plus costs of online searching;
- Plus Value Added Tax (VAT).

As stated in the Web site most searches take at least 30 minutes and therefore cost J 41.00 for staff time + costs for online searching + VAT. The site also mentions that the average list of references costs J 80.00 for medical subjects, and between J 100.00 and J 150.00 for other subjects.

Users are also charged a fee if the results are to be faxed. In order to obtain an STM search service, the user has to fill in a form that has three parts. In the first part users need to fill in their personal details, etc., in the second part, users need to enter the query, and in the third part they need to specify the modes of delivery, payment, etc. In the second part of the form, users can enter the detail specification of the query using Boolean operators and specifying date, language, etc., as limiting factors.

DIGITAL REFERENCE SERVICES FOR USERS OF ACADEMIC LIBRARIES

Academic libraries have also begun to offer Web-based reference services. Wasik and Wasik and Lankes discuss the value of digital reference and AskA services in the K-12 educational environment. They described how AskA services are built and maintained, and also explain how the service works in the classroom.

Archer and Cast emphasised the importance of the personal touch in reference services and discussed how Web technology and the personal element of reference services can be combined to provide Web-based reference services. Tenopir and Tenopir and Ennis reported a survey of the current practices of digital library services in 70 academic libraries in the USA.

These studies noted that the university libraries allow their patrons to pose reference questions in a variety of ways: 99 per cent offer e-mail reference, 96 per cent offer reference services by appointment, and 29 per cent of the libraries offer real-time virtual reference. Breeding briefly described the various customer relationship management (CRM) software, such as eGain, LivePerson and WebLine, that are used by libraries for providing Web-based reference services. He also suggested that while the CRM software offer a great deal of sophistication to the virtual reference environment, they are more complex and expensive compared to lower-cost chat-based utilities that allow a managed two-way text conversation between the reference provider and the remote library user, thus replacing the need for a face-to-face communication.

Smith discussed the current technologies, such as chat and video conferencing software used by libraries for providing digital reference services. Richardson *et al.* examined the information technology aspects and the key organisational issues involved in establishing an electronic reference desk service in a library. They also reviewed the usefulness of some electronic reference services. Breeding provided an overview of some methodologies and collaborations currently in use to extend assistance to patrons in learning to use virtual resources and in finding the information they need.

DIGITAL LIBRARY SERVICE BY CO-OPERATIVE LIBRARY SYSTEMS

In order to deal with the rising cost of reference sources and staff and also of the huge initial investment required for introducing new services in libraries, many have gone for a co-operative model of digital reference services. Oder and Weissman described the 24/7 Reference Project at Metropolitan Cooperative Library System, a consortia around Los Angeles, and the Bay Area Libraries Project at San Francisco that are co-operative projects for providing Web-based reference services to customers.

One of the advantages of Web-based reference services is that users can ask for such services from a remote location at any time of the day. However, Rogers presented an interesting report of a study analysing Web-based reference services in academic libraries in Illinois.

This study shows a usage pattern that is quite similar to the timing of usage of traditional reference services in libraries, for example, 80 per cent of all usage occurred between 8 a.m. and 10 p.m.; evening use was higher than morning use, and the busiest hour was between 2 p.m. and 3 p.m.

REFERENCE AND INFORMATION SERVICES ON THE WEB

A number of reference and information services are now available on the Web. Interestingly, many of these services are provided by non-library and commercial organisations. While some are free, others need payment.

Detailed discussions on such services are available in a number of publications, McKiernan maintains a site that provides categorised listing of libraries that offer real-time reference services using chat software, live interactive communication tools, call centre management software, bulletin board services and other Internet technologies. Most of these services are designed for registered users of the libraries concerned.

Researchers categorised online reference and information services into three broad groups:

- Reference and information services from publishers, database search services, and specialised institutions;
- Reference services provided by libraries and/or experts through the Internet; and
- Reference and information services where users need to conduct a search and find information through theWeb.

Researchers discussed several online information services that belong to the first category.

They have listed various current awareness and SDI services such as: the contents page service from commercial publishers, such as Elsevier's

- Contents Direct Service, IDEAL Alert from Academic Press, and so on;
- Information on new books available free from publishers and vendors, such as the *Wiley Book Notification Service* and Amazon.com;
- SDI services fromonline search service providers, such as Dialog;
- *Current Contents* and *ISI Alerting Services* from ISI, and so on.

Some of these services, particularly the contents page services from publishers of journals, are free, while for others, such as *Dialog Alerts* or *Current Contents* from ISI, users need to register and pay.

It provides the following facts about theWeb-based reference services listed there:

- The listed Web-based reference services are offered by dotcom companies;
- These services use the Web only for communication between the user and the system/answer provider, while the information service is provided by a human expert;
- While most services are free, some charge as high as $250 per question;
- in many cases services are provided by (self-proclaimed?) volunteer experts;
- There are some services offered in specific subject fields.

In addition to those in table, there are also some Web-based reference services where users need to conduct a search for a reference query. Such services provide free access to various online reference sources, and allow users either to select a specific source or conduct a search on a range, or all, of the reference sources.

Examples of such services include the following:

- Internet Public Library.
- Infoplease

- Britannica
- Bartleby Reference.
- Internet Library for Librarians.
- Electric Library.
- Mediaeater Reference Desk.
- ReferenceDesk.
- Xrefer.

While most of these Web-based reference services are available free, some charge a small fee. For example, the Electric Library charges $79.95 for an entire year of unlimited access. Janes *et al.* reported a study of 20 Web-based "expert services". By asking 240 questions to 20 selected expert services, they noted that the sites gave verifiable answers to 69 per cent of factual questions. An interesting observation of this study was that the kind of reference interview that takes place in traditional reference service environments is non-existent in Web-based reference services.

In fact, the sites did not come back for any discussion or clarification after receiving the initial queries. As a justification, the authors suggested that Web-based information services have been built mainly to answer factual questions, and therefore the experts concerned do not need to go through the reference interview process. Nevertheless, the high rate of success of factual questions shows that more and more end-users will move towards these expert services rather than to libraries for answers to simple types of questions.

SEARCH ENGINE SERVICES

Although Ask Jeeves is basically a search engine, many researchers also see it as aWeb-based information service because of two reasons:

- Unlike in other search and metasearch engines, users can ask a question in Ask Jeeves, and in many cases can get an answer right away; and
- Users can ask a question on a given topic, and Ask Jeeves comes up with a list of questions on the same or similar topics; the user can select any of the those predefined questions, and then Ask Jeeves provides answers to that.

This is an interesting service and may be considered as a useful model for digital library reference and information services.

The Ask Jeeves site maintains that:

- Ask Jeeves is a unique question-answering system that allows users to ask questions in plain English, and then delivers the answer. As one of the most sophisticated navigation systems on the Internet, Ask Jeeves combines a unique natural language engine with a proprietary knowledgebase.Taken together, this mechanism processes the meaning and grammar of real questions in plain English; provides intelligent responses for user confirmation; links directly to relevant, high-quality answers; and, perhaps most exciting of all, becomesmore intelligent as its knowledgebase expands with each question asked and each answer delivered.

The site further says that Ask Jeeves processes each query syntactically and semantically, and then Ask Jeeves' answer-processing engine provides the question template response. When the user clicks on a response, the answer-processing engine retrieves the answer template that contains links to the answer locations. Thus, Ask Jeeves helps users select a query from a pre-defined set of queries on a given topic.

However, there is a debate on whether the kind of service provided by Ask Jeeves matches reference services provided by libraries. Kresh reported an interesting finding: "One consortial system in northern California conducted an informal test of Ask Jeeves by sending it 12 questions its libraries had answered. There were no trick questions, none were arcane, just questions typically received by those libraries. Jeeves was unable to answer any of the questions".

Nevertheless, the techniques and the technology used by Ask Jeeves may be very useful for introducing reference services in digital libraries. Webhelp.com is another service that claims to offer "real-time search assistance with a real live expert I any time, day or night". About.com is a service that shows a number of pre-defined categories related to a search topic given by the user. For example, a simple search on "e-commerce" not only produces a list of sites, but also provides a set of topics related to "e-commerce", such as e-commerce definition, e-commerce security, advantages of e-commerce, e-commerce disadvantages, e-commerce statistics, etc.

EVALUATION OF DIGITAL LIBRARIES AND THEIR SERVICES

Evaluation data of digital libraries and their services are not yet widely available. In fact, very few evaluation studies of digital libraries have taken place so far. The most prominent publications reporting some digital library evaluation experiments appear in *Library Trends.* Saracevic discusses a number of issues related to the methodology and criteria for evaluation of digital libraries. Arguing that digital libraries were still at the stage of research and evolution, he commented that the best practice standards have yet to develop against which the performance levels are to be measured. Carter and Janes reported a study that analysed the log of over 3,000 reference questions asked of the Internet Public Library (IPL), which is one of the most widely used reference services on the Web.

This study has identified different categories of reference questions, such as common questions, quick questions, regular questions and unanswered questions, which were handled by IPL. The study revealed that users seem to have difficulties in assigning subject categories to their questions, and also in determining whether they are factual or require detailed information searching.

Since, the greatest part of reference and information services in the past has revolved around assisting users in their information search, and because of the fact that in a digital library environment end users need to search information resources all of which are online, it may be wise to take a quick look at some recent studies involving end-users' search behaviour in the online and Web search environment.

Pending any data from large-scale digital library evaluation experiments involving users, findings of these studies may help us assess the users' online information search behaviour.

Gordon and Pathak compared the retrieval effectiveness of eight search engines: Yahoo!, Excite, Magellan, HotBot, AltaVista, Lycos, Infoseek and Open Text, and noted, among other things, that there were no statistical differences in the retrieval effectiveness among users for recall, though there were for precision.

Although this study talks about the performance of the selected search engines, this observation is very important as far as the need for personalised help in digital library searching is concerned. It shows that the Web search tools differ in terms of search precision, and who can argue that in an online search environment of today, precision is a very important issue since, no one will ever have time to sift through the hundreds of thousands of documents retrieved by an online search tool at any given instant.

One million Web queries to discern how the public searches the Web and had some astonishing findings, as follows:

- A great majority of Web queries are short, not much modified, and very simple in structure;
- Very few queries incorporate advanced search features, and when they do so, half of them are mistakes;
- Despite gathering a large number of Web sites as answers to their queries, users do not view beyond the first or the second page of results;
- Web users are notmuch interested in relevance feedback.

Yet another study reveals similar findings. The usage of the MelvylWeb catalogue at the University of California at Berkeley. During the 479-day study period users conducted about 2.5 million search sessions, during which about 7.4 million search statements were executed.

The findings of this study reveal that:

- The length of time research searchers spent at a session grew from six to ten minutes during the 16 month study period;
- During the study period, about 7.4 million database selections were made, out of which the catalogue database accounted for 32 per cent (about 2.4 million uses), Medlars for 22 per cent, magazine database for 10 per cent, periodicals database for 8 per cent, Inspec for 4 per cent and *Current Contents* for 4 per cent;

- The time users spent on each database also varied: about 3 minutes per search in the Medlars database, while 2.2 minutes for the catalogue database;
- Users displayed about four to five citations for each search they performed;
- The length of time users spent displaying results was 30-40 seconds.

The observations of these studies are very useful for designing digital library services. One of the major problems of a digital search environment is the absence of human intermediaries who play a major role in traditional online search services. Appropriate online support for query formulation and modification may improve digital library search results. Again, since, most users do not look at more than a handful of records, appropriate mechanisms have to be developed for filtering retrieved output.

CONCLUSION

The reference librarian in the new millennium will need the ability to read the situation a user is in and find the right information for that situation. Considering this view and also to keep in pace with the rapid appearances and developments of Web-based reference and information services provided by non-library organisations, many library and information science professionals have now turned their attention to the provision of e-reference services. Oder and Weissman suggested that "the year 2000 brought the advent of live reference.

Several libraries, especially academic ones, have used or adapted chat or commercial call centre software to communicate with surfers in real time and send Web resources to their browser. Indeed, this is a time when digital library researchers should think of the best ways and means to make the optimum use of the technology and experience and expertise of human intermediaries in improving digital libraries from mere access centres to information service providers.

Many recent projects have taken the approach to building software agents to do much of the work of reference librarians. While this is a useful approach, and such programmes will reduce the workload of human experts, it is doubtful whether digital libraries can totally replace human experts and personalised services.

So far as the information filtering aspect of the personalised services is concerned, the personal digital library approach of automatic filtering based on user nature, and the DWE approach of information filtering based on user categories and tasks, seem to be quite promising.

Recent research on online search behaviour of users re-emphasises the need for user training and assistance in online searching. This is in contrast to the views of Arms, who proposed that information retrieval tasks can now be successfully performed by end users without the assistance of reference librarians. User training, or information literacy programmes, may be conducted regularly and sophisticated online tutorial programmes using digital video technology may be developed to assist users. For assistance in conducting complex subject searches, the current practice of e-mail communications, online chat, videoconferencing, etc., are useful and may be deployed depending on the nature, number, location, available IT resources, etc., of the end users.

The approach taken by Ask Jeeves in the use of templates for storing queries, and the knowledgebase for storing the queries and their answers may be adopted by digital libraries. The strength of Ask Jeeves is the knowledgebase which, according to the site, "contains links to more than 7 million answers, which contain information about the most frequently asked questions on the Internet". Library and information professionals are trained in organising information and a new research may be conducted for finding the best way to organise reference queries and answers on various topics.

A facet analysis technique may be used in formulating different templates around a given search topic and they may be stored in a knowledge base. A knowledge base, developed on such an approach, will grow fast initially, but after a certain time the growth rate will be minimum. Only when new aspects of a given topic appear in the research and literature will there be a new impetus.

Co-operation in providing ready reference and subject-specific reference services may be a useful cost-cutting measure. Indeed, the high cost of staff in libraries has been a major problem.

However, since, digital libraries can be accessed and queries easily dealt with from remote locations, co-operative mechanisms based on subject specialisation and other criteria may be considered. Specialised search and other forms of assistance need not always be free. In fact, especially where specialised and reliable searches can save end-users' valuable time. Payments for such services may not always necessarily come from the end users. They may be recovered from research projects, business projects and so on. Holmes-Wong suggested that, by combining Internet technology and electronic commerce, libraries may be able to offer customisable electronic reference services to users.

Nevertheless, new research for testing e-commerce models for digital library reference services needs to be undertaken. To sum up, this study re-emphasises the need for, and provision of, personalised information services in the next generation digital libraries.

The current research projects aiming at finding the best means of providing such services through digital libraries are trying a variety of techniques and technologies, including:

- Information filtering mechanisms based on users' personal characteristics and tasks;
- Agent technology for automatic information discovery, organisation, filtering and retrieval based on user nature, need, etc.;

- Co-operative models for sharing the resources and specialisations I both the content and staff;
- Internet technologies such as Internet chat, call centre management software, video conferencing, etc.

These research projects will definitely bring some useful models and approaches that the second generation digital libraries may adopt.

Further research may be carried out in a number of areas, including:

- Building appropriate packages for end-user training involving the best practices for digital library use suitable for specific user needs, characteristics, etc.;
- Testing the query template and knowledge-based approaches in a digital library environment
- Testing e-commerce models for handling the payment and cost management aspects of sophisticated and resource-intensive personalised services;
- Tracing the techniques of expert information problem-solving processes, and building models for other users in a given domain; and
- Testing traditional library classification tools and facet analysis techniques for creating question templates and knowledge bases for storing answers in specific subject fields.

8

Challenges of Internet Research in Data Quality

The preceding part highlighted the ways in which online research can reduce the cost of psychological research on traditional topics and open up new phenomena to the psychologist's lens. These opportunities sometimes entail risks to both the quality of the research itself and to the human subjects who participate in it. In this part we discuss concerns about data quality associated with conducting research online.

SAMPLE BIASES

Although the majority of Americans now have access to the Internet, they are by no means representative of the nation as a whole. While the large differences between Internet users and non-users in terms of gender, income, and age that existed in the 1990s have shrunk, people with and without computers still differ on many demographic and social dimensions. For example, Internet users are more likely to be white, to be young, and to have children than the nation as a whole.

There is some evidence that they differ in psychological characteristics as well; users, for example, are both more stressed and extroverted than non-users. There is currently no sampling frame that provides an approximate random sample of Internet users, unlike the case of random digit dialing of telephone numbers, which provides an approximate sample of the U.S. population. The problem of representativeness is compounded because many online surveys and experiments rely on opportunity samples of volunteers. As a result, it is not clear exactly how to go about the task of appropriate generalization.

For psychologists, who often value internal validity over generalizability, the large and diverse samples online are preferable to the college sophomores on whom much psychological theory rests. But for sociologists, political scientists, and others who attempt to track the pulse of the nation or to generalize to broader groups beyond the participants, these self-selected samples are problematic. Even if a sampling frame of all Internet users could be constructed, or in specialized populations where such frames exist, problems of non-response may threaten the generalizability of the findings.

Response rates to online surveys are typically lower than comparable mail or telephone surveys and, when given a choice of Internet or paper questionnaires, respondents still overwhelmingly choose paper. The problem of biased sample selection for surveys is especially problematic for longitudinal or panel designs. It is more difficult to maintain contact with respondents in online surveys than in telephone or mail surveys because e-mail address change much more frequently than phone numbers or postal addresses.

CONTROL OVER THE DATA-COLLECTION SETTING

Previously, we noted that conducting research online *enhances* control for random assignment of participants to conditions and for the selection and ordering of questions in a questionnaire. On the other hand, the researcher typically has less control over the environment in which the research is conducted than in other experimental settings. As Nosek, Banaji and Greenwald note, in the laboratory, the experimenter stage-manages the physical environment, controlling to a degree the participant's visual, auditory, and social stimuli.

Moreover, in the laboratory, an experimenter can verify some of the identities that participants claim, can tailor instructions to ensure that each participant understands them, can monitor participants' behaviour to ensure that they are involved and serious, can make appropriate decisions about retaining or removing participants once a study has commenced, can assess the effect of the research experience on them, and can intervene if the researcher perceives undesirable effects. While an experimenter may not perform many of these actions in any particular laboratory experiment, they represent options when designing and executing the research. When the researcher decides to conduct an experiment online, many of these actions are not possible or are more difficult to put into effect.

The anonymous nature of the Internet may encourage some people to participate for the express purpose of damaging data. This could involve multiple submissions by the same individual, widespread dissemination of the URL for the purposes of flooding the site, and other nefarious behaviours designed to undermine the integrity of the research. There are some technical protections for this, such as the use of cookies or tracking IP addresses to guard against multiple responses, if the survey or experiment is an open one. Nevertheless, these solutions are not perfect, especially when computers are shared, as among students in a university computer lab. If the research is by invitation only with respondents given IDs and passwords or individually tailored URLs, one can exert better control over participation.

Even if the distortions are not deliberate, online subjects may simply invest less time and energy in the research task than those involved in a telephone survey or laboratory experiment. For example, in the experiments described in Sidebar 4, Williams and his colleagues report substantially higher dropout rates than they have observed conducting similar research in the laboratory. Withdrawal from the experiment undermines the value of random assignment of subjects to an experimental condition.

The fact that such behaviours may more readily occur on the Internet is in itself an interesting topic for study, but for many research enterprises, such practices may at best add noise to the data and more likely damage the entire study. In online communities that are the subject of naturalistic observation, anonymity also can have an effect. When people are not identified, they feel less accountable for their actions and are more likely to engage in deviant behaviour. While this is an interesting phenomenon in itself, it has the potential to generate misleading generalizations about behaviour off-line from the behaviour observed online.

ONLINE RESEARCH AND DATA-COLLECTION – WHY

Feedback is a vital part of any organizations growth. Weather you conduct regular focus groups to elicit information from key players or, your account manager calls up all your marquee accounts to find out how things are going – essentially they are all processes to find out from your customers' eyes – How are we doing? What can we do better? Online surveys are just another medium to collect feedback from your customers, employees and anyone your business interacts with. With the advent of Do-It-Yourself tools for online surveys, data collection on the internet has become really easy, cheap and effective.

SENDING OUT A SURVEY TO CUSTOMERS CAN DOUBLE SALES

We all are well aware of a simple fact in marketing - Acquiring a new customer is 10 times more difficult and expensive than retaining an existing one. This is one of the fundamental driving forces behind the wide-spread adoption and interest in CRM and related customer retention strategies. In a research study by Rice University Professor Dr. Paul Dholakia and Dr. Vicki Morwitz, published in Harvard Business Review, the experiment concluded that the simple fact of asking customers how a company was performing by itself proved to be a great customer retention strategy.

In the research study, conducted over the course of a year, one set of customers were sent out a satisfaction and opinion survey and the other set was not surveyed. After a year, twice the number of people continued and renewed their loyalty towards the company in the group that took the survey.

The research study offered a couple of interesting rationales based on consumer psychology, behind this phenomenon:

- *Satisfaction Surveys Reinforce the Customers Desire to be Coddled and Reinforce Positive Ffeelings*: This stems from part of the human psychology that wants to "appreciate" a product or service they already like. The survey feedback loop is merely a tool to express this. The survey is a vehicle to "interact" with the company and reinforces the customer's commitment to the company.
- *Surveys may Increase Awareness of Auxiliary Products and Services:* Surveys can be considered vehicles of communication - both inbound as well as outbound. Most people consider surveys as a data collection exercise. When conducting consumer surveys, they can also serve as a medium for disseminating information. It is important to note a few caveats here.
- In most countries including the US, "selling under the guise of research" is illegal.
- However, we all know that information is disseminated while collecting information.
- Additional disclaimers may be added to the survey to make users aware of this fact. Eg: "As suggested, be collecting your opinion and informing you about products and services that have come online in the last year..."
- Induced Judgements:
- The very process of asking people their opinion can induce them to form an opinion on something they otherwise would not have considered. This is a very subtle and powerful argument. This argument is analogous to the "Product Placement" strategy currently used for marketing products in mass-media like movies and television shows. One example is the extensive and exclusive use of the "mini-Cooper" in the blockbuster movie "Italian Job." This strategy is questionable and should be used with great caution.
- Surveys should be considered as a critical tool in the customer relationship dialog. The best thing about surveys is its ability to carry "bi-directional" information. The research conducted by Paul Dholakia and Vicki Morwitz shows that surveys not only get you the information that is critical for your business, but also enhances and builds upon the established relationship you have with your customers.
- Recent advances in technology have made it incredibly easy to conduct real-time surveys and opinion polls. Online tools make it easy to frame questions and answers, and create surveys on the Web. Distributing surveys via e-mail, website links or even integration with online CRM tools like Salesforce.com have made online surveying a quick-win solution.

SURVEY MODE: PHONE VS. ONLINE VS. IN-PERSON INTERVIEWS

Essentially there are four choices for data collection – in-person interviews, mail, phone and online.

There are pros and cons to each of these modes:

- In-Person Interviews
- *Pros:* In-depth and a high degree of confidence on the data
- *Cons:* Time consuming, expensive and can be dismissed as anecdotal
- Mail Surveys
- *Pros:* Can reach anyone and everyone – no barrier
- *Cons:* Expensive, data collection errors, lag time
- Phone Surveys
- *Pros:* High degree of confidence on the data collected, reach almost anyone
- *Cons:* Expensive, cannot self-administer, need to hire an agency
- Web/Online Surveys
- *Pros:* Cheap, can self-administer, very low probability of data errors
- *Cons:* Not all your customers might have an e-mail address/be on the internet, customers may be wary of divulging information online.

In-Person interviews always are better, but the big draw-back is the trap you might fall into if you don't do them regularly. It is expensive to regularly conduct interviews and not conducting enough interviews might give you false positives. Validating your research is almost as important as designing and conducting it. We've seen many instances where after the research is conducted – if the results do not match up with the "gut-feel" of upper management, it has been dismissed off as anecdotal and a "one-time" phenomenon.

To avoid such traps, we strongly recommend that data-collection be done on an "ongoing and regular" basis. This will help you compare and contrast how perceptions change depending upon how you market your product or service. The other issue here is sample size. To be confident with your research you have to interview enough people to weed out the fringe elements.

A couple of years ago there was quite a lot of discussion about online surveys and their statistical validity. The fact that not every customer had internet connectivity was one of the main concerns. Although some of the discussions are still valid, the reach of the internet as a means of communication has become vital in the majority of customer interactions. The US Census Bureau the number of households with computers has doubled between 1997 and 2001.

In 2001 nearly 50 per cent of the households had a computer. Nearly 55 per cent of all households with an income of more than 35,000 have internet access, and this jumps to 70 per cent for households with an annual income of 50,000. This data is from the US Census bureau for 2001. There are primarily three modes of data-collection that can be employed to gather feedback – Mail,

Phone and Online. The actual mode used for data-collection is really a cost-benefit analysis.

There is no slam-dunk solution but you can use the table to understand the risks and advantages associated with each of the mediums:

Survey **Medium**	Cost Per **Response**	Data **Quality/Integrity**	Reach (All **US Housholds)**
Paper	$20 – $30	Medium	100%
Phone	$20 - $35	High	95%
Online/ E-mail	$1 - $5	Medium	50-70%

Keep in mind, the reach here is defined as "All US Households." In most cases, you need to take a look at how many of your customers are online and make a determination. If all your customers have e-mail addresses, you have a 100 per cent reach of your customers. Another important thing to keep in mind is the ever-increasing dominance of cellular phones over land-line phones. United States FCC rules prevent automated dialing and calling cellular phone numbers and there is a noticeable trend towards people having cellular phones as the only voice communication device. This introduces the inability to reach cellular phone customers who are dropping home phone lines in favour of going entirely wireless. Even if automated dialing is not used, another FCC rule prohibits from phoning anyone who would have to pay for the call. Almost all cellular phone services in the US charge for incoming airtime.

Multi-mode Surveys

Surveys where the data is collected via different modes (online, paper, phone etc.) is also another way of going. It is fairly straightforward and easy to have an online survey and have data-entry operators to enter in data (from the phone as well as paper surveys) into the system. The same system can also be used to collect data directly from the respondents.

CONDUCTING AND ONLINE SURVEY – EFFECTIVELY

So, you've decided to conduct an online survey. There are a few questions in your mind that you would like answered and you are on the lookout for a fast and inexpensive way to find out more about your customers, clients etc. The first and foremost thing you need to decide what the objectives of the study are. Ensure that you can phrase these objectives as questions or measurements. If you can't, you are better off looking at other means of gathering data like focus groups and other qualitative methods. Online Surveys tend to focus in on more on "Quantitative" data collection. Review the basic objectives of the study. What are you trying to discover? What actions do you want to take as a result of the survey? This helps you double check the validity of the data collection mechanism.

Online Surveys are just one way of collecting and quantifying perspectives:

- Visualize all of the relevant information items you would like to have.

What will the output report look like? What charts and graphs will be prepared? What information do you need to be assured that action is warranted?

- Rank each topic in items 1 and 2 according to the value of the topic. List the most important topics first. Revisit items 1 and 2 again to make sure the objectives, topics and information you need are appropriate. Remember, you can't solve the problem if you ask the wrong questions.
- How easy or difficult is it for the respondent to provide information on each topic? If it is difficult, is there another way to obtain the information by asking another question? This is probably the most important step. Online Surveys have to be Precise, Clear and Concise. Due to the nature of the "Web" and the fickleness associated, if your questions are too complicated and are not easy to understand, you will have a high "drop out" rate.
- Create a sequence for the topics that is unbiased. Make sure that the questions asked first do not bias the results of the next questions. Sometimes providing too much information, or disclosing purpose of the study can create bias. Once you have a sequence of topics, you can have a basic layout of a survey. It is always prudent to add an "Introductory" text to explain the project and what is required off the respondent. It is also professional to have an ending "Thank You" text as well as information about where to find the results of the survey, when they are published.
- Determine the type of question that is best suited to answer the question and provide enough robustness to meet analysis requirements. This means do you use open-ended text questions, dichotomous, multiple choice, rank order, scaled, or constant sum (ratio scale) questions. There is a fine line you need to walk here - Generally tougher analysis requirements will lead to more complicated questionnaire design. However there are a couple of tools available to make life easier: -
- Page Breaks - Avoid having a huge scrolling survey. Introduce page breaks as necessary. Please also refrain from just having one question per page. This increases the time to complete the survey as well as increases the chances for "drop outs".
- Branching - Use Branching and Skip Logic to make your surveys "Smart". Avoid using text like, "If you answered No to Q1 then Answer Q4" - this causes respondent frustration and increases the "drop out" rate. Design the survey using Branching Logic so that the correct questions are automatically routed based on previous responses.

- Write the questions. You may need to write several questions for each topic, selecting the best one. You might also be better off dividing the survey into multiple parts.
- Sequence the questions so that they are unbiased.
- Repeat all of the steps above to find any major holes. Are the questions really answered? Have someone review it for you.
- Time the length of the survey. A survey should take less than five minutes. At three to four questions per minute, you are limited to about 15 questions. One open end text question counts for three multiple choice questions. Most online software tools will record the time taken for the respondents to answer questions.
- Pretest the survey to 20 or more people. Obtain their feedback... in detail. What were they unsure about? Did they have questions? Did they have trouble understanding what you wanted? Did they take a point of view not covered in your answers or question?
- An easy way to do this is to create another survey, with a few "open ended" essay questions along with your main project. Let's call this the "feedback survey".
- E-mail the "Project" survey to your test group and then e-mail the "feedback" survey also after that.
- In that way, you can have your test group send you comments regarding the functionality as well as usability of your "Project" survey by using you "feedback survey"!
- Revise your online questionnaire using incorporating the feedback that you got.
- Send the Survey out to all your respondents!

Online surveys are a great alternative to expensive mail or telephone surveys. There are a few caveats to online surveys however that you must be aware of. If you are trying to survey a representative sample of the general population, please bear in mind that not everyone is online. Moreover, not everyone is receptive to online survey also. Our research has shown that the demographic that responds to online survey invitations is generally biased towards younger people.

SURVEY DESIGN

- *Writing Great Questions for Online Surveys*: Writing great questions is an art that like all arts requires a great amount of work, practice, and help from others. The following discussion is one that identifies some of the common pitfalls in creating a great questionnaire.
- *Avoid Loaded or Leading Words or Questions:* Slight wording changes can produce great differences in results. Could, Should, Might all sound almost the same, but may produce a 20 per cent difference in agreement to a question (The supreme court could.. should.. might..

have forced the breakup of Microsoft Corporation). Strong words that represent control or action, such as prohibit produces similar results (Do you believe that congress should prohibit insurance companies from raising rates?) Sometimes wording is just biased: You wouldn't want to go to Rudolpho's Restaurant for the company's annual party would you?

- *Misplaced Questions*: Questions placed out of order or out of context should be avoided. In general, a funnel approach is advised. Broad and general questions at the beginning of the questionnaire as a warm-up. Then more specific questions, followed by more general easy to answer questions like demographics.
- *Mutually Non-exclusive Response Categories*: Multiple choice response categories should be mutually exclusive so that clear choices can be made. Non-exclusive answers frustrate the respondent and make interpretation difficult at best.
- *Nonspecific Questions:* Do you like orange juice? This is very unclear...do I like what? Taste, texture, nutritional content, Vitamin C, the current price, concentrate, fresh squeezed? Be specific in what you want to know about. Do you watch TV regularly? (what is regularly?).
- *Confusing or Unfamiliar Words:* Asking about caloric content, bits, bytes, mbs, and other industry specific jargon and acronyms are confusing. Make sure your audience understands your language level, terminology and above all, what you are asking.
- *Non-directed Questions Give Respondents Excessive Latitude:* What suggestions do you have for improving tomato juice? The question is about taste, but the respondent may offer suggestions about texture, the type of can or bottle, mixing juices, or something related to use as a mixer or in recipes.
- *Forcing Answers*: Respondents may not want, or may not be able to provide the information requested. Privacy is an important issue to most people. Questions about income, occupation, finances, family life, personal hygiene and beliefs (personal, political, religious) can be too intrusive and rejected by the respondent.
- *Non-exhaustive Listings*: Do you have all of the options covered? If you are unsure, conduct a pretest using the "Other (please specify) __________" option. Then revise the question making sure that you cover at least 90 per cent of the respondent answers.
- *Unbalanced Listings:* Unbalanced scales may be appropriate for some situations and biased in others. When measuring alcohol consumption patterns, One study used a quantity scale that made the heavy drinker appear in the middle of the scale with the polar ends reflecting no

consumption and an impossible amount to consume. However, we expect all hospitals to offer good care and may use a scale of excellent, very good, good, fair. We do not expect poor care.

- *Double Barreled Questions:* What is the fastest and most convenient Internet service for you? The fastest is certainly not the most economical. Two questions should be asked.
- *Dichotomous Questions*: Make sure answers are independent. For example the question "Do you think basketball players as being independent agents or as employees of their team?" Some believe that yes, they are both.
- *Long Questions*: Multiple choice questions are the longest and most complex. Free text answers are the shortest and easiest to answer. When you Increase the length of questions and surveys, you decrease the chance of receiving a completed response.
- *Questions on Future Intentions:* Yogi Berra once said that making predictions is difficult, especially when they are about the future. Predictions are rarely accurate more than a few weeks or in some case months ahead.

SURVEY QUESTION AND ANSWER TYPES

So you've decided that you need a better understanding of the characteristics of people who visit your website, or of some other business-related question. Developing a focused and effective questionnaire will help you to efficiently and accurately pinpoint the information that will help you make more informed decisions. Developing a questionnaire is as much an art as it is a science. And just as an artist has a variety of different colours to choose from in the palette, you have a variety of different question formats with which to question an accurate picture of your customers, clients and issues that are important to them.

The Dichotomous Question

The dichotomous question is generally a "yes/no" question. An example of the dichotomous question is: Have you ever purchased a product or service from our website?

- ☐ Yes
- ☐ No

If you want information only about product users, you may want to ask this type of question to "screen out" those who haven't purchased your products or services. Researchers use "screening" questions to make sure that only those people they are interested in participate in the survey.

You may also want to use yes/no questions to separate people or branch into groups of those who "have purchased" and those who "have not yet purchased" your products or services. Once separated, different questions can be asked of each of these groups. You may want to ask the "have purchased" group how satisfied they are with your products and services, and you may want to ask the "have not purchased" group what the primary reasons are for not purchasing. In essence, your questionnaire branches to become two different sets of questions.

The Multiple Choice Questions

The multiple-choice question consists of three or more exhaustive, mutually exclusive categories. Multiple choice questions can ask for single or multiple answers. In the following example, we could ask the respondent to select exactly one answer from the 7 possible, exactly 3 of the 7, or as many as 3 of the 7 (1,2,or 3 answers can be selected).

Example: A multiple-choice question to find out how a person first heard about your website is:

How did you first hear about our web site?

- ☐ Television
- ☐ Radio
- ☐ Newspaper
- ☐ Magazine
- ☐ Word-of-mouth
- ☐ Internet
- ☐ *Other:* Please Specify _______________

For this type of question it is important to consider including an "other" category because there may be other avenues by which the person first heard about your site that you might have overlooked.

Rank Order Scaling

Rank order scaling questions allow a certain set of brands or products to be ranked based upon a specific attribute or characteristic. Perhaps we know that Toyota, Honda, Mazda, and Ford are most likely to be purchased. You may request that the options be ranked based upon a particular attribute. Ties may or may not be allowed. If you allow ties, several options will have the same scores.

Example

Based upon what you have seen, heard, and experienced, please rank the following brands according to their reliability. Place a "1" next to the brand that is most reliable, a "2" next to the brand that is next most reliable, and so on.

Remember, no two cars can have the same ranking:

- __ Honda
- __ Toyota

- __ Mazda
- __ Ford

The Rating Scale

A rating scale question requires a person to rate a product or brand along a well-defined, evenly spaced continuum. Rating scales are often used to measure the direction and intensity of attitudes. The following is an example of a comparative rating scale question:

Which of the following categories best describes your last experience purchasing a product or service on our website?

Would you say that your experience was:

- ☐ Very pleasant
- ☐ Somewhat pleasant
- ☐ Neither pleasant nor unpleasant
- ☐ Somewhat unpleasant
- ☐ Very unpleasant

The Semantic Differential Scale

The semantic differential scale asks a person to rate a product, brand, or company based upon a seven-point rating scale that has two bi-polar adjectives at each end. The following is an example of a semantic differential scale question.

Example: Would you say our web site is:

- ☐ (7) Very Attractive
- ☐ (6)
- ☐ (5)
- ☐ (4)
- ☐ (3)
- ☐ (2)
- ☐ (1) Very Unattractive

Notice that unlike the rating scale, the semantic differential scale does not have a neutral or middle selection. A person must choose, to a certain extent, one or the other adjective.

The Constant Sum Question

A constant sum question permits collection of "ratio" data, meaning that the data is able to express the relative value or importance of the options (option A is twice as important as option B).

Example:

The following question asks you to divide 100 points between a set of options to show the value or importance you place on each option. Distribute the 100 points giving the more important reasons a greater number of points. The computer will prompt you if your total does not equal exactly 100 points.

When thinking about the reasons you purchased our TargetFind data mining software, please rate the following reasons according to their relative importance:

- Seamless integration with other software ________
- User friendliness of software ________
- Ability to manipulate algorithms ________
- Level of pre- and post-purchase service ________
- Level of value for the price ________
- Convenience of purchase/quick delivery ________
- Total 100 points

This type of question is used when you are relatively sure of the reasons for purchase, or you want input on a limited number of reasons you feel are important. Questions must sum to 100 points and point totals are checked by javascript.

The Open-Ended Question

The open-ended question seeks to explore the qualitative, in-depth aspects of a particular topic or issue. It gives a person the chance to respond in detail. Although open-ended questions are important, they are time-consuming and should not be over-used.

An example of an open-ended question might be:

- (If the respondent indicates they did not find what they were looking for...)

What products of services were you looking for that were not found on our website? If you want to add an "Other" answer to a multiple choice question, you would use branching instructions to come to an open ended question to find out What Other.

The Demographic Question

Demographic questions are an integral part of any questionnaire. They are used to identify characteristics such as age, gender, income, race, geographic place of residence, number of children, and so forth. For example demographic questions will help you to classify the difference between product users and non-users. Perhaps most of your customers come from the Northeast, are between the ages of 50 and 65, and have incomes between $50,000 and $75,000.

Demographic data helps you paint a more accurate picture of the group of persons you are trying to understand. And by better understanding the type of people who use or are likely to use your product, you can allocate promotional resources to reach these people, in a more cost effective manner. Psychographic or life style questions are also included in the template files. These questions provide an in-depth psychological profile and look at activities, interests and opinions of respondents.

CHALLENGES OF INTERNET RESEARCH: PROTECTION OF HUMAN SUBJECTS

Conducting research online raises challenges in protecting human subjects as well as in protecting the quality of the data. We believe that online research is not inherently more risky than comparable research conducted through other venues, but that conducting research online may change the nature of the risk and the investigators' ability to assess it. Some of the challenges arise because fundamental concepts for assessing informed consent and risk, such as the nature of individual identifiably or public behaviour become ambiguous when research is conducted online. Other challenges arise because of the researcher's reduced control over the research environment, which makes it more difficult to insure participants' identity or to assess their reactions to the research situation. The basic ethical principles underlying research involving human subjects are contained in the Belmont Report, prepared by the National Commission for the Protection of Human Subjects of Biomedical and Behavioural Research in 1979.

These include:

- *Respect for Persons:* Individuals should be treated as autonomous agents who can make informed decisions to become or refuse to become participants in research. Potential participants who are not capable of self-determination, because of diminished capacity, need protection.
- *Beneficence*: Researchers are obligated to secure the well-being of human subjects, maximizing possible benefits from their participation in research and minimizing harm.
- *Justice:* The burdens of being a research participant and the benefits of the research should be fairly distributed.

These principles have been formalized into the Federal Policy for the Protection of Human Subjects. The regulation sets standards for assessing the degree of risk to human subjects and trade-offs between risk and benefit, for establishing voluntary, informed consent before people participate in research and documenting their consent, and for the treatment of minors and other vulnerable populations. It established an oversight process called the *Institutional Review Board* (IRB) system, which assists those conducting research involving human subjects to comply with the spirit and the letter of the regulation.

AMBIGUITIES IN KEY CONCEPTS WHEN RESEARCH IS CONDUCTED ONLINE

Both the broad ethical principles articulated by the Belmont Report and the detailed Federal regulations about the protection of human subjects depend upon key concepts such as risk, expectations of privacy, pre-existing records, and identifiability, whose complex meanings are affected when research is conducted online. To illustrate this point, a flow chart outlining some of the criteria that a researcher or Institutional Review Board needs to consider in determining whether the research needs to gain informed consent from a research participant and whether that consent must be documented. In a later part, as suggested, explicitly discuss obtaining and documenting informed consent online. It should be clear from an examination of figure that assessing whether informed consent is required involves determining whether a research project is classified as human subjects research, whether the project is exempt from the Federal regulations, and whether an IRB can waive the consent requirement or its documentation.

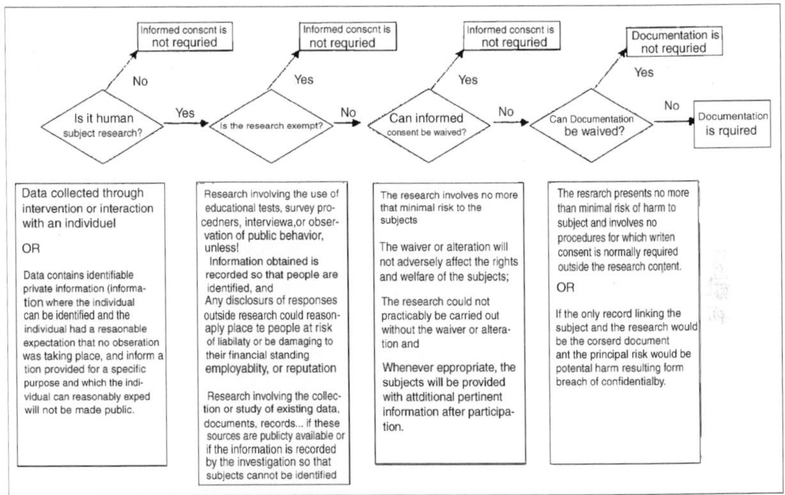

Fig. Some Factors Relevant to Internet Research Influencing Whether Informed Consent is Required and must be Documented

Figure lists criteria for making these determinations, which are likely to change when research is conducted online.

These criteria include the following:

- Whether individuals are identifiable or anonymous
- Whether behaviour is public or involves reasonable expectations of privacy
- Whether individuals expected that records were being created or expected that their behaviour was ephemeral
- Whether subjects expected that records about them would be made public or kept private
- And the degree of risk associated with the research experience

Conducting Internet research increases the ambiguities in assessing each of these criteria. We expand on these ambiguities in following parts, illustrating them with the case of online communication forums, like chatrooms and listservs. When conducting research online, researchers need to contend with changes in the technology, the ways the technology is typically used, and the norms surrounding this use, because this context is integral to assessing anonymity, privacy, risk and the like. For example, the concept of minimal risk depends upon a comparison of the risk associated with research participation to risk in everyday life. The concept of privacy depends upon participants' reasonable expectations about whether others will be allowed access to information about them. As online behaviour and norms change, the nature of minimal risk and the very concept of privacy themselves change.

Identifiable Versus Anonymous Information

Determining whether an individual is identifiable or anonymous has implications for the risks participants are exposed to, whether the research is exempt from Federal humansubjects regulations, and whether the research even involves human subjects at all. The greatest risk associated with online research centers on breaches of confidentiality, in which private, identifiable information is disclosed outside of the research context. In the case of online survey and experimental research, the researcher can often reduce this risk by explicitly not asking for identifying information or by recording personal identifiers separately from the research data.

In observations of naturally occurring online behaviour, the very nature of anonymity versus identifiably is ambiguous. Consider the question of whether a researcher can quote dialog from an online conversation, identifying excerpts by the pseudonyms by which participants identify themselves. Many participants in a chat room use a pseudonym to simultaneously mask and express their identities. As such, the choice of a pseudonym itself represents data of which the scientific audience may need to be aware. The use of pseudonyms does not guarantee anonymity and may not prevent participants from being identified. Internet users may choose online pseudonyms that contain part or all of their real names. Additionally, in the online conversation, participants often disclose information that publicly links their pseudonym to their real identities.

In some cases, where an unusual name or rare demographic category exists, small amounts of information can lead to identification of the respondent. In e-mail-based discussion forums, known as list servers, participants' identifiers invariably include their electronic mail addresses, making it easy to trace and contact them. Moreover, many Internet users employ the same pseudonym for an extended period of time and at multiple Internet sites. Consequently, they care about the reputation of that pseudonym. Thus disclosing information from a purportedly "anonymous" pseudonym in many cases has the potential to identify and to harm its owner.

Public Versus Private Behaviour

Some have argued that scientists can record Internet-based communication without the knowledge or consent of participants, because this constitutes unobtrusive observation of unidentifiable people in public places. His federal regulations, research involves human subjects only if data is collected through interaction with a subject or if it collects "identifiable private information". The regulation bases its definition of "private information" on the "reasonable expectation" of privacy. Expectations about privacy are likely to be shaped by a number of features of online settings. In Yahoo Groups, for example, participants' expectations of privacy are likely to be influenced by whether archives of their conversations are open to the public or only to available only to members, even though researchers can easily become members with access to the archives. In other cases, the presence of explicit policies posted on websites or online discussions are likely to influence expectations of privacy.

For example, one text-based virtual reality environment announced at its login screen:

- *"Notice for Journalists and Researchers*: The citizens of LambdaMOO request that you ask for permission from all direct participants before quoting any material collected here."

People are also likely to have higher expectations of privacy if the discussion is among a small, stable group rather than a large one with substantial turnover in membership. In general, in an online setting, participants may often have expectations of privacy because they cannot see the "eavesdroppers." In a face-to-face setting like a cafe, the presence of an idle stranger is likely to be noticed, and people may adjust their behaviour accordingly. In a chat room, however, a lurker, that is, a person who reads messages, but doesn't contribute, is much more likely to go unnoticed. Waskul and Douglass, *"the blurring of public and private experience is particularly characteristic of on-line research"*. Whether a person conversing online can reasonably expect the communication to be private depends upon legal regulation, social norms, and specific details of implementation, all of which are changing. Researchers and IRBs need to explicitly decide whether communication among individuals on an electronic mail distribution list, such as the soap-opera distribution list studied by Baym or an Internet chatroom, such as the sexuallyoriented ones studied by Bull and McFarlane is public behaviour.

In these settings, people disclose opinions and facts that they would likely not disclose in a physical public location. Their perceptions and expectations are often that the encounter includes only other participants in the chat room who are simultaneously present. The ethical considerations should be influenced by relevant legislation. Laws about the privacy of computer-based electronic communication are still evolving. The recently passed Electronic Communications Privacy Act states that it is illegal to intercept electronic communications. Private electronic mail and instant messaging exchanged between individuals are considered protected communication.

However, this does not include most group-oriented communication, such as bulletin boards, public distribution lists, and chat rooms, even ones where members must enter a password before participating, if the person recording the information is considered a "party to the communication." It is also not illegal in the case that "the electronic communication system ... is configured so that such electronic communication is readily accessible to the general public." Whether behaviour should be considered public or private also depends upon changing features of technology. For example, many websites often automatically create logs showing the *Internet Protocol* (IP) address of the machines that someone used to visit the site.

When a person has exclusive use of a personal computer with a fixed IP address, knowing the IP address is tantamount to know the identify of its users. IP addresses did not translate into individual identifiers in the earlier minicomputer era, when many people had accounts on a single computer, or now, if the system uses dynamic IP addresses in which one of a fixed number of addresses is assigned to a machine on the fly. In the case of dynamic IP addresses, tracing the address only identifies the machine pool, not the actual machine or its user.

Ambiguities in Defining "Existing Public" Records

According to federal regulation, research is exempt from IRB regulations if it consists of the collection of existing and publicly available data, documents, and records. Existing public records include newspaper articles, letters to the editor, birth announcements, public voter lists, and telephone books. The rules concerning the use of such data were constructed, however, prior to the existence of the Internet.

The distinctions are often fuzzy both about:

- Whether something can be said to "exist" prior to the study or
- Whether the record is indeed "public."

For example, when individuals interact, browse and buy online, their behaviour often leave traces. Yet, at times, there is ambiguity about the status of these traces as pre-existing records. Market research firms, such as Doubleclick have created technology that compiles a history of a single machine's traversal of cooperating Internet sites, selling this information to its subscribers and using it to place targeted advertisements. One might argue that the widespread use of such technologies, often revealed in a website's privacy policy, makes these transaction logs public records, even though many Internet users are unaware of them and consider their Web behaviour private. The issue continues to be complicated even when research participants voluntarily publish information online and know, in a sense, that the information is a public record.

For example, many people post family pictures online, intending them for their family and friends. A recent college graduate created a personal web page with her resume, pictures of her sorority sisters and members of her families. When asked who she thought was looking at this website, she replied, "Well, see I don't think anybody would look at it unless I told them it was there. So I kind of view it, I guess, as the same thing as like if you, if someone came over to your house. ... You might show them your photo albums of your family, your friends, or your cat, or whatever." Technically, these photos and her resume, including her name and address, were a matter of public record, and the poster should have realised this.

In the interview just described, however, the poster considered the records private, like a photo album in ones living room. For researchers who comb the Internet for scientifically relevant data, it is not clear whether the use of such data is ethical. It is an enduring record, but in the expectation of the person who posted it, the record may be private. It may be that in the future, better education about the scope and access of information available on the Internet will align the assumptions of various parties more closely with each other.

RISK TO SUBJECTS FROM INTERNET RESEARCH

Both general ethical principles and federal regulation require that the risks to subjects from participating in research should be minimized. When the Belmont Report was first developed, after the disclosure of the Tuskegee syphilis experiments, the major concern was for the risks of physical injury or death associated with medical studies. Risks, however, also include social, psychological, economic, and legal outcomes, which are more typical of behavioural research. Evaluation of risk must weigh both the magnitude and the probability of harm to the subjects against the value of the research outcome to the individual and society. Research that results in unreliable or invalid data can have no benefit and, as such, is not worth any risk it may pose to participants. Researchers have a different set of options available to them when conducting minimal risk research as opposed to research with greater risk.

For example, when conducting minimal risk research, they can request the waiver of informed consent or its documentation, and IRBs can conduct expedited reviews when evaluating such research. According to the federal regulations, research has minimal risk when "...the probability and magnitude of harm or discomfort anticipated in the research are not greater in and of themselves than those ordinarily encountered in daily life...".

Internet research involves two potential sources of risk:

1. Harm resulting from direct participation in the research
2. Harm resulting from breach of confidentiality

The nature of the potential risks varies with the particular research method used and the particular implementation decisions made within a choice of method.

For example, it is easier to anonymize data in quantitative surveys and experiments than in observations of online conversations, where participants may reveal information about themselves. The risk to subjects if they leave a research setting before receiving debriefing information is greater for deception studies than in many online communication forums or surveys.

Harm as a Consequence of Participation in Online Research

Much online research involves minimal risk. It exposes participants to innocuous questions and benign or transient experiences with little lasting impact. In general, online research is no more risky than any offline surveys, experiments, or observations. In some respects, it may be less risky, because the reduced social pressure in online surveys or experiments compared to their face-to-face counterparts makes it easier for participants to quit whenever they feel discomfort.

This freedom to withdraw is no trivial benefit, given the strong pressures to continue in face-to-face studies. Although risk in online settings is typically low, the actual risk depends upon the specifics of the study. For example, some questions in a survey or feedback from an experiment may cause participants to reflect on unpleasant experiences or to learn something unpleasant about themselves. Banaji, Greenwald, and Nosek's research on implicit attitudes, for instance, provides some participants with feedback that they may have prejudices of which they were unaware.

Similarly, participating in a survey may make a respondent confront unpleasant or disturbing issues, which can lead to distress. Experiments that deliberately manipulate a subject's sense of self-worth, reveal a lack of cognitive ability, challenge deeply-help beliefs or attitudes, or disclose some other real or perceived characteristic, may result in mental or emotional harm to some participants. For example, Williams' research on ostracism deliberately exposed participants to situations in which they were socially excluded. Theory predicted and the data confirmed the negative effects of exclusion.

A cost/benefit analysis of the gains to knowledge and the human condition generally versus the costs to the individual participants are no different here than in medical research or in traditional psychological research. Although not explicitly covered in the common rule, research participants may be harmed if the welfare of the online groups in which they participate is damaged by the research. Consider the case of online social-support groups, such as Breast Cancer Support, where people who confront a common problem share information, empathy and advice. Research may damage communication and community in those forums. King quotes a member of an online support group who wrote that she was not going to participate actively because of a researcher's presence in the group.

"When I joined this I thought it would be a *support* group, not a fishbowl for a bunch of guinea pigs. I certainly don't feel at this point that it is a "safe" environment, as a support group is supposed to be, and I will not open myself up to be dissected by students or scientists. I'm sure I'm not the only person who feels this way". When conducting cost-benefit analysis for research, investigator and IRB alike must anticipate these subtle consequences of their decisions.

Debriefing

APA ethical guidelines call for debriefing participants—providing an explanation of the nature, results, and conclusions of the research, delivered as soon after their participation as practical. If deception was involved, the researcher needs to explain the value of the research results and why deception was necessary. If investigators become aware during the debriefing that research procedures have caused harm to a participant, they are to take reasonable steps to ameliorate the harm. In addition, since many psychology experiments, including those conducted online, recruit subjects from psychology classes, they have an obligation to make the experience educational.

Even when subjects are not students, educating participants should be considered a public good. Debriefing is a way to give something back to the public, affirming the Belmont Report's principle of justice. Studies online have the advantage that researchers can post debriefing materials at a website, and can automatically update these material as new data and results come in. By providing participants with a code, debriefing materials can be tailored to particular experimental conditions and be made personally relevant.

As suggested earlier, however, debriefing in online research may be difficult. The absence of a researcher in the online setting makes it difficult to assess a participant's state, and therefore to determine whether an individual has been upset by a experimental procedure or understands feedback received. In contrast to a face-to-face setting, the online researcher is less likely to know if intervention is needed, how to adjust messages for a particular recipient, or how to fix problems caused by the research experience. In addition, participants in online research may leave the setting before receiving debriefing.

Although it is hard to debrief a participant who leaves the session early, Nosek, Banaji and Greenwald have suggested some solutions:

- Subjects enter an e-mail address before the study begins, so that at the end of the study debriefing material is e-mailed to them.
- A "leave the study" button, available at all times, brings up a debriefing statement when selected.
- When the subject closes the window, a new window appears with the debriefing statement, much as various advertisements appear after a window is closed in some websites.

Breach of Confidentiality

Probably the greater risk of harm in online research comes not from the experience of participating, but from possible disclosure of personal information at a later time. Researchers must ensure adequate provisions to protect the privacy of subjects and to maintain the confidentiality of data. The identifying information can include names, e-mail addresses, partially disguised pseudonyms, or other distinguishing personal information. Identifying information may be inadvertently disclosed either as the data is being collected, or, more commonly, when it is stored on a networked computer connected to the public Internet. Data in transit is vulnerable, for example, if a participant or automated process sends data to the investigator by electronic mail.

The store-andforward nature of electronic mail means that the message may rest in temporary directories on intervening computers before it is finally delivered to the addressee. The danger is less for data collected through automated Web surveys, although "sniffing" programmes can eavesdrop on data in transit to search for known patterns, such as social security numbers, credit card numbers, or e-mail addresses. These risks can be avoided by not transmitting information that will permit identification or by separating this data from other research data. Although analogous risks can occur with paper forms, they are higher when data is shipped over the Internet, because of the openness of the networks and the possibility of automated pattern detection. Greater risks result from outsiders gaining access to stored data files, either through deliberate hacking or because the investigator mistakenly distributed them.

This risk is not unique to online research but is a challenge for all data stored on networked computers. Researchers should regularly check the permissions associated with computer directories. Directories can be password protected, and sensitive files can be encrypted. However, many investigators fail to take these precautions to protect their data. The standard approach to dealing with problems of confidentiality is to separate personal identifiers from other data describing participants.

Thus, one often keeps names and addresses in one file and data in a second, with an arbitrary code number to link the two files. Tourangeau, Couper and Steiger illustrate some techniques used to maintain separation of identity from data in survey research involving sensitive data. A special complication in maintaining a participant's anonymity arises when an investigator conducting online research must match different pieces of information from the same respondent. For example, the HTML protocol, in which most Web surveys are authored, is stateless, meaning that it does not keep history from one page view to another. If an investigator separates questions from a survey into multiple pages, the HTML protocol does not automatically link the responses from a single respondent. To link the questionnaire, programmers sometimes use cookies, small text files stored on a respondent's computer.

There are a variety of other ways to keep track of a respondent's answers across several Web pages, such as session cookies, which are stored in memory, hidden values embedded in the HTML, or environment variables such as IP address. As long as these techniques use an arbitrary code to link the questionnaire parts, they may pose fewer confidentiality threats than the use of cookies. Paying online subjects for their participation may also link participants' responses to their identities. Some researchers have severed this link by buying gift certificates from online retailers, such as Amazon.com, and displaying the unique certificate number to a respondent at the completion of a questionnaire.

Thus, participants can redeem their certificates without revealing their identity. The degree of concern over confidentiality should be directly related to the sensitivity of the data being collected. One should be less concerned when the information about the participants is innocuous or if participants are anonymous. Many online surveys and experiments fall into one or both of these categories. When participants are identifiable and the research involves data that places them at risk of criminal or civil liability or that could damage their financial standing, employability, insurability, reputation, or could be stigmatizing, investigators must be especially concerned about breaches of confidentiality.

Under these circumstances, standard security measures in place for e-commerce transactions, such as encryption and *secure socket layer* (SSL) protocols, are likely to be sufficient. Numerous tutorials exist describing the options. The level of security should be appropriate to the risk. As research by Singer, Hippler and Schwarz demonstrates, overly elaborate assurances of confidentiality may actually heighten rather than diminish respondents' concern, causing participants to be less willing to provide sensitive information. In addition, using SSL potentially adds burden to the respondent, depending on their server settings and degree of interactivity required of the task. Some subjects may be excluded from participating because of the complexity required in interacting with the high level of encryption required.

INFORMED CONSENT

Investigators must typically obtain voluntary informed consent from research participants, in which they freely agree to participate after they understand what the research involves and its risks and benefits. As indicated earlier, investigators conducting online research may have difficulties in establishing whether participants are truly informed or even whether they are who they purport to be. Children and other vulnerable groups such as the mentally handicapped are not empowered to give consent for themselves. Their parent or guardian must consent, and the child may optionally be asked to assent. Here the inability to establish the participants' identity is especially problematic, because it is so easy for children to pretend to be their parents.

These problems necessarily raise the possibility that the consent will not be valid. Depending on the risk involved in the research, the researcher may either accept the possibility of uninformed consent or insist that a legally verified signature accompany the consent form. Getting informed consent online may not be suitable for high-risk studies. Note that researchers working with children online are subject not only to human subjects regulations, but also to the *Children's Online Privacy Protection Act* (COPPA). Among other constraints, this regulation applies particularly to operators of a website directed towards children or those who know they are collecting information from children.

We believe that these restrictions apply to research projects designed to collect information from children. They are prohibited from collecting personal information from a child without posting notices about how the information will be used and without getting verifiable parental consent. Researchers can increase the likelihood that participants are granting truly informed consent or that they are who they purport to be. For example, it is possible to get better feedback from participants about whether they understand the consent statement by breaking a consent form into segments and requiring a 'click to accept' before continuing, or by administering short quizzes to establish that a participant understood one part before administering the next. Similarly, one can more reliably distinguish children from adults by having participants enter information that is generally available only to adults or by requiring that they register with a trusted authority, such as VeriSign.

Many of these techniques have been developed to deal with problems of fraud in electronic commerce applications or for protecting online communications. They will be evolving in response to business and security needs. These techniques often come at a cost to the participants. The extra effort is likely to reduce response rates, increase non-response to sensitive items and possibly produce biased data. In addition, these techniques may require specialized technologies and knowledge, which may exclude some types of subjects from the research. Therefore these techniques are appropriate only when there is more than minimal risk to the participant. Federal human-subjects regulation requires that informed consent be documented by the use of a "...written consent form approved by the IRB and signed by the subject".

It is difficult to obtain legally-binding signatures online. However, *Institutional Review Boards* (IRBs) can waive the requirements for written documentation of informed consent for minimal risk research, and many IRBs permit research participants to click a button on an online form to indicate they have read and understood the consent form. Table lists methods of obtaining consent for Internet-based studies from strongest to weakest. The weakest method of consent, simple click to accept electronic forms, is most vulnerable to misrepresentation.

There is no reliable way to know who is clicking, or whether a child or parent is the one clicking. As digital signatures become more commonly used, there may be new ways to obtain consent with relative ease. The table illustrates the tradeoffs inherent in each of these methods for obtaining consent. In particular, anonymity is often traded off when strong forms of consent are used, especially when documentation is kept.

Table. How Method of Interaction Influences the Ability to Protect the Research Participants

Method of Interaction between Investigator and Research Participant	Research Issue					
	Insuring Informed Consent	Documenting Informed Consent	Insuring Debriefing	Protecting Anonymity	Preventing Coercion	Ease and Cost of Interaction
Face-to-face dialog with signed forms	++	++	++		--	--
Telephone conversation	++	--	++	-	-	-
Postal mail	--	++	0	++		0
Electronic forms signed by verifiable digital signature.	--	++	0	--	?	++
Electronic forms signed by simple "click to accept" method	--	+	0	++	++	++

Note:

Cells represent a rough estimate of the value of interaction techniques against several criteria.

++ = very good; + = good; 0 = neutral;

– = deficiencies; — = serious deficiencies.

ADVICE TO RESEARCHERS AND INSTITUTIONAL REVIEW BOARDS

The Internet allows researchers to collect data in new ways and to observe phenomena that might be rare in other settings. Psychologists need to become educated in the possibilities and caveats, so that they can capture advantages of conducting online research while reducing risks to research quality or to human participants. In general, research on the Internet is not inherently more difficult to conduct or inherently riskier to participants than other, more traditional research styles.

But because the Internet is a relatively new medium for research, where online behaviour, norms, technology, and research methods are all evolving, conducting online research raises ambiguities that have been long settled in more conventional laboratory and field settings. Until conducting online research becomes routine, it is likely to require more forethought and self-reflection than conventional research in the discipline. The parts provide some guidance to researchers and the Institutional Review Boards, which monitor their conduct.

START SMALL

By opening up research populations, through sampling and observation of online groups, and by automating research processes, such as random assignment or survey distribution and collection, the Internet enables researchers to work with larger samples and more complex designs, potentially allowing them to examine more subtle psychological phenomena or higher-order statistical interactions. If one thinks of users of the Internet, the online groups they inhabit, and the conversations and transactions they leave behind as public goods available for researchers to study, then the very economies and ease of access that make the Internet an attractive research medium give rise to a dilemma of the commons. Poor online research can potentially contaminate a large number of participants.

Low quality academic research conducted online is having some of the same consequences as commercial electronic mail and telemarketing—undermined the ability of legitimate researchers to collect data online. Researchers should restrain themselves and supervise their students, so that they only consume resources appropriate to the importance of their research problem. People who have run surveys and experiments online also recommend starting with small pilot projects to identify how online data collection methods differ from conventional ones.

Nosek, Banaji, and Greenwald, for example, recommend that a pilot project explicitly attempt to replicate a well-known phenomenon in the off-line setting. Once comparability of subject behaviour can be established, then new variables can be addressed with greater confidence.

UNDERSTAND AND GUARD AGAINST SOURCES OF POOR DATA

One of the earliest considerations has to do with ensuring that the data collection effort is worth the cost and effort. Sampling biases, aberrant subject behaviour from being anonymous, and protections against fraudulent data are all issues to be addressed before the study begins. Investigators can reduce fraudulent data by tracking IP addresses, putting cookies on participants' computers, and tracking sign-ons from those who were invited to participate. They can improve the validity of data from experiments and surveys by programming input forms to check for anomalous values or suspicious patterns of data.

USE TECHNIQUES FOR PROTECTING HUMAN SUBJECTS COMMENSURATE WITH RISKS

No purpose is served when researchers or their IRBs place hurdles in front of research involving minimal risk. One should not use over-elaborate informed consent statements, encryption, digital signatures, or extensive assurances of confidentially when risks are minimal. These features discourage participation and are likely to harm the quality of the data collected and provide little benefit to human subjects. Instead, one can guard against risk with lower keyed approaches. Because experimenters get no feedback from participants, they need to pre-test instructions and informed consent statements so they are clear to the wide-ranging populations from which subjects may come. IRBs should waive documentation of informed consent, by agreeing to a "click to assent" button on websites.

For low risk surveys and experiments, debriefing material can be customised to participants' behaviour and delivered as an updated set of Frequently Asked Questions. Because the most likely risk for data collected online is the breach of confidentially, where research data is disclosed outside of the research context, investigators should use good data management practices to lessen this risk.

In particular, stripping identifiers from data, storing identifiers and data in separate files, and auditing the security of data directories should be routine practice for all research involving human subjects. On the other hand, research that places human subjects at greater risk, either as a direct consequence of the research experience itself or from disclosure of sensitive data, requires stronger safeguards or may not even be appropriate for the Internet. Because investigators have reduced ability to assess a participant's state or to respond to evidence of distress when conducting online research, deception experiments and research that exposes participants to stressful events may be problematic if conducted online.

Researchers should consider screening respondents, either through sample selection or through preliminary data collection, to eliminate vulnerable populations.

The greater freedom of participants to withdraw from online research is a mixed benefit. Compared to laboratory settings, they are more likely to leave before experiencing severe distress, but also before they can be adequately debriefed.

To counteract early withdrawal, researcher can arrange their study so that participants are sent to a debriefing site automatically at the end of a session, and debriefing material can be customised to their behaviour. If the data collection involves highly sensitive information, engage extra precautions. In addition to the standard practice of separating identifying information from the data itself, a researcher might consider engaging a service to acquire subjects, collect the data and arrange for payment, if appropriate.

In this way, the researcher is never in possession of the identifying information that would harm the subject. Under some circumstance, researchers might apply for a Certificate of Confidentiality, allowing the investigator and others who have access to research records to refuse to disclose identifying information on research participants in civil, criminal, administrative, legislative, or other government proceedings. With sensitive topics, such schemes as certified digital signatures for informed consent, encryption of data transmission, and technical separation of identifiers and data, may be warranted. Research with sensitive topics may require strong verification that the assent is from the person who purports to be answering, including digital signatures or mailed consent.. There are special difficulties if the research involves minors. Depending on the sensitivity of the information collected, parental consent may have to be acquired on paper, to ensure the parents are fully informed about the experience their child will have in the research.

Bibliography

Ajit Singh Siwatch: *Encyclopedic Dictionary of Library and Information Science, Vols. I to III*, Shree Publishers, 2010.

Amjad Ali: *Ane's Encyclopedic Dictionary of Library and Information Science*, Ane Books India, 2006.

Bhupendra Narayan Singh: *Encyclopaedia of Library and Information Science in the Digital Age Vols. I to III*, Anmol Pub, 2011.

Bikika Laloo Tariang: *Essays on Library and Information Science Education*, Ess Ess Publications, 2012.

C.D. harma: *Advances in Library and Information Science Vol. 1: Computer Applications*, Scientific, 1995.

C.K. Sharma: *Encyclopaedic Dictionary of Library Information Science and Network*, JBD, 2002.

D.B. Patil and M.M. Kooganuramath: *Library and Information Science*, APH, 2011.

G. Devarajan: *Applied Research in Library and Information Science*, Ess Ess Pub, 2005.

H.K. Srivastava, Mohit: *Foundation of Library and Information Science*, 2011.

I.M. Goswami: *Encyclopaedia of Library and Information Science (5 Vols-Set)*, Commonwealth, 1997.

Jogender Singh Burman: *Encyclopaedic Survey of Library and Information Science : Principles and Practices (5 Vols-Set)*, Rajat Publication, 2006.

Khalid K. Faruqi and Mehtab Alam: *Library Information Systems and E-Journal Archiving*, Authorspress, 2005.

Kundan Godia: *Electronic Services in Library and Information Science*, Adhyayan, 2007.

L.S. Ramaiah: *Images and Perceptions in Library and Information Science*, Ess Ess, 1998.

Mahendra Singh Sodhi: *Advancement in Library and Information Science*, Adhyayan Pub, 2006.

P. Kaushik: *Library Information Services and Systems*, Anmol, 2006.

P.P. Rawat, O.P. Gupta and V. Venkatappaiah: *Current Developments in Library and Information Science : Papers presented in honour of Prof. P.N. Kaula on his 71st Birthday*, Reliance, 1998.

P.S.G. Kumar: *A Student's Manual of Library and Information Science 2 Volumes*, B.R. Pub., 2012.

P.S.G. Kumar: *Foundations of Library and Information Science: Paper 1 of UGC Model Curriculum*, B.R. Publishing Corporation, 2012.

Poonam: *HRD in Library and Information Science*, ACE Books, 2010.

Punit Ralhan: *Advancement in Library and Information Science*, Oxford Book Company, 2009 .

R P Bajpai: *Current Trends in Library and Information Science*, Shree Pub, 2007.

Raghunath Pandey and M.N. Velayudhan Pillai: *History of Library and Information Science*, Jnanada Prakashan, 2011.

Ram Shobhit Singh: *Encyclopaedia of Library Information Systems and E-Journal Archiving, Vols. I-II*, Anmol, 2008.

Ravikanth Sangwan: *Encyclopaedia of Library and Information Science*, Anmol, 2006.

S.P. Agrawal: *Directory of LIS Education in India : All in one Compendium on Library and Information Science Stud*, Reliance, 1996.

Santosh Patel: *Library Information : Preservation and Access*, Authors Press, 2003.

Shiv Ram Verma: *Foundations of Library and Information Science*, Shree, 2005.

Shri Umesha, Mahesh Mudhol and K.M. Khan: *A Handbook On Distance Education with Special Reference to Library and Information Science in India*, Ess Ess Publications, 2004.

Shyama Balakrishnan and P.K. Paliwal: *Library Information Procedure*, Anmol, 2001.

T. Nasirudheen: *A Comprehensive Course in Library and Information Science*, Ess Ess Publications, 2012.

Tariq Ashraf and Sanjay Kumar Jha: *Handbook of UGC Net for Library and Information Science*, Bookwell, 2008.

Tariq Ashraf and Sanjay Kumar Jha: *Handbook of UGC Net for Library and Information Science*, Synergy Books India, 2014.

Vaishali Khaparde: *Advancement in Library and Information Science*, Ess Ess Publications, 2012.

Index

G

I

L

M

O

P

R

S

T

U

V

W

X